POSTCARD HISTORY SERIES

Vineland

ON THE COVER: As the largest single building on Landis Avenue, the three-story Baker House Hotel dominated the business district and offered visitors and potential settlers a welcome respite at the end of their journeys. Leather-bound guest registers from the hotel not only include signatures of those travelers but also feature an enlightening assortment of advertisements from local businesses. (Courtesy of the Ingraham postcard collection.)

POSTCARD HISTORY SERIES

Vineland

Arjorie Moniodis Ingraham and the
Vineland Historical and Antiquarian Society

ARCADIA
PUBLISHING

ISBN 978-1-4671-2177-4

Published by Arcadia Publishing
Charleston, South Carolina

Printed in the United States of America

Library of Congress Control Number: 2013952359

For all general information, contact Arcadia Publishing at:
Telephone 843-853-2070
Fax 843-853-0044
E-mail sales@arcadiapublishing.com
For customer service and orders:
Toll-Free 1-888-313-2665

Visit us on the Internet at www.arcadiapublishing.com

This book is dedicated to Arjorie Moniodis Ingraham's late husband, Horace Robert Ingraham, and her children, Diane Ingraham-Villar and Robert Louis Ingraham, who inspired her passion for preserving Vineland's history, and to the people of Vineland, who care about its past.

Contents

Foreword

Postcard collectors are a dedicated group of people. I know because I have been collecting postcards since I was 10 years old, when my mother gave me my first postcard, sent to her by her brother, Gurino. It was also the first postcard that she had ever received. Later in life, my father-in-law, Claude Raymond Ingraham, gave me several real-photo postcards that had been made from the glass slides of photographs that he had taken as a young man while roaming around Vineland. Thankfully, his interest in local sites documented many places and people who have long since disappeared.

As a Vineland native, I have enjoyed studying the history of my hometown, and postcards have been an interesting window into the past. But, as any real collector can tell you, photographic postcards are just one type that has been produced over the years. Other types include colorful linen and chrome postcards, which are included here and show scenes of Vineland's downtown shopping district, as well as its parks, churches, and residential neighborhoods.

For more than 100 years, Vineland postcards were produced by local businesses as well as firms located in Philadelphia and Boston. George Daynor, creator of the infamous Palace Depression, invested heavily in postcards, which served as an effective advertising tool for his unusual "palace of junk." Unfortunately, local businesses and the Vineland Chamber of Commerce stopped producing postcards in the late 1970s, a time when changing technology meant that folks no longer looked to paper and the written word as a means of communication. No further effort was made locally after that time to mass-produce postcards, but that did little to deter the interest of collectors like me, who find them an interesting glimpse into the history of their hometown.

My collection includes images of local schools, defunct businesses, and unusual homes like the George Arbuckel house on South Main Road. Best known for the immense granite statues that Arbuckel, a plumber, constructed on the grounds, it also featured a five-acre hedge maze behind the house—a kind of miniature Disneyland that drew a lot of attention from the public for many years. His home is just one of the many buildings unique to Vineland that are pictured here.

I hope you enjoy your "visit" to Vineland as seen through these postcards.

—Arjorie Moniodis Ingraham

Acknowledgments

We are grateful to the following people, who expended a lot of effort to make this book a reality: Diane and Carlos Villar, Ruth A. Shropshire, Lauren Valentine, Allan Black, Jennifer Navarrete, Kevin Lopez, Brittney Place, Kim Sauerwald, and Sara Silva. All images in this title are courtesy of the Ingraham postcard collection.

Introduction

The route to Vineland is as follows: From New York and Philadelphia: From New York City—Take Ferry at foot of Cortlandt street for Jersey City. Thence per New Jersey Railroad, to Philadelphia direct. Thence take Ferry at foot of Market street, at 8 a.m. and 3:15 p.m. for Camden. Thence per West Jersey Railroad to Vineland direct, arriving here at 10:02 a.m. and 5:14 p.m.

—B.F. Ladd, editor, *Evening Journal*

It is not easy to tell the story of a town like Vineland. In some ways, it is the story of every American town that sprang up in the mid-19th century—a turbulent time when the country was bursting with energy and promise and also torn apart by war. In other ways, its story is unique, filled with individual personalities whose lives left a mark not just on their community but on the country as well.

Vineland was founded in 1861 by an ambitious 28-year-old Philadelphia attorney named Charles Kline Landis, a man who was both a devoted humanitarian and a staunch capitalist. On the one hand, he was a visionary who was determined to create Vineland as a place that embodied all the highest ideals of America. On the other, he was happy to receive a substantial profit in exchange for his efforts.

Landis had been involved in real estate development before, but he saw Vineland as a place where he could imprint his own beliefs. In his new "village," as the town was originally called, one's race or religion did not matter as much as respecting the rights of others, including women, who were tired of being treated as second-class citizens. To ensure that his new town thrived in a productive fashion, Landis also declared it dry from the onset; no liquor was sold or publicly imbibed, although it is likely that some residents occasionally enjoyed a sip of medicinal bitters (which were often at least 40 percent alcohol). While a scattering of settlers were already living in the region he chose to develop, their presence did nothing to impede his plans. In 1861, Landis bought about 20,000 acres from Richard Wood of nearby Millville, who was at that time the property's official owner, and proceeded to clear the land. He created a one-square-mile central area as the town, which was ringed by Landis Township, a section set aside for farming. To Landis, the region was ideal for growing different types of fruit.

Growth was slow and steady in the early years. In 1862, the first permanent house in town was erected by C.P. Davis on North East Boulevard (a structure that currently sits on the grounds of the Vineland Historical and Antiquarian Society's museum). According to B.F. Ladd, a newspaper editor who lived in Vineland during its early days, "There were only about a dozen people living in Vineland when the Civil War erupted. However, Landis was unwilling to release any of the men to go and fight. So, he paid the required bounty to have replacements found, ensuring that he would have enough manpower to carve his community out of the New Jersey Pine Barrens. Landis advertised the town so skillfully that pioneers were quickly attracted from throughout the United States and Europe. He had brochures printed in the native languages of Italian, German, and Swiss immigrants. By the end of the war, the town had become the home of scholars, business owners, inventors, and artists. Shoe factories, rug makers, lumber mills, and button manufacturers were among the industries that opened there." By 1865, more than 1,000 acres of land had been sold and 500 buildings had been erected in the town and the surrounding township.

The Vineland Historical and Antiquarian Society, founded in 1864, has been collecting pieces of Vineland's past for almost as long as the town has existed. While Vineland's story has been told before, we decided it was time to approach the subject from a new perspective. As a result, when Arjorie Moniodis Ingraham graciously offered to loan local postcards from her extensive collection as the foundation for the book, we realized this would be a novel way to look at different aspects of our town's past. Some of the scenes depicted in the postcards are familiar, like images of Landis Avenue at a time when it was the primary shopping destination for local residents. Others are of long-lost businesses and homes that once graced Vineland's streets but are little more than a memory now.

Whenever possible, we have tried to use the words of the people who once lived in Vineland to give the reader a better sense of the times.

While several generations have passed since the last of these postcards were first produced, Vineland itself has essentially remained unchanged. Like most American towns, its residents struggle with a fluctuating economy, rising medical costs, and a host of other concerns. However, for many present-day immigrants, it still remains the promised land—a place where new opportunities are available to anyone who is not afraid of a little hard work, just as Charles Kline Landis planned for all those years ago.

—Patricia A. Martinelli, curator
Vineland Historical and Antiquarian Society

One

Landis Avenue

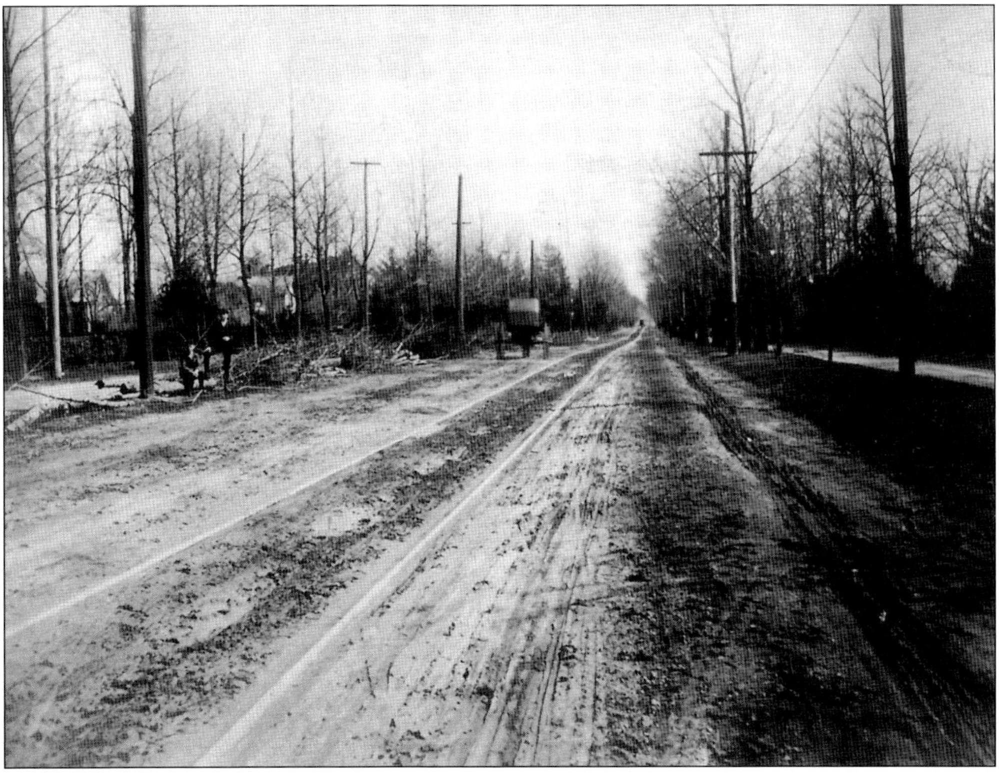

In the mid-19th century, the territory upon which Vineland was founded was the western edge of the New Jersey Pine Barrens, a forest of oaks and pines that was harvested by early settlers as a source of lumber and coal. After Charles K. Landis founded Vineland in 1861, he worked with a handful of men to cut down trees to create new roads. Its heart was Landis Avenue, a 100-foot-wide thoroughfare modeled on the grand boulevards of Paris.

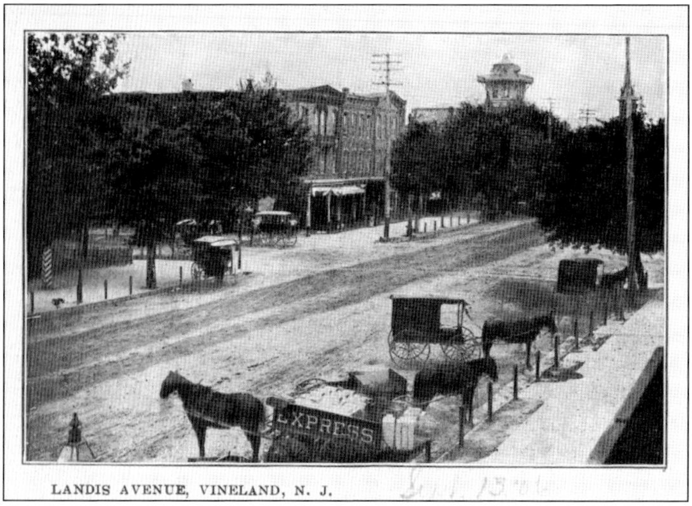

After investing in Elwood and Hammonton with business partners, Landis created the "village of Vineland" as a place where his unique vision could come to life. Originally just one square mile in size, the town was surrounded by roughly 20,000 acres that became Landis Township. Early settlers quickly built homes on Landis Avenue, many of which included front rooms set aside for all types of business.

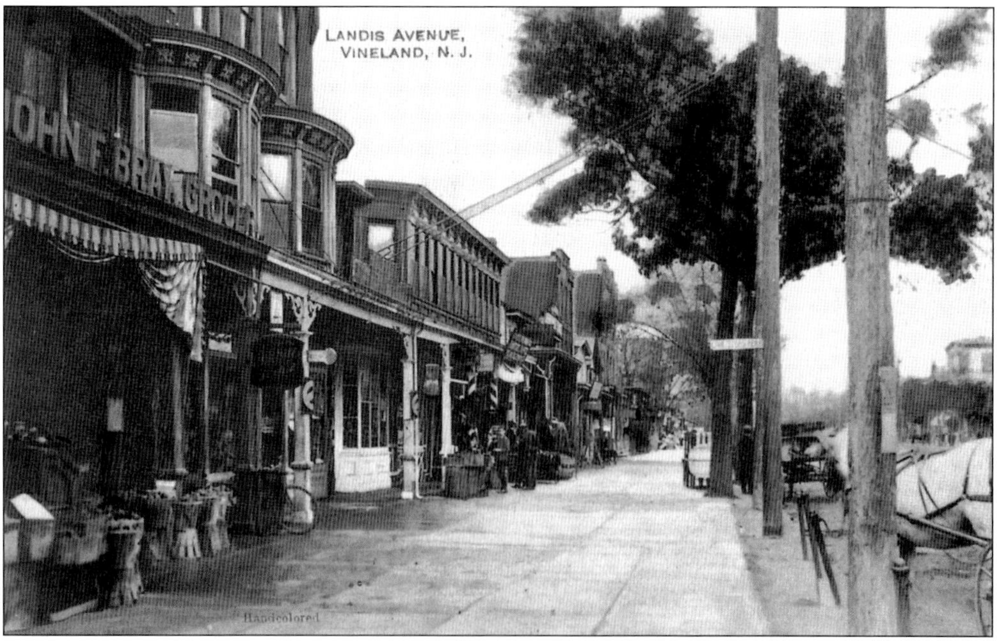

Those early days of settlement were very gratifying to Charles K. Landis. He wrote, "In the Autumn of 1861 the population of Vineland consisted of four families. It now (in 1869) consists of over ten thousand thriving and industrious people. The town plot in the centre has a population of three thousand people. Improvements are going on in all directions. New buildings, stores, and manufactories are being erected, and new farms and orchards cleared and planted."

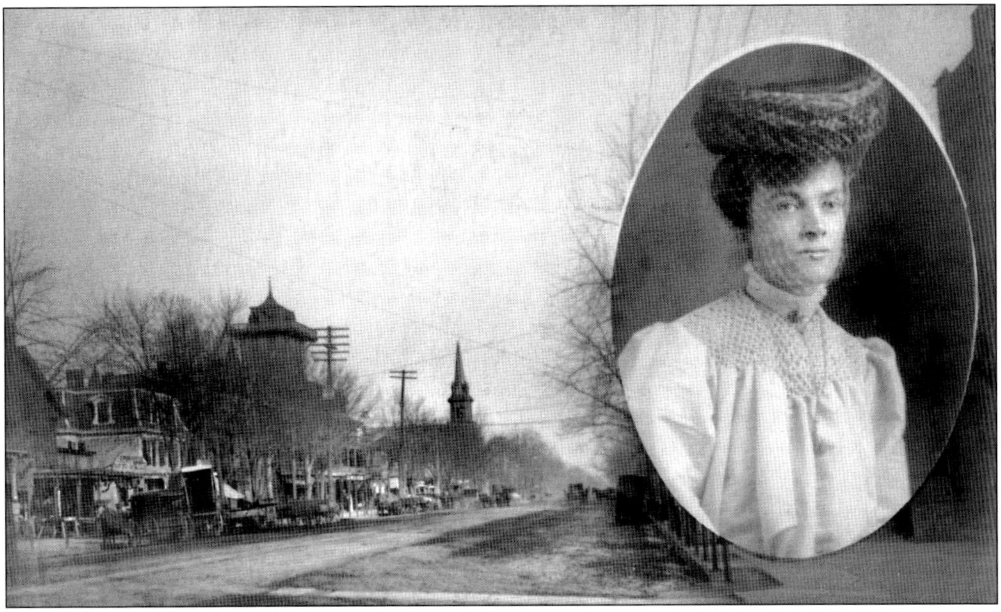

According to local newspaper editor B.F. Ladd, "Vineland society is made up largely of enterprising business men, manufacturers and farmers from New England, New York, Pennsylvania and the Western States. Many invalids who have suffered elsewhere from pulmonary and other chronic complaints, have regained their health here. In fact, Vineland has attained an enviable reputation as a health resort."

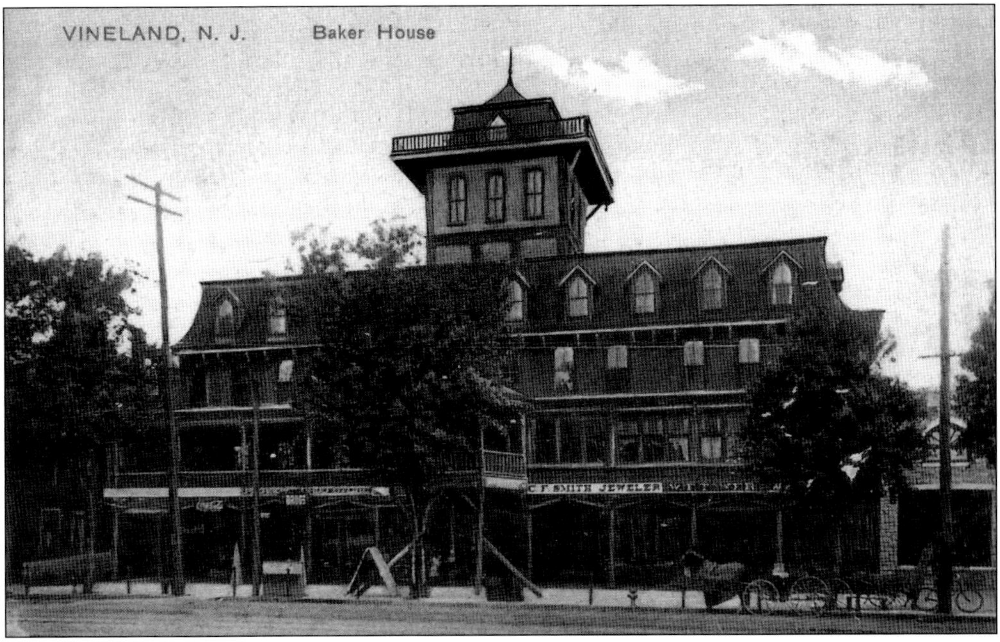

In the 1860s, a huge three-story hotel was opened by C.B. Webb on Landis Avenue in the heart of Vineland. The elegant frame structure featured accommodations for 100 guests at an average price of $1 per night. In 1869, the Baker brothers moved to Vineland from Louisburg, Pennsylvania, and purchased the hotel, which they renamed the Baker House. In the years that followed, the hotel was operated by other owners, including W.F. Bowman and Seaman R. Fowler.

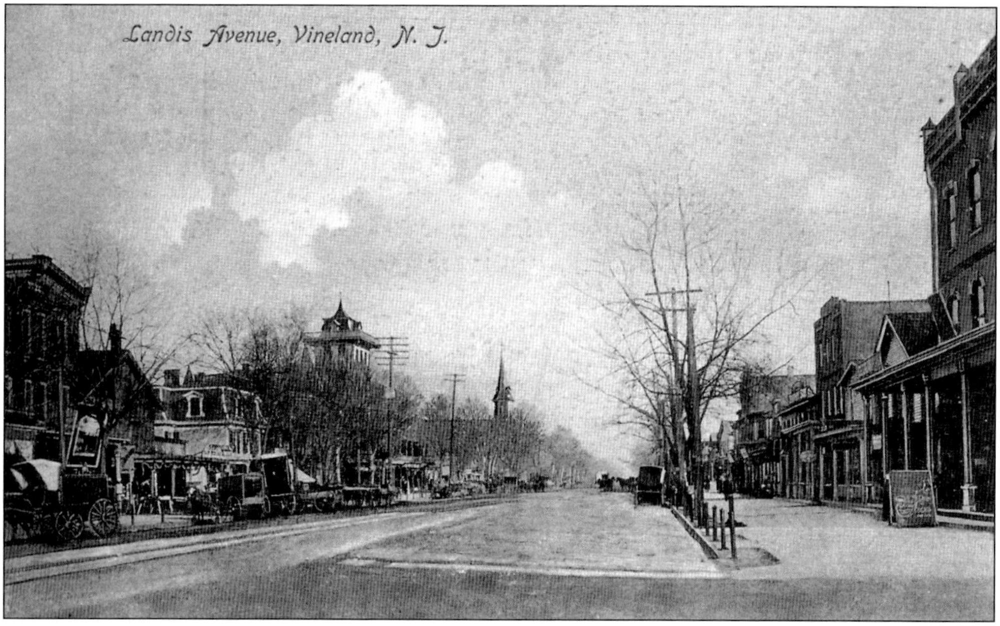

Even before Charles Landis established Vineland, he had already planned "the broad design of the settlement was that it should be agricultural, manufacturing, commercial and educational." He also noted, "I decided that all the roads should be broad and straight and at right angles, making up for the want of the picturesque in the straight line and right angle by requiring trees for shade in single or double rows, to be planted along all the roads."

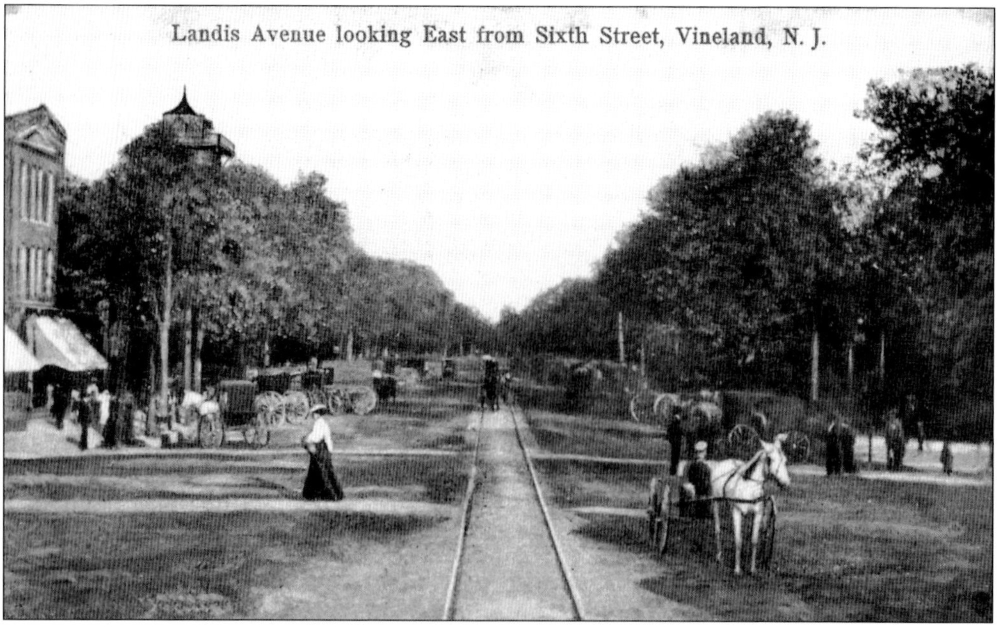

By 1880, the population of Vineland had grown to more than 6,000 residents. The town was divided into lots that were 600 feet by 300 feet in size. Streets running east and west were named Peach, Pear, Plum, Wood, Grape, Almond, Quince, and Cherry, while cross streets were numbered from Second to Eighth. The town was bounded by Park Avenue on the north, Chestnut Avenue on the south, and East and West Avenues on the east and west sides.

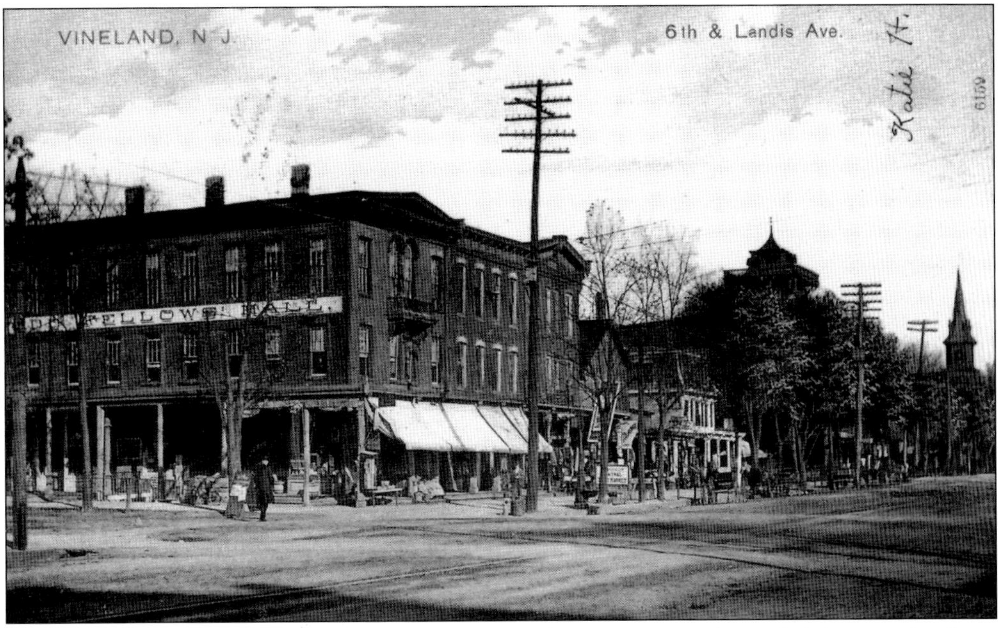

In addition to businesses, Landis Avenue became home to a number of civic organizations, including the Independent Order of Odd Fellows, a philanthropic organization that traces its roots to 18th-century England. It is not surprising that the Odd Fellows, which was the first club to welcome both men and women as members, became extremely popular with the liberal-minded residents of Vineland.

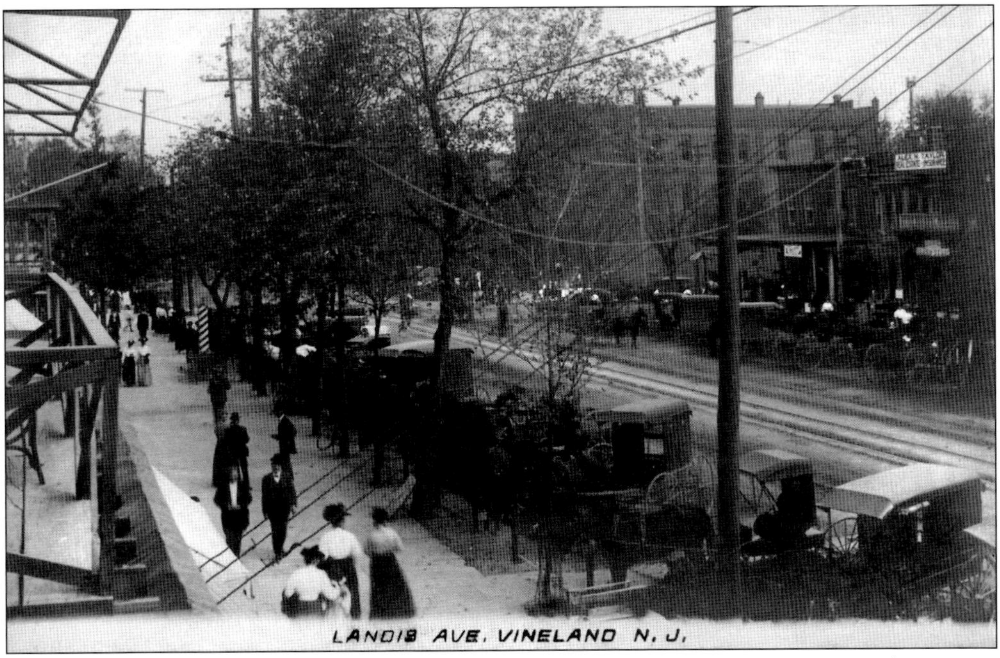

Some of the first successful businesses that were established in brick buildings on Landis Avenue included Merchants', Leavitt & Sherburne's, Dyer & Hale's, Robinson's, Swing's, Sykes', Roberts', Pearson's, Liberty, Sylvester's, the Bank Building, Mechanics', Central, Brown's, Flood's, Baker House, Parkinson's, Prouty's, Stevens', Russell's, Erickson's, and Moran's.

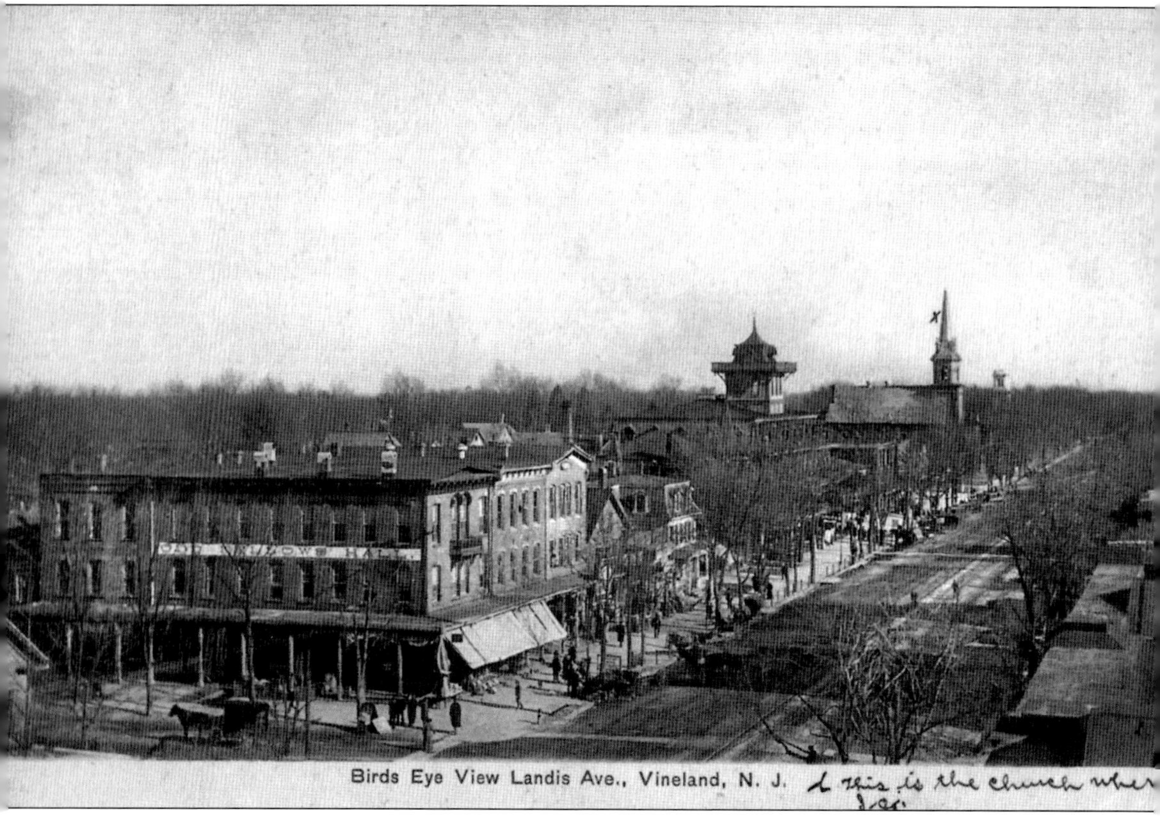

This bird's-eye view of Landis Avenue shows the variety of businesses that had sprung up between Sixth and Seventh Streets by the late 1800s. Within a few years, this main artery—just bare dirt for many years—would be covered in brick to facilitate transportation by horse-and-wagon and feature a trolley line at its center. Visitors often sent postcards like this to family members and friends to show what life was like in the thriving town.

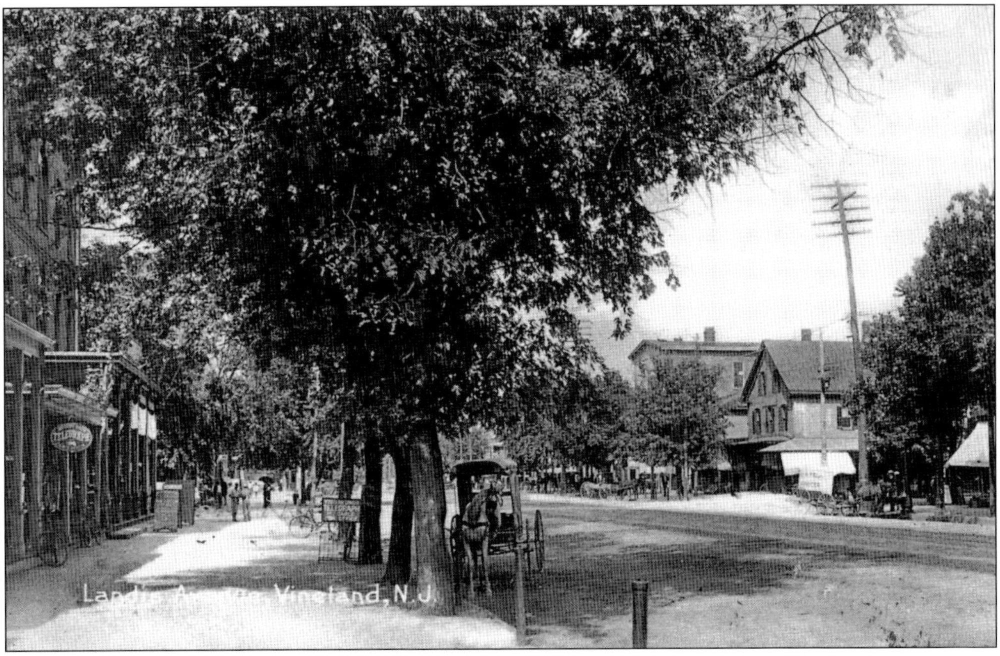

Vineland residents, like most Americans in the 19th century, enjoyed a love affair with technology that allowed them to send telegraphs, make telephone calls, and flip a switch to turn on the electric lights. Local entrepreneurs quickly established businesses on Landis Avenue to introduce these modern marvels to the townspeople.

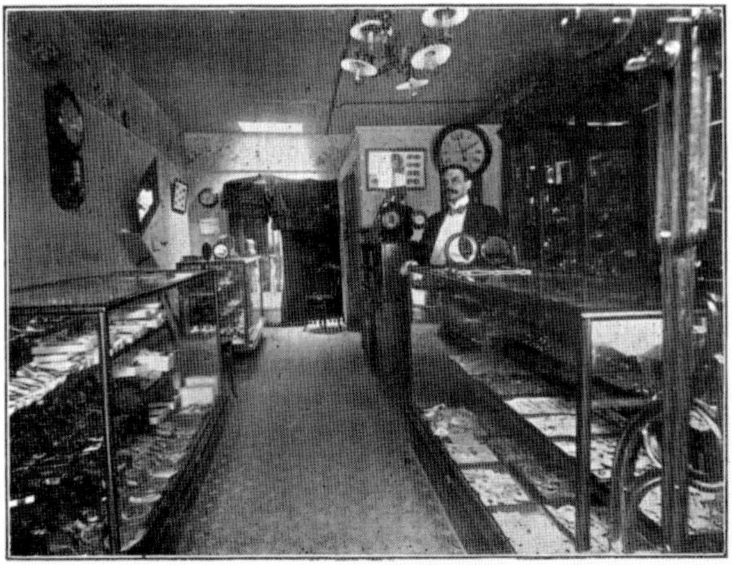

The Jewelry Store of F. P. Donahey Vineland N. J.

Opened in 1894, F.P. Donahey's jewelry store quickly became one of the most popular businesses in town. However, besides offering the usual lines of gold and silver jewelry for men and women, Donahey's was also the place where local residents could have their eyes checked by optician H.W. Blaisdell. The cast-iron clock erected outside of Donahey's store at 614 Landis Avenue still stands today.

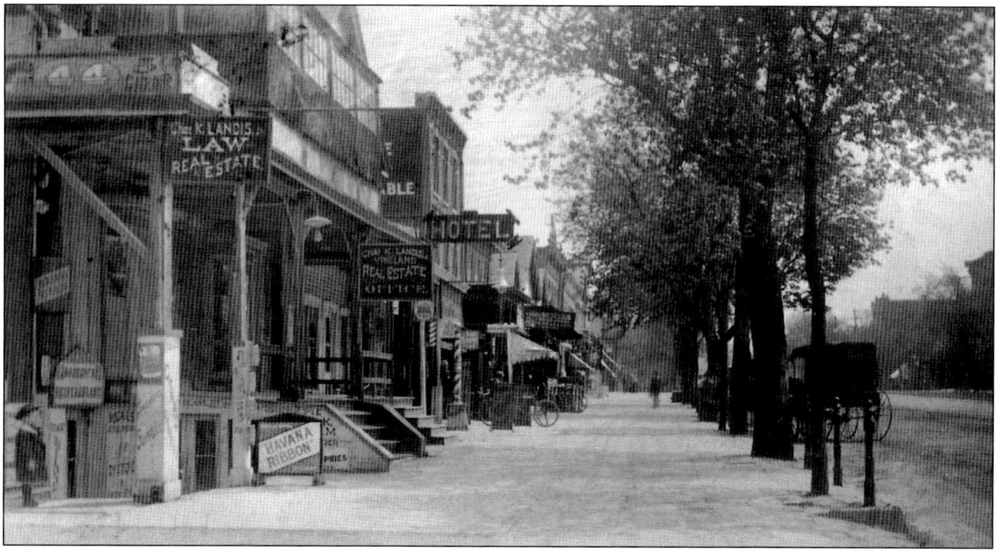

Charles K. Landis established a successful law practice in Philadelphia while still a young man. But, like many other businessmen, he saw advantages to investing in land in South Jersey, and he soon established himself as the new town's sole real estate agent. Both his law office and his land office were located at the intersection of Landis Avenue and Railroad Boulevard, at the center of town.

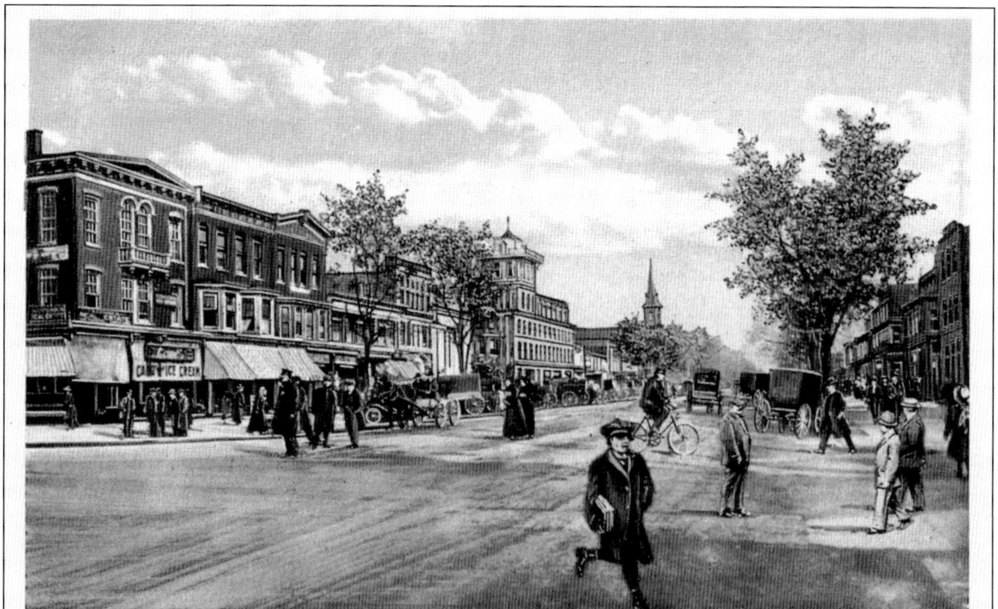

By the spring of 1862, many new settlers began clearing land and erecting dwellings. The new settlers spent their money on improving their properties, while also purchasing goods at the businesses that developed on Landis Avenue. Landis decreed that each buyer "should erect a habitation not nearer than twenty feet from the side of the street in the city plot, or seventy-five feet from the roadside in the country. The stipulation about setting houses back removed them from dust, and induced great attention to the ornamenting of front gardens with flowers and shrubbery."

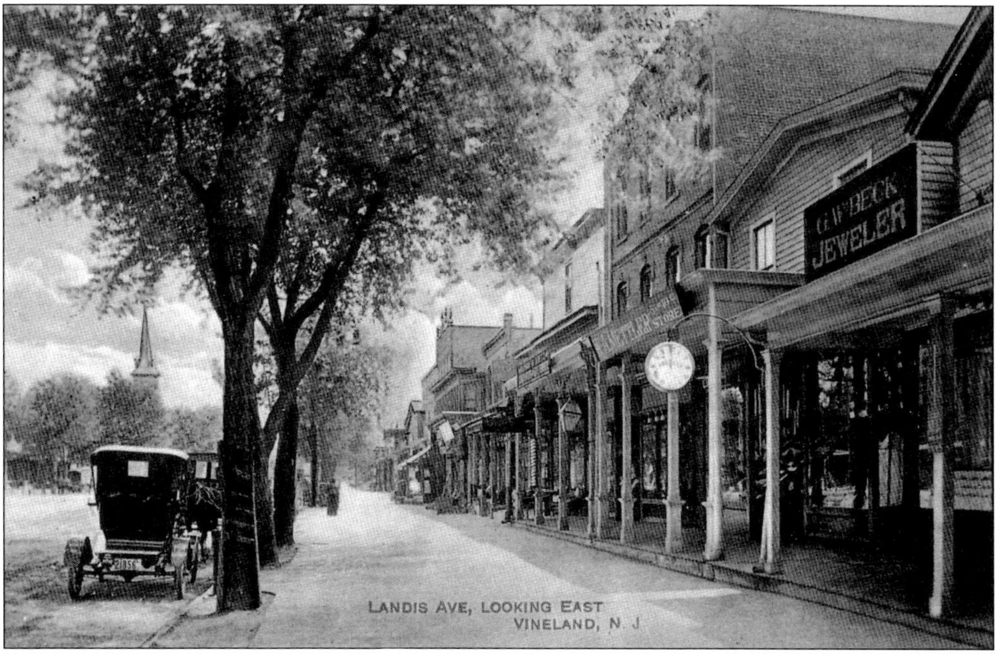

Vineland was extensively advertised, and its advantages were set forth in such glowing terms that it soon became well known in all parts of the country as a desirable place to settle. One businessman, John Gage of Chicago, settled there with his family in 1864. In addition to inventing a carpentry plane that was used by builders nationwide, Gage and his family were very community oriented. Portia Gage was one of the first women in town to support the women's suffrage movement, by staging demonstrations with other feminists.

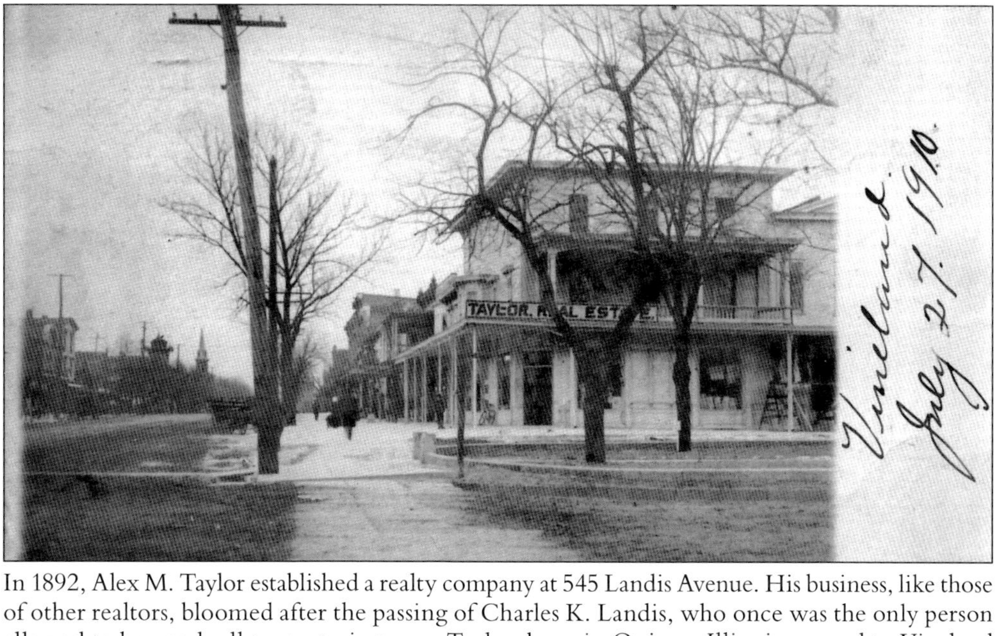

In 1892, Alex M. Taylor established a realty company at 545 Landis Avenue. His business, like those of other realtors, bloomed after the passing of Charles K. Landis, who once was the only person allowed to buy and sell property in town. Taylor, born in Quincy, Illinois, moved to Vineland as a child in 1866. He later became an active member of different organizations, including the Vineland Historical and Antiquarian Society and the First Presbyterian Church.

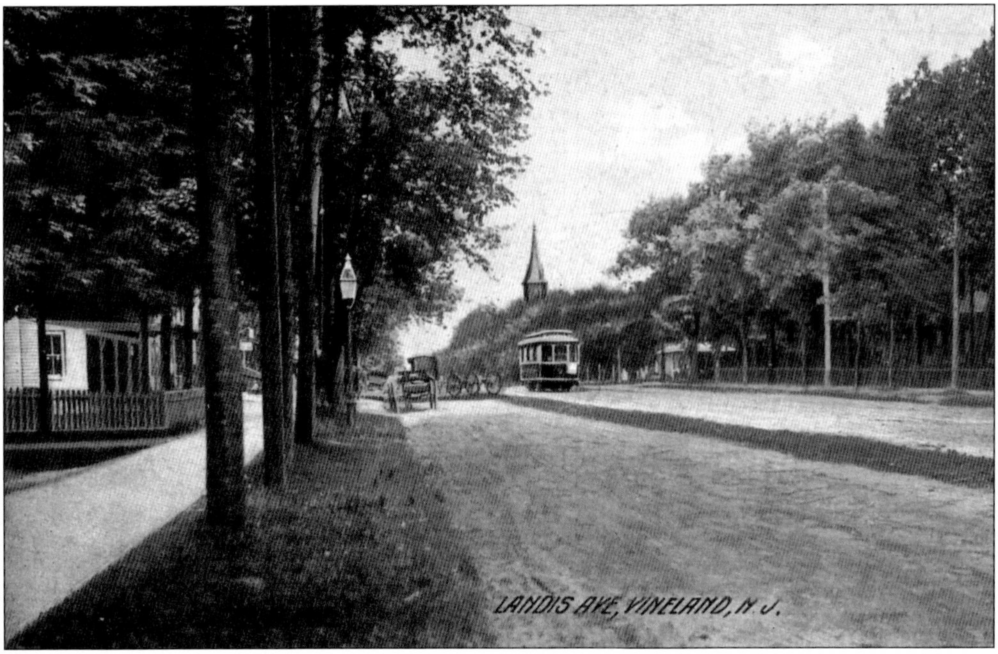

After the electric motor was perfected in the late 1800s, the horse car commonly used for transportation in cities and smaller towns was quickly replaced by a new motorized form known as the trolley. Like many Americans, Vineland residents seized on this innovation as a convenient way to travel through the downtown to do their shopping, and to neighboring towns such as Millville and Bridgeton. Unfortunately, the advent of the automobile eventually led to the demise of the trolley in many towns.

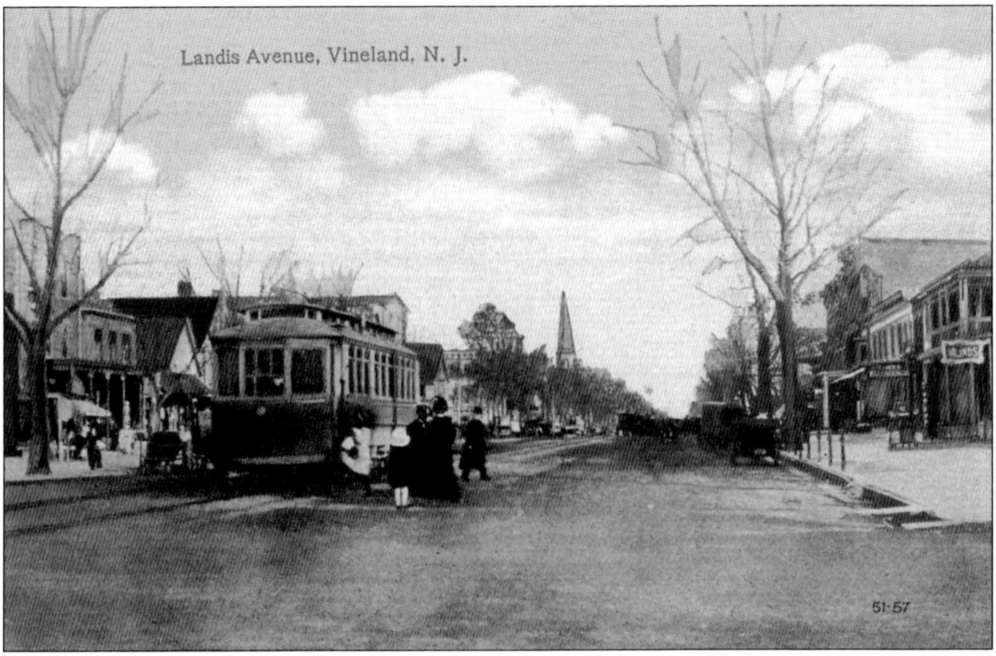

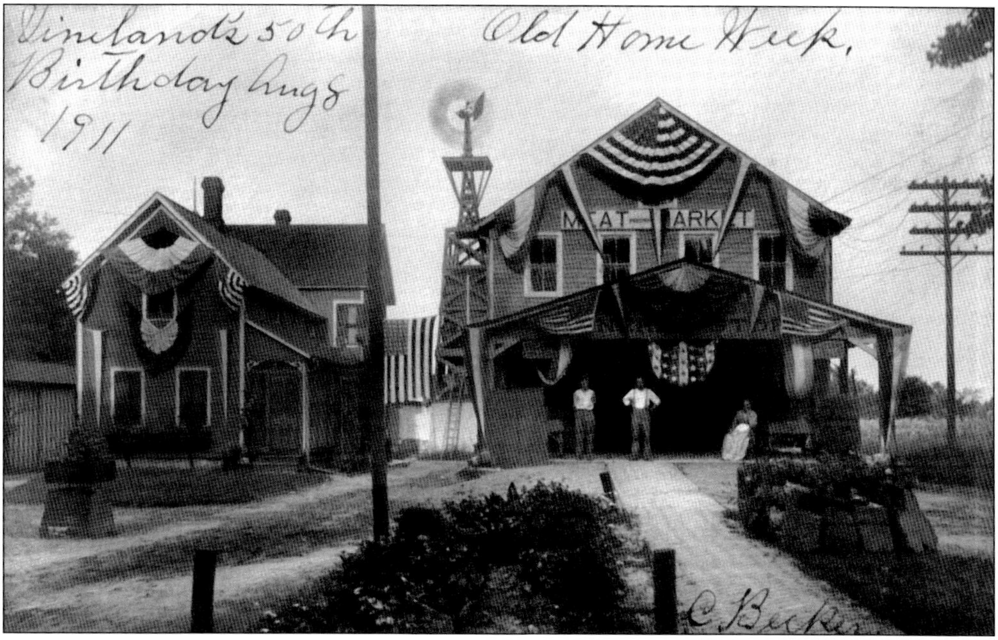

Cuno Becker was a Vineland merchant who sold a variety of goods at his store at 617 East Landis Avenue, including produce, tea, fabric, and other household merchandise. Other downtown businesses ranged from smoke shops, where men could buy their favorite cigars, to women's clothing stores that offered the latest Paris fashions.

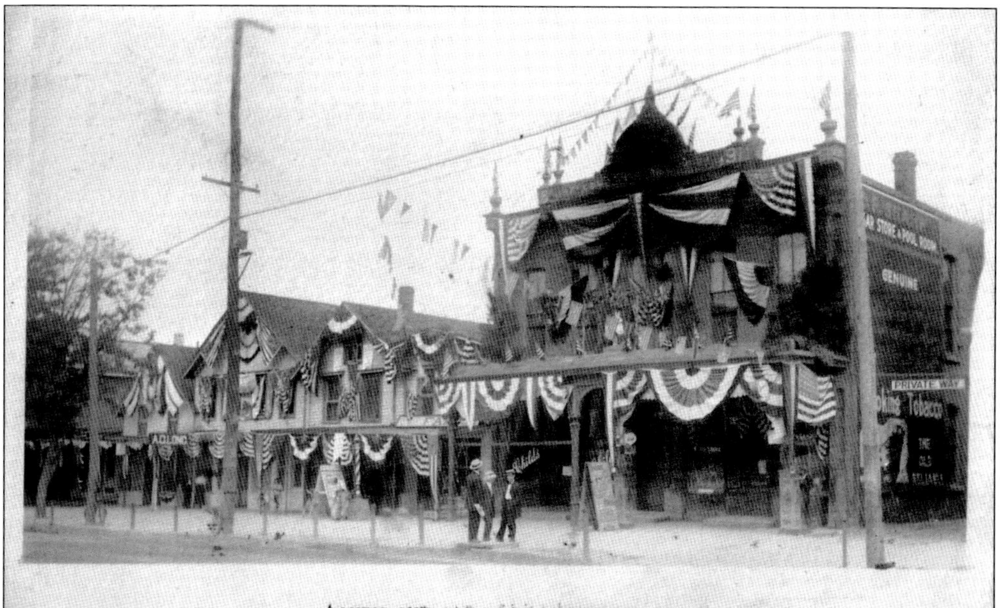

Patriotic fervor was on display everywhere during Vineland's 50th anniversary celebration, and Landis Avenue was no exception. Merchants decorated their stores with flags, banners, and red-white-and-blue swags to show their support for their town, which thrived in the early years of the 20th century.

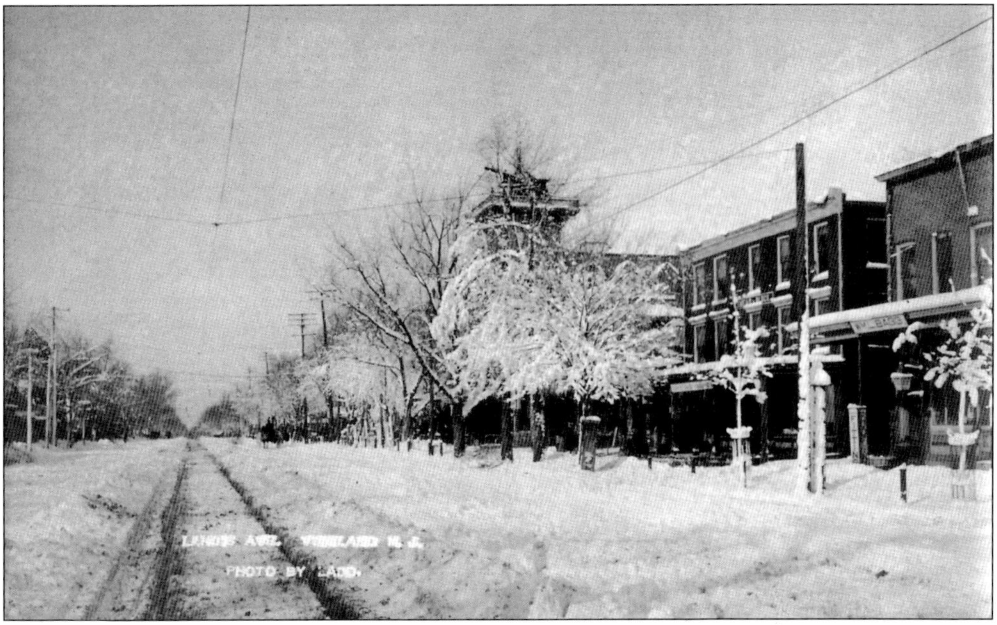

Despite being promoted for its "healthful" climate, Vineland periodically endured a number of severe snowstorms over the years that literally closed businesses on Landis Avenue. One of the worst nor'easters to hit not just the town but also the whole region occurred in 1899, with winds gusting close to 50 miles per hour and a snowfall of more than three feet.

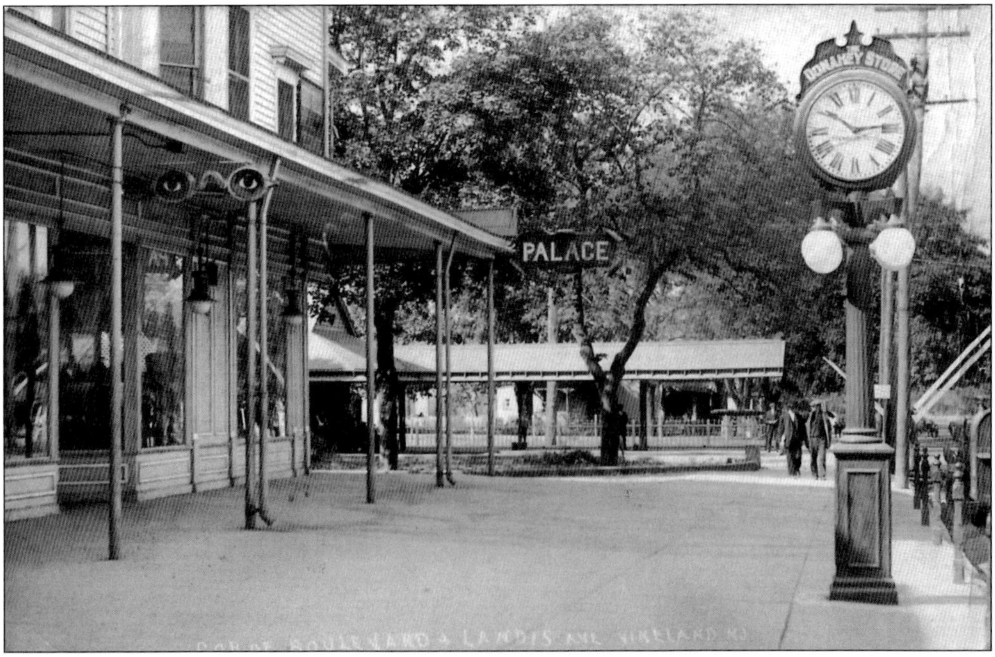

Located at the intersection of Landis Avenue and Railroad Boulevard, the Palace Theater was built on the property where the Landis family had once resided. For 5¢, local audiences could enjoy a matinee or evening performance of silent films such as Biograph Pictures' *A Drama on the Reef.* Other early theaters on Landis Avenue included the Globe and the Grand, which were eventually replaced by the Landis Theater.

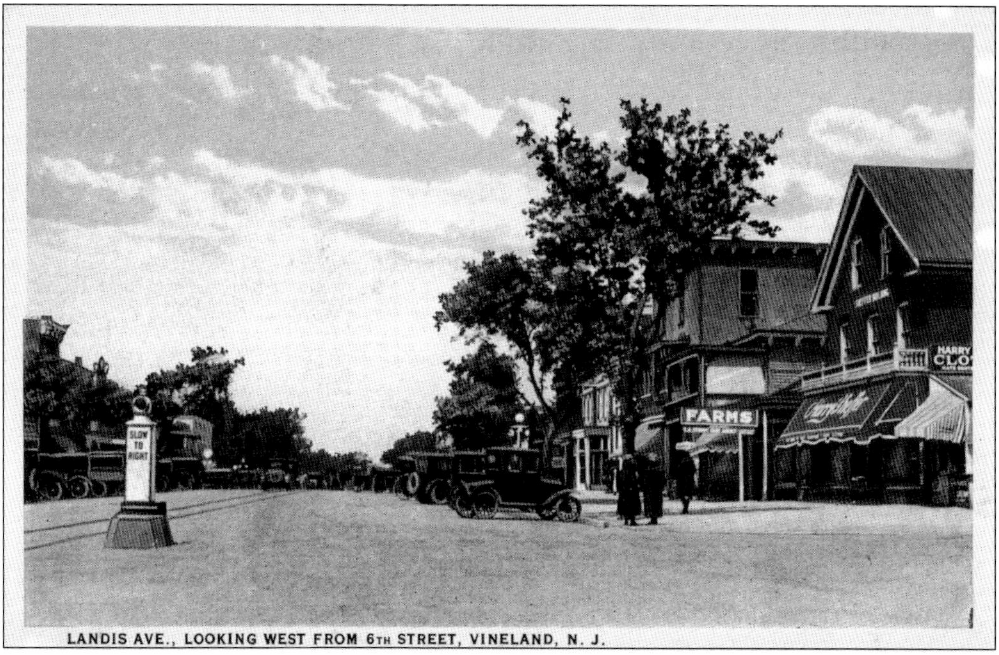

The newfangled invention known as the automobile was quickly adopted by many Vineland residents. By the 1920s, there were automobile dealerships on Landis Avenue, with gasoline pumps conveniently close by. Signal lights were placed on concrete islands at the center of the street in an effort to keep traffic under control.

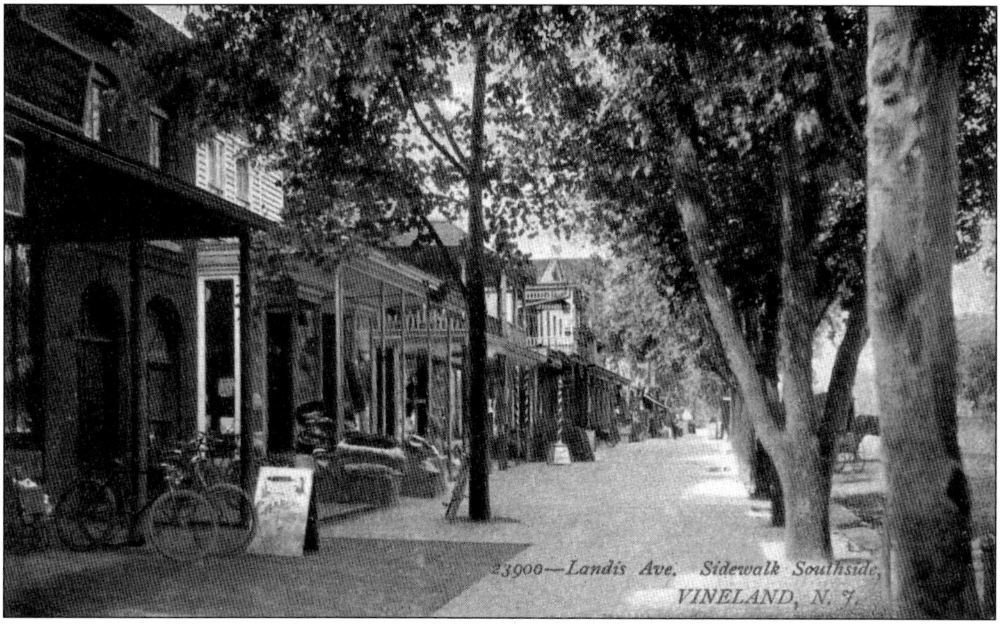

By the early 1900s, Landis Avenue drew new generations of shoppers, who could purchase everything from groceries to clothing there, visit their dentist, get legal advice, and even get a haircut, all within walking distance. Cycling was so popular that the city had to post speed limit signs throughout the downtown area to keep the wheelmen, as they were known, from becoming a danger to pedestrians.

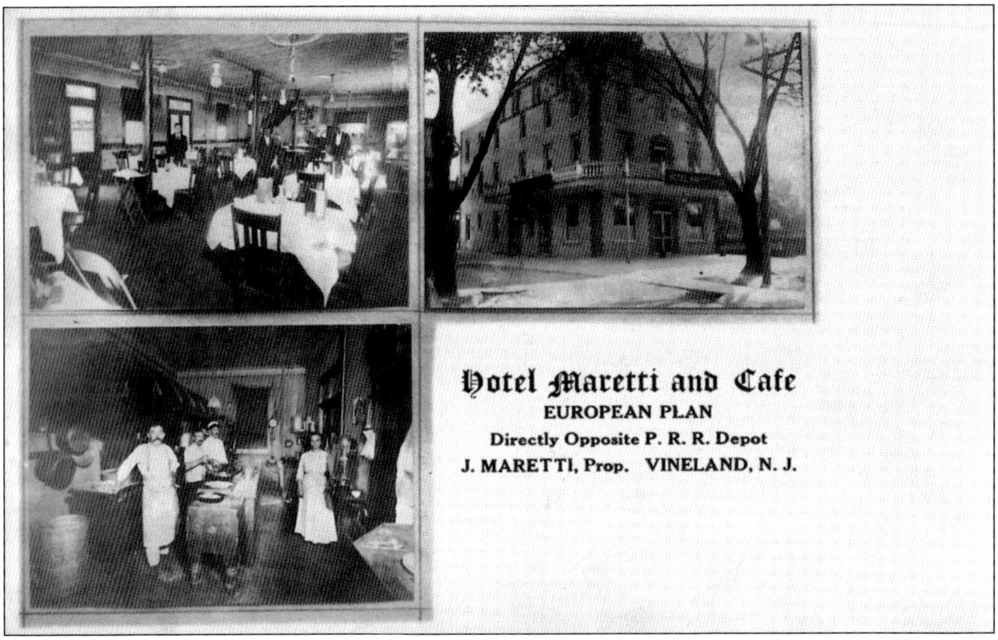

After the first Italian immigrants settled in the town in the 1870s, some of them chose to operate businesses, like the Hotel Maretti and Café, situated across from the Pennsylvania Railroad depot at Landis Avenue and Railroad Boulevard. The four-story brick hotel competed with many other hotels and boardinghouses for the patronage of new settlers and visitors to Vineland. The Maretti family became well-respected residents of the town, whose children continued to successfully operate businesses and remain involved in community affairs in the years that followed.

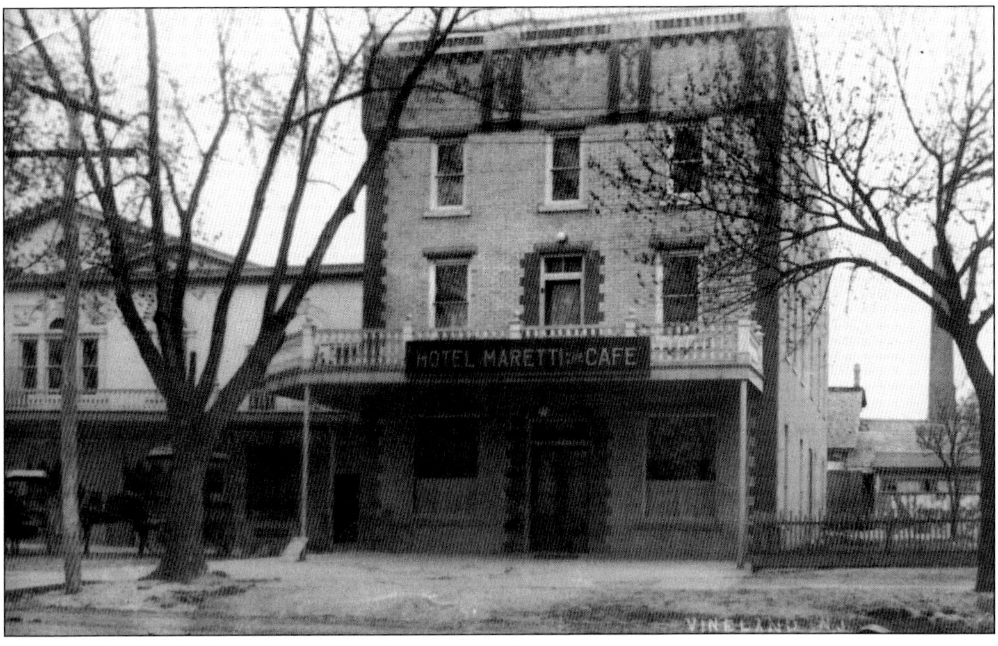

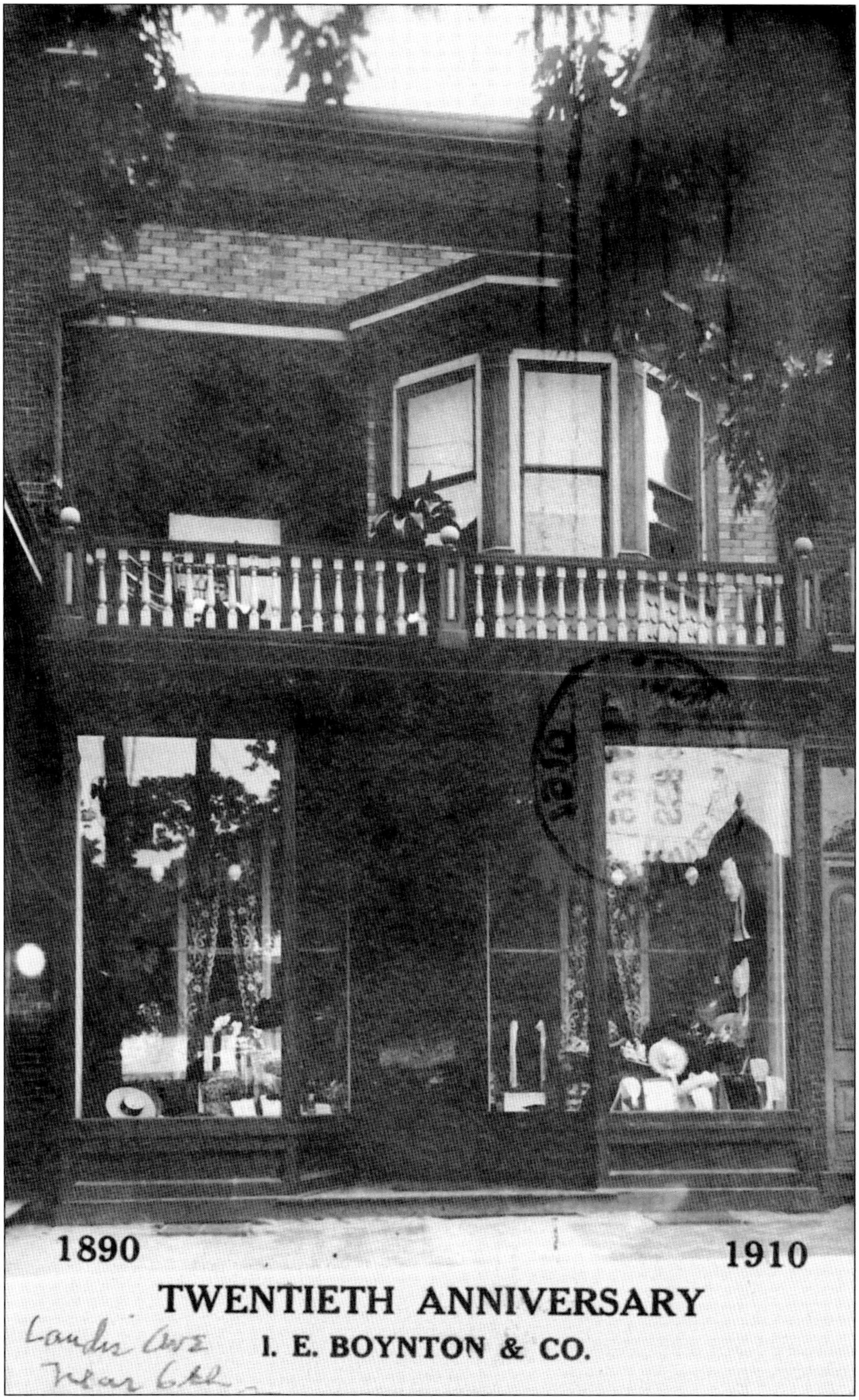

Since Vineland did not discriminate against women owning and operating businesses, a number of dress shops and millinery stores sprang up on Landis Avenue. They ranged in size from small family-run shops, owned by women like Louisa Bennett, to Zambone's Corner, where a number of different merchants offered their wares for sale under one roof.

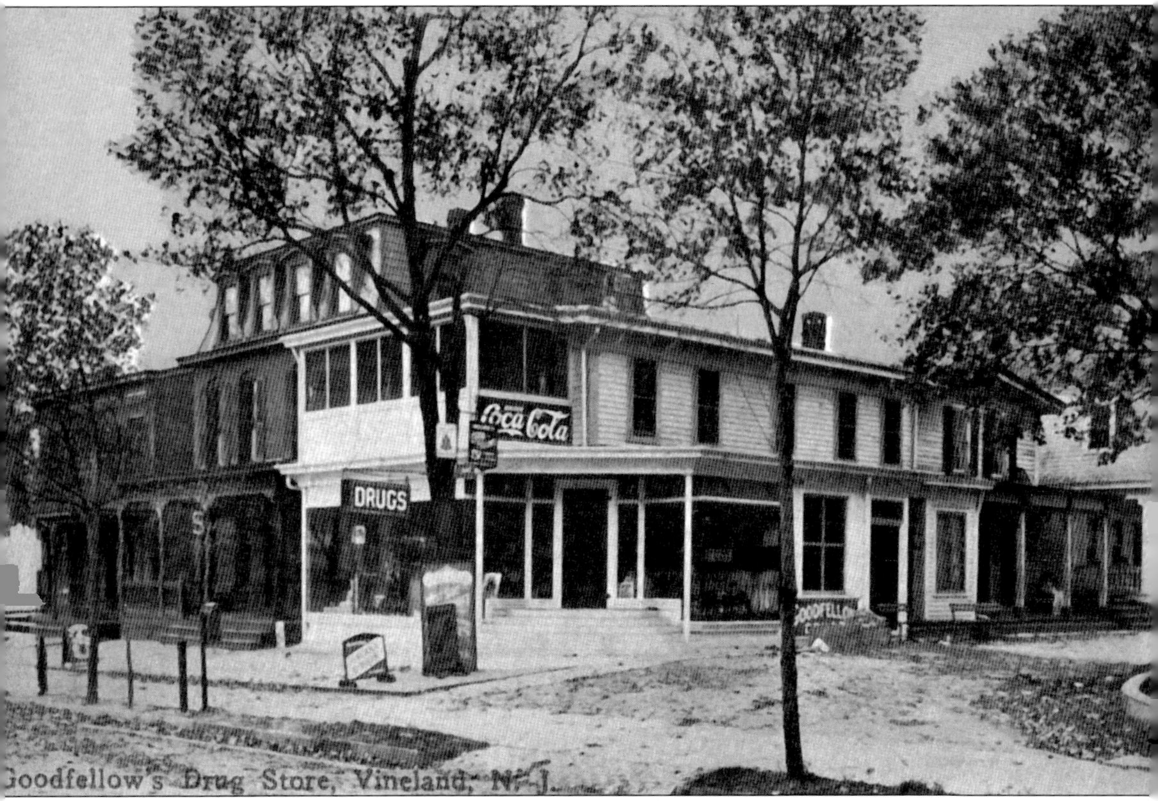

Goodfellow's Pharmacy, at the intersection of Landis Avenue and Railroad Boulevard, was just one of many drugstores operating in Vineland by the late 19th century. Like other pharmacies such as Conwell's, Matlack's, and Winslow's, Goodfellow's offered a range of often homemade medications that were sold in locally produced bottles that bore their names and logos.

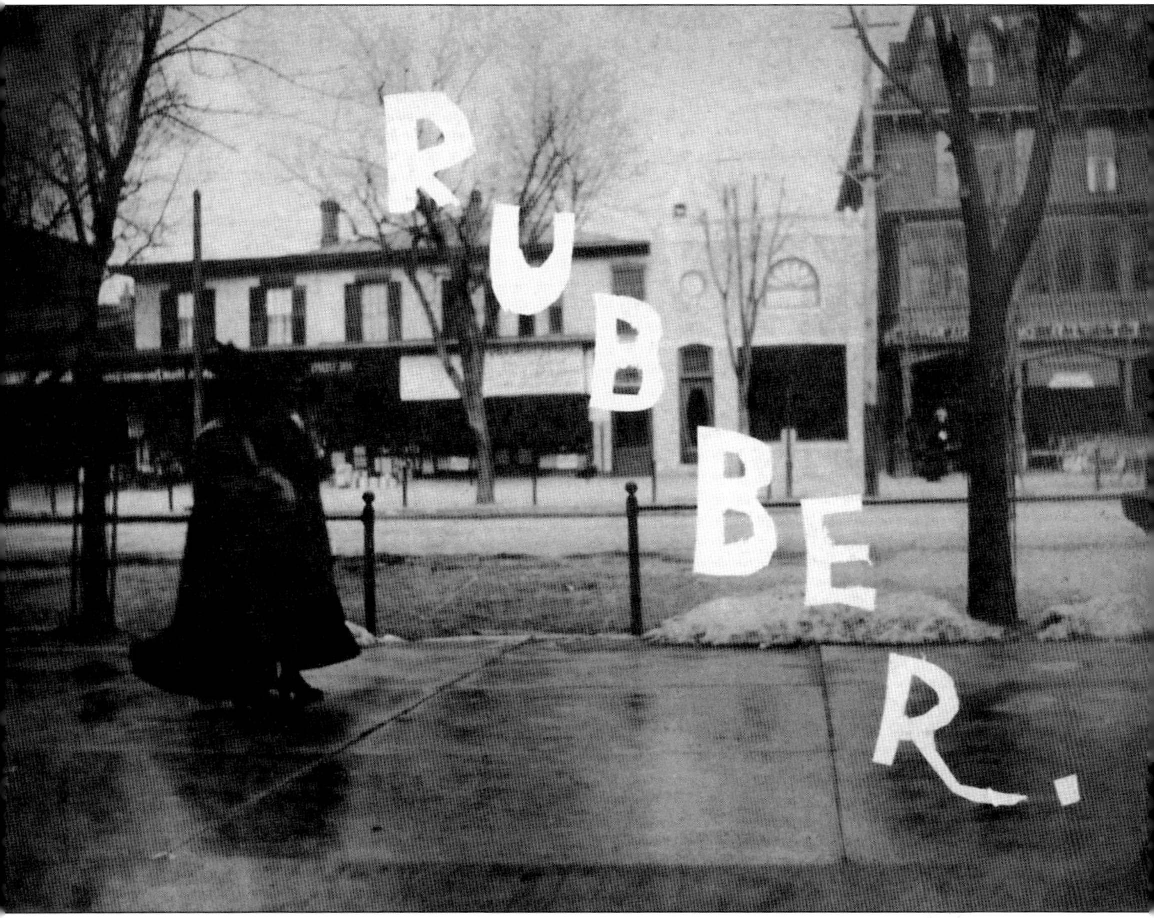

As the popularity of bicycles, motorcycles, and the automobile continued to spread throughout South Jersey, specialty shops such as F. Earl Rickerd's business on Landis Avenue offered a variety of rubber products, including tires and tubes in the 1920s. In addition, they often employed mechanics who could repair or replace different parts.

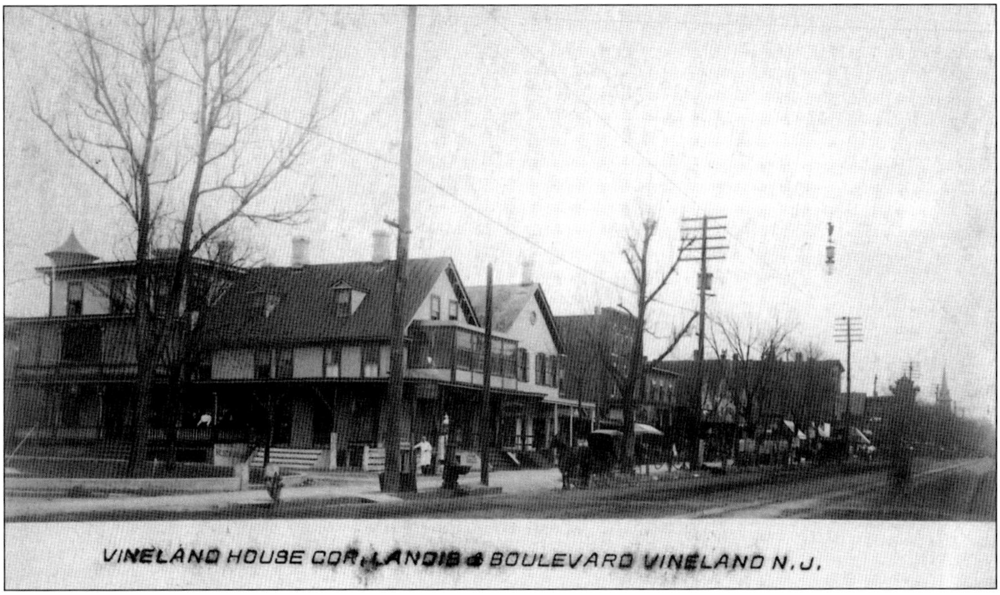

With all of the activity humming on Landis Avenue in the 19th century, a few local residents decided to try their skill at running restaurants. Between the visitors who were curious to see the new town and settlers who arrived to make Vineland their new home, there was never any shortage of customers.

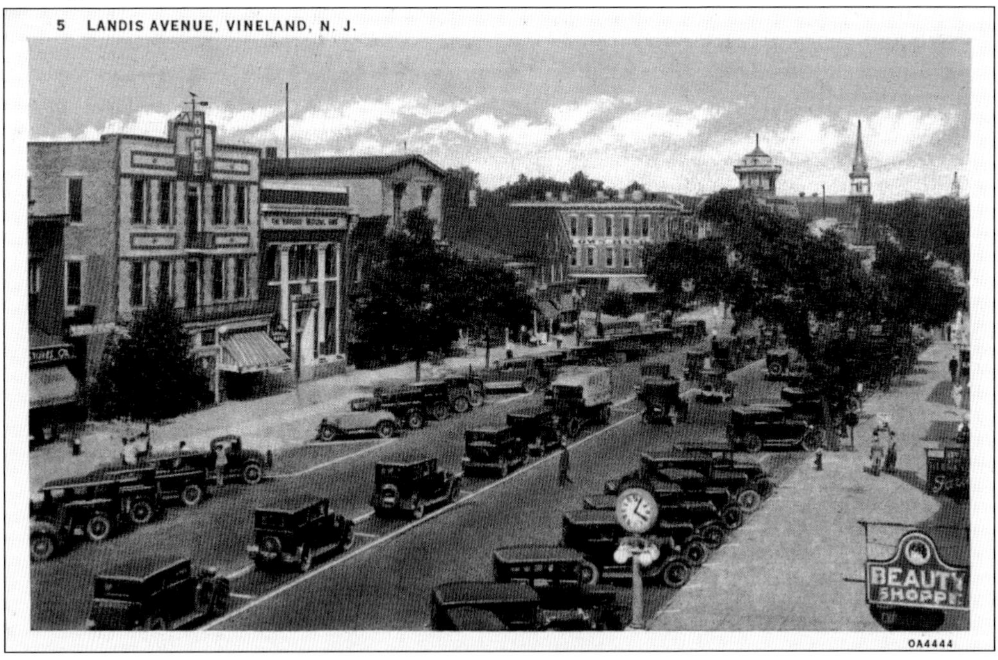

New businesses continued to open in the 1920s and 1930s on Landis Avenue, where the automobile eventually replaced the horse-and-wagons that once paraded there. By then, the street was paved and the sidewalks were broadened to accommodate shoppers, who could still find virtually everything they needed downtown. Longtime businesses such as Sears, Roebuck and Co. grew so quickly that they later had to expand or move to entirely new locations to accommodate their growing customer base.

Two

Business and Agriculture

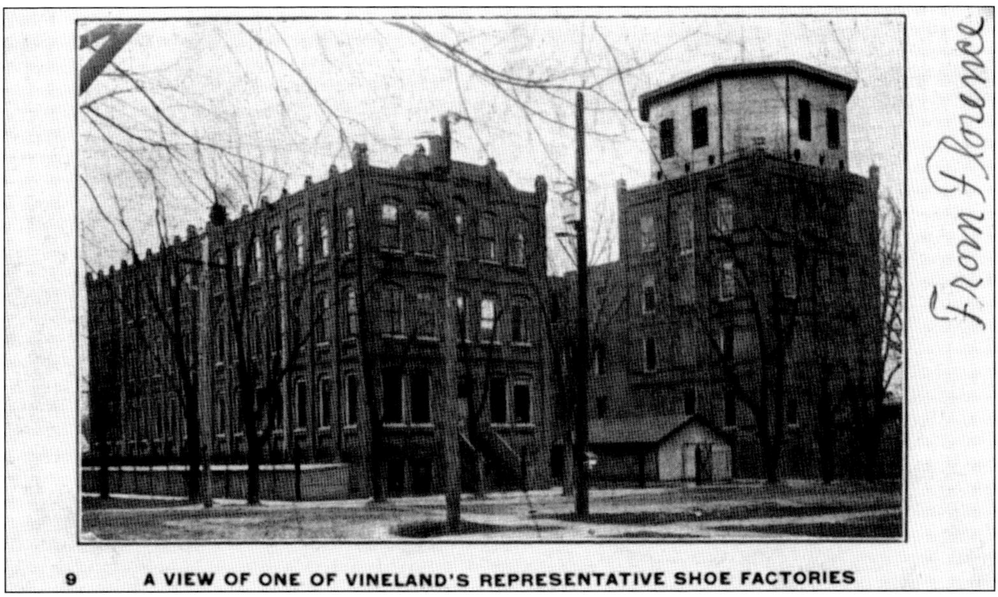

The Charles P. Keighley shoe factory, located at Sixth and Montrose Streets, was the foremost manufacturer of shoes in Vineland. In the late 1800s, the company produced 1,500 pairs of shoes per day, which were shipped to department stores all along the East Coast. Keighley also made shoe manufacturing equipment that was sold to other factories throughout the United States.

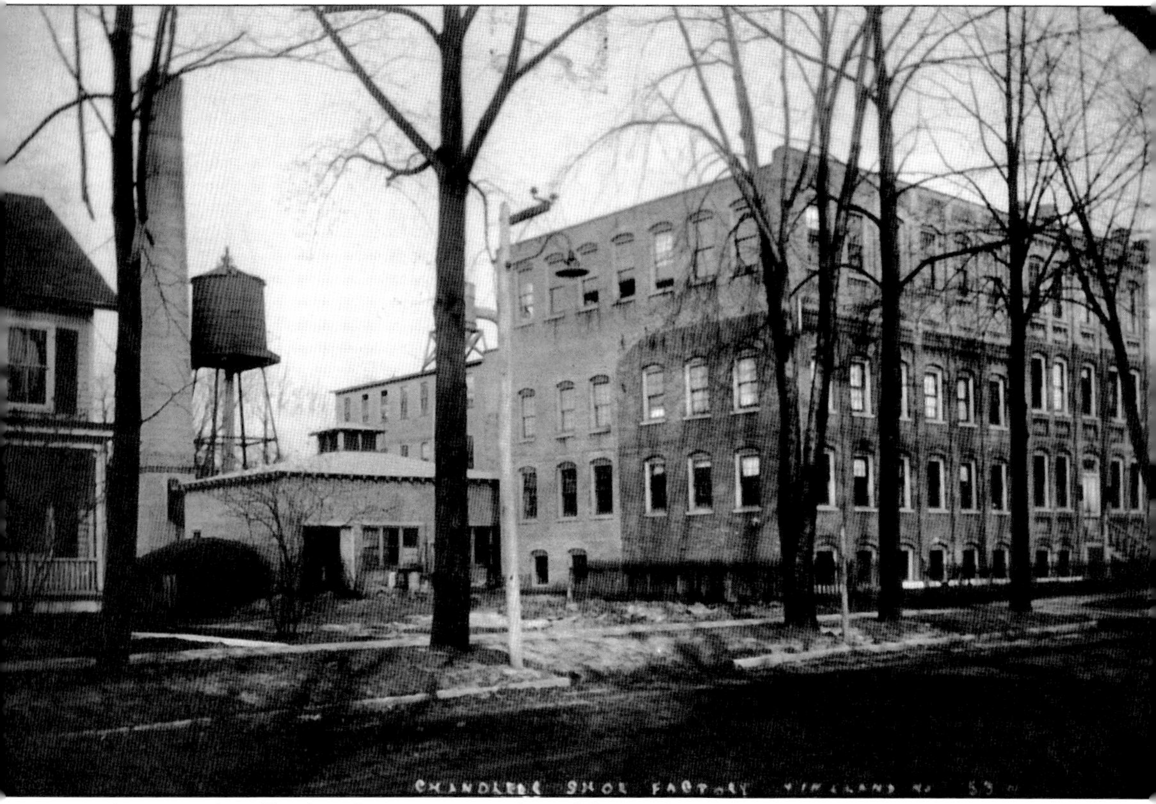

The D.H. Chandler shoe factory was another of the six shoe companies once located in Vineland. Like Charles P. Keighley, Chandler was an experienced shoemaker before he opened his factory on Montrose Street in Vineland. The business grew quickly and, before long, Chandler was producing about 1,000 pairs of shoes per day that were sold to department stores in Philadelphia and New York.

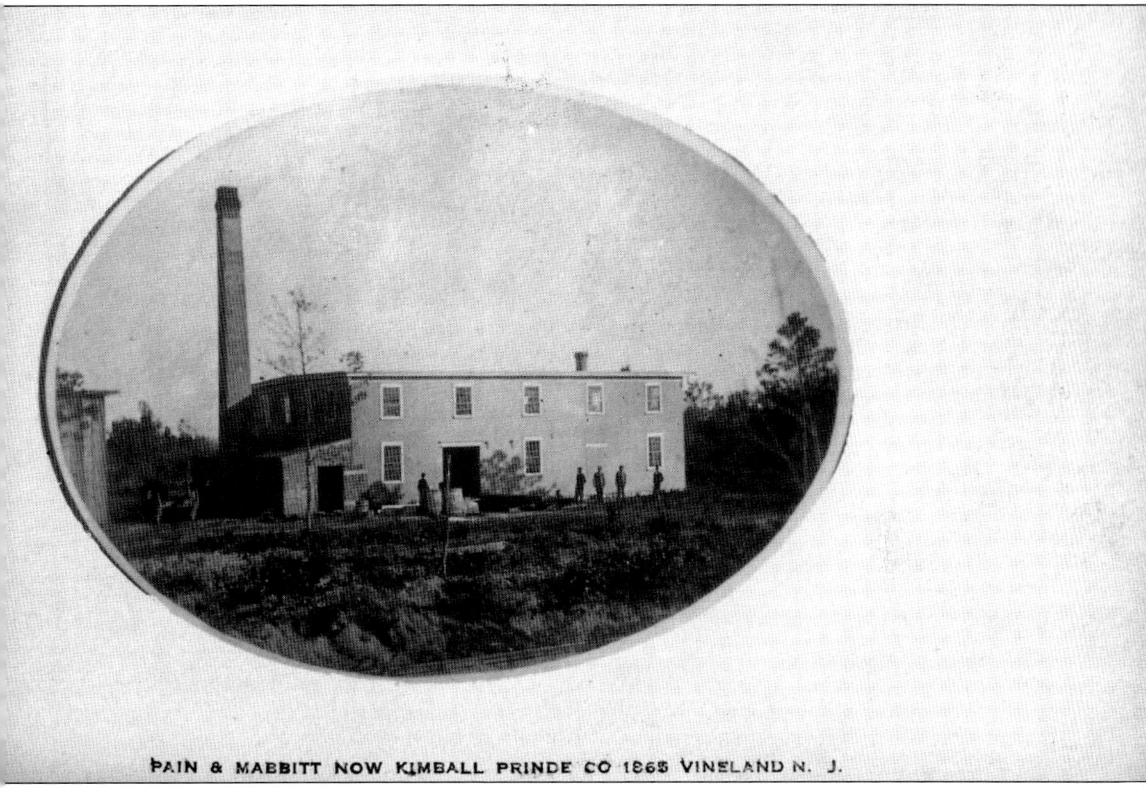

Truman Mabbett was another early Vineland entrepreneur; he built this sash factory on the corner of Railroad Boulevard and Almond Street in 1865, where it produced window and door sashes until 1870. The following year, the company was sold to the Kimball & Prince Lumber Company, which remained in business at that location well into the 20th century.

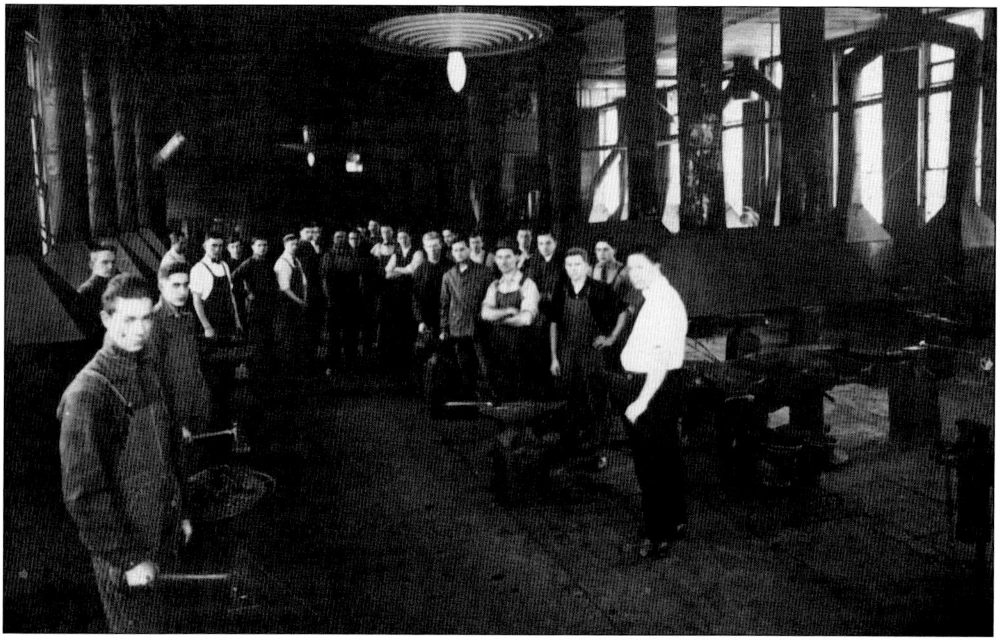

Three iron foundries were known to have operated in Vineland in the late 19th and early 20th centuries. Although South Jersey's iron industry had reached its height in the early 1800s, such local foundries had success crafting products for area residents ranging from grave markers to decorative fencing. Proximity to the railroad at the center of town also allowed them easy access to markets up and down the Eastern Seaboard.

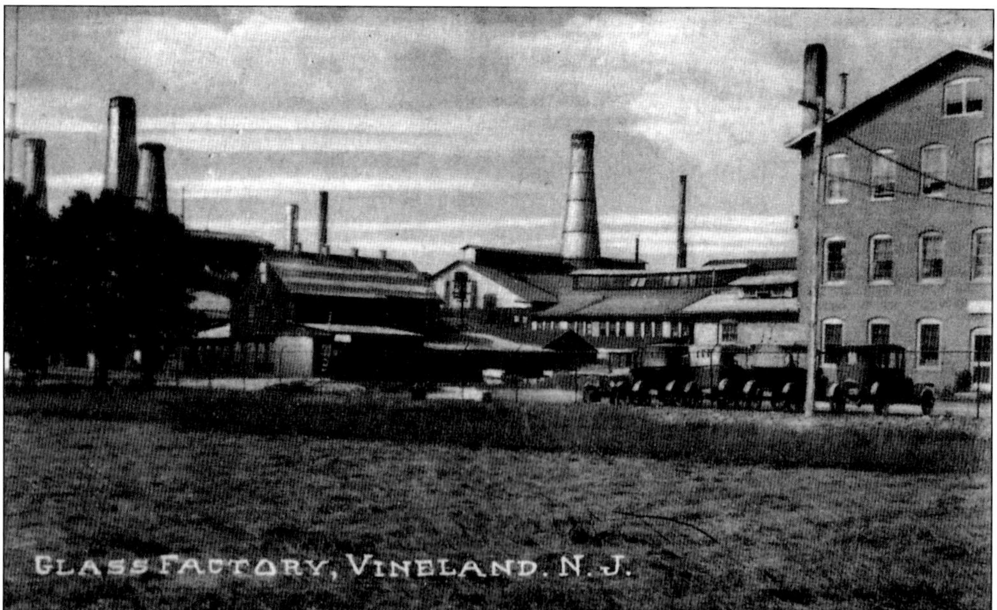

In 1924, the Vineland Flint Glass Works, owned by Victor Durand Jr., embarked on a new venture that would result in the creation of Durand art glass. Although the "fancy shop" division of the company was only in operation for seven years, the glass artisans employed there created elegant decorative glassware and tableware that is still prized today by collectors.

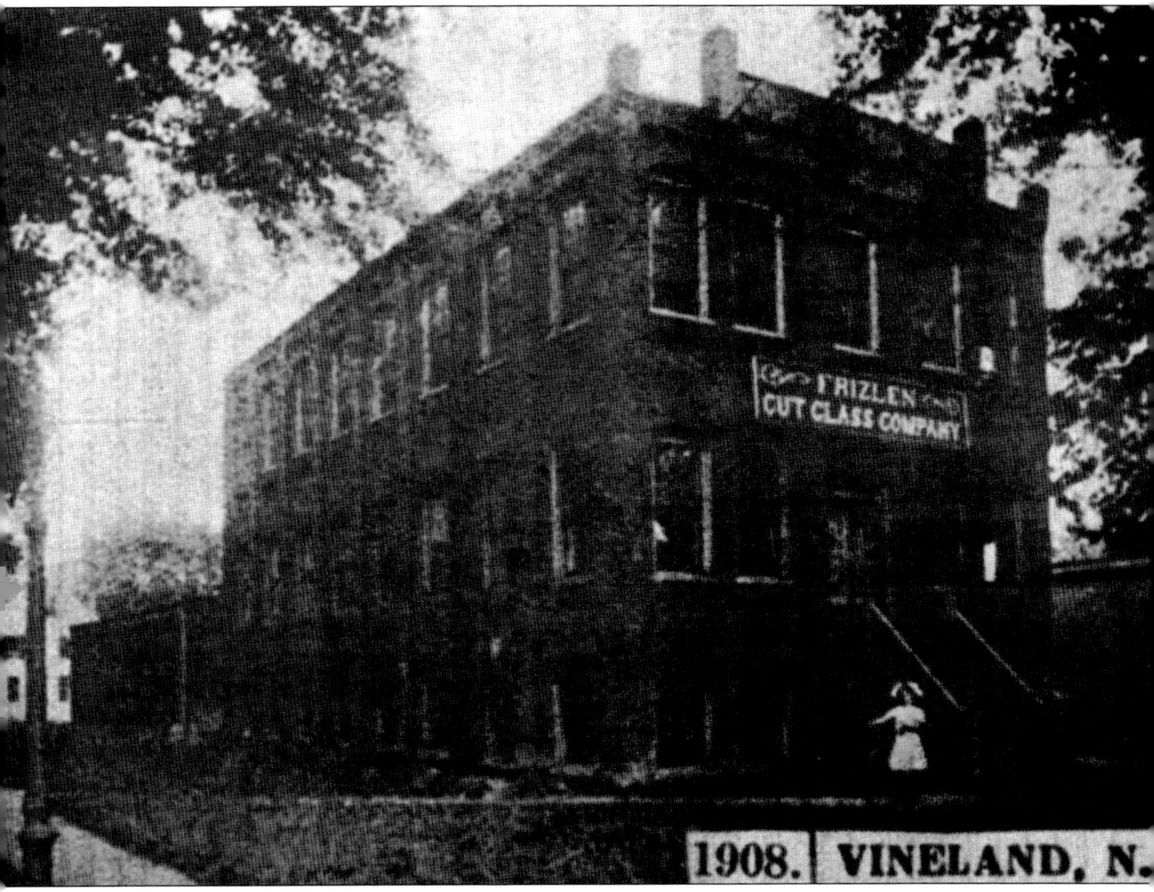

The glass industry thrived in South Jersey because the natural ingredients needed to create glassware—silica sand and trees from the Pine Barrens, which was used to fuel the glasshouse furnaces—were nearby. One of Vineland's best-kept secrets was the Frizlen Cut Glass Company, which started there in 1905 but moved a few years later to neighboring Cherry Hill. Unfortunately, since the company had no signature pattern, it is difficult to identify the glassware produced there.

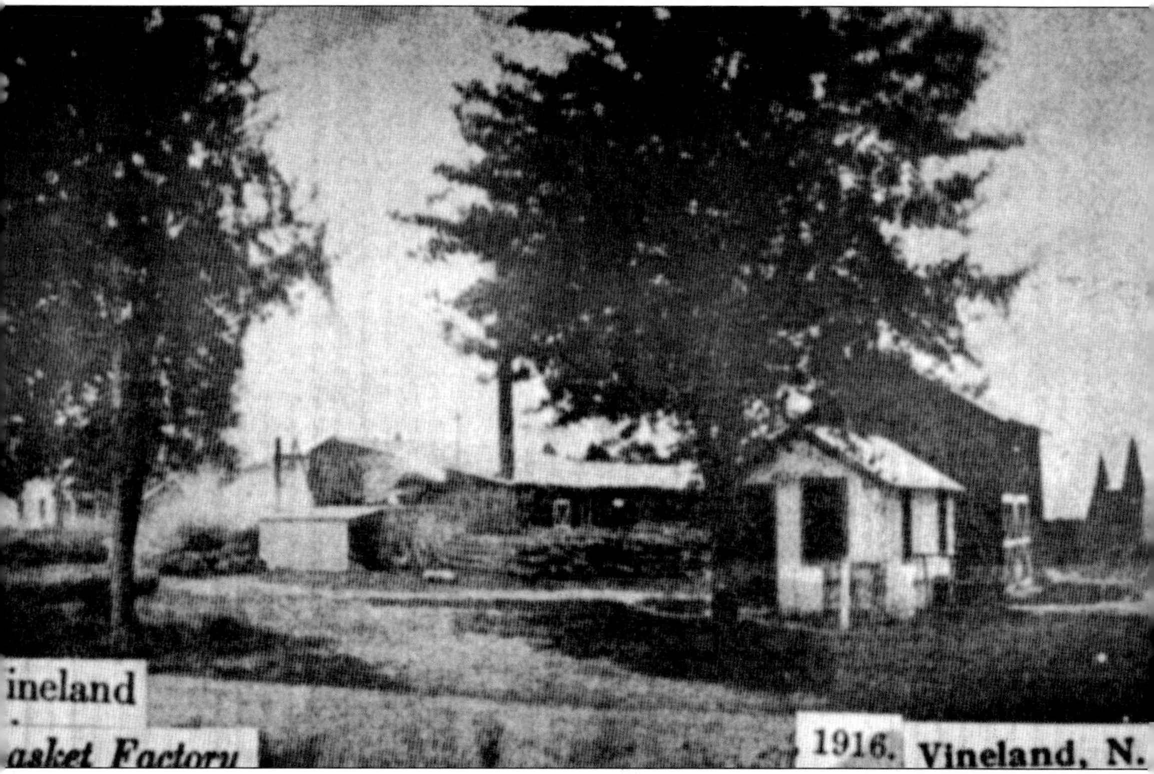

The Vineland Basket Company, which employed about 30 people, was rechristened in 1912 after Dr. Thomas B. Welch bought partial interest in George Blizzard's Jersey Package Company. Located at the corner of Fourth and France Streets, it was the first company of its type in New Jersey to use machines to produce its fruit baskets, truck baskets, and hamper baskets.

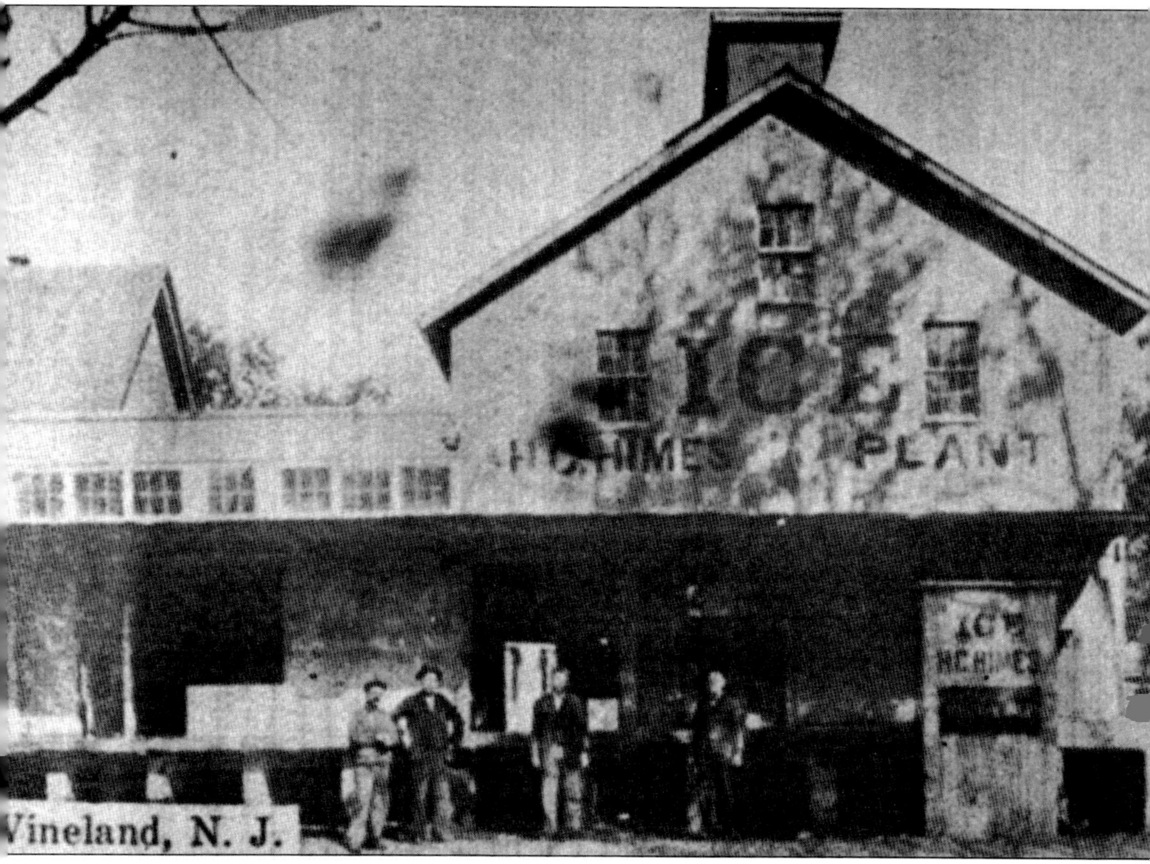

Another innovation, the icebox, caught the attention of local Vineland residents in the late 19th century. After moving to Vineland in 1898, H.C. Himes bought a refrigerating plant at 522 Elmer Street from W.G. Marshall. Himes operated the company until 1920, when he sold his interest to another firm. He remained active with the business until it was sold again in the 1950s.

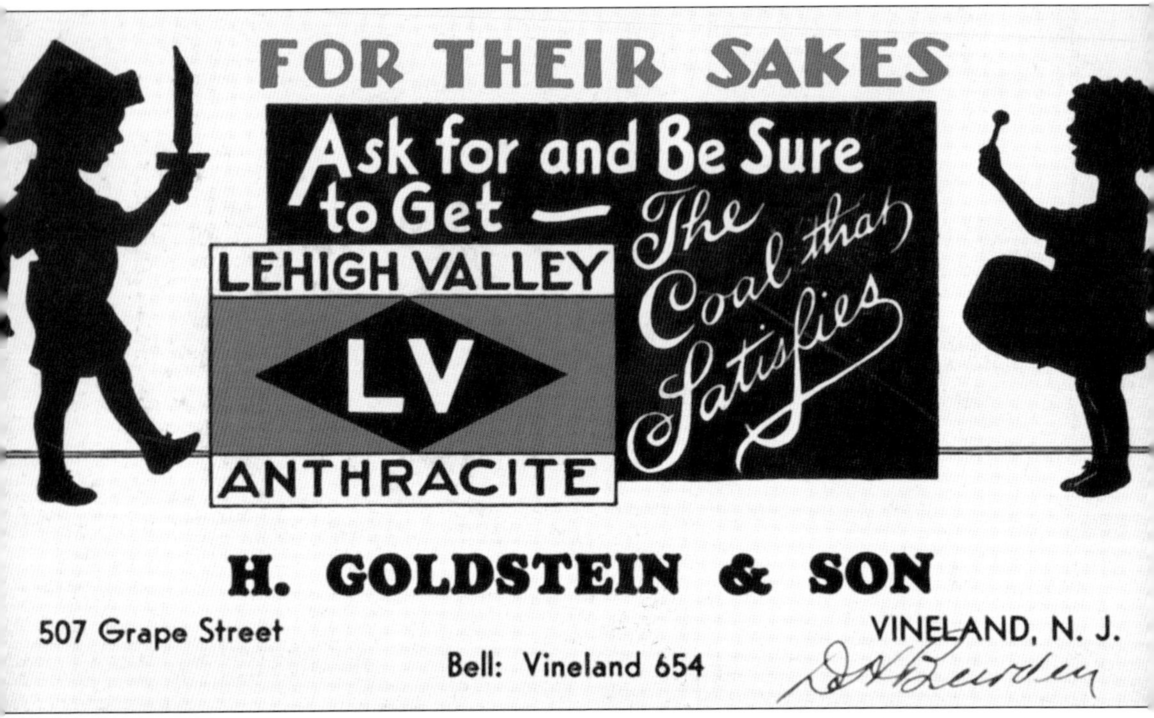

Coal dealers like H. Goldstein & Son, headquartered on Grape Street, offered Vineland residents Lehigh Valley anthracite coal, transported to town by rail from Pennsylvania. The company competed with other local businesses such as S. Weintraub & Son and Cheli & Son for customers in Vineland, where coal was an important source of heating for homes and businesses in the late 19th and early 20th centuries.

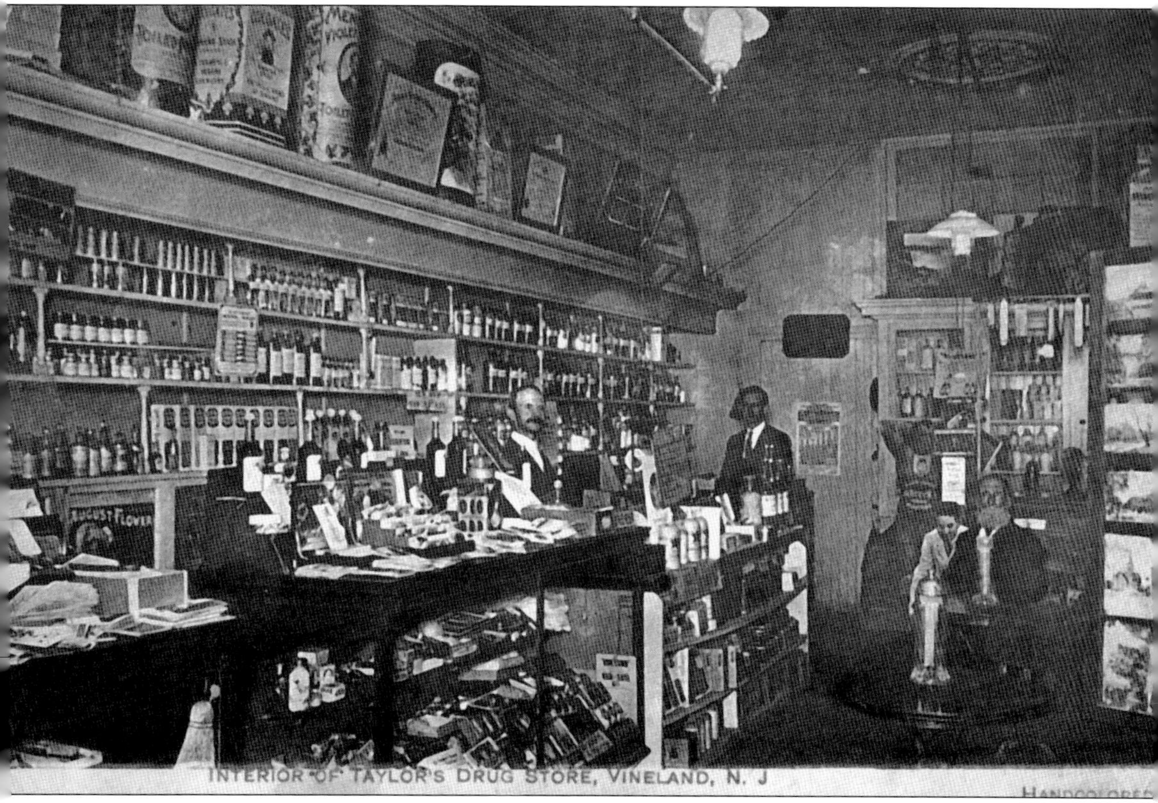

In addition to a real estate agency, Alex Taylor owned and operated Taylor's Drug Store on Landis Avenue, which was just one of many pharmacies that operated in Vineland in the late 19th and early 20th centuries. Local pharmacists often compounded their own medications, which could include everything from cocaine or mercury mixed with a splash of alcohol.

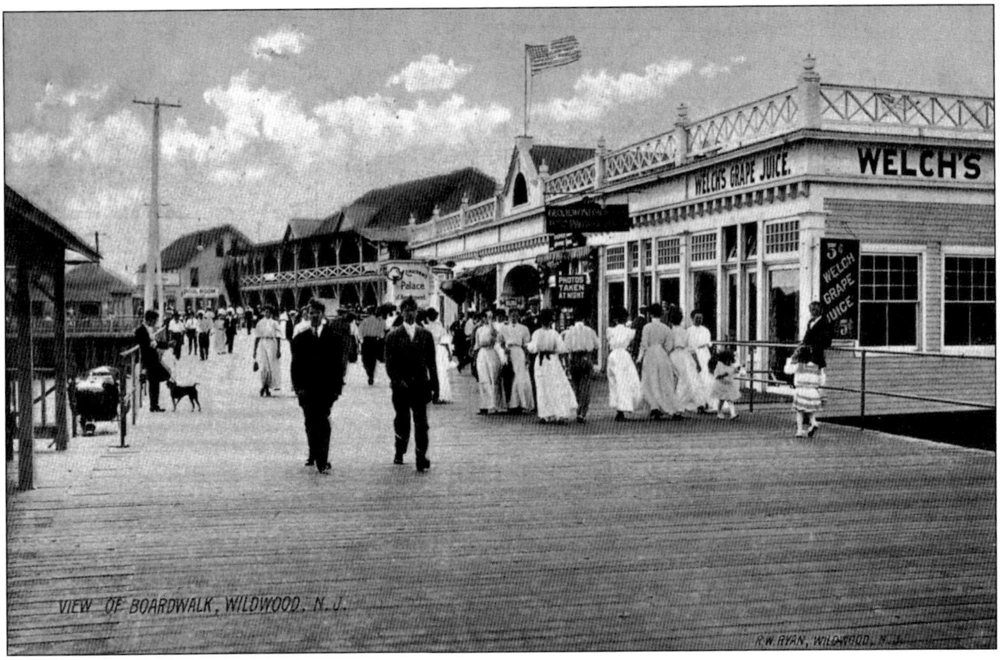

In 1869, Dr. Thomas B. Welch, a dentist who was an early settler in Vineland, invented his formula for making juice instead of wine from grapes. His new company was so successful that before long, he was promoting the drink to health-conscious Americans who visited resorts like nearby Wildwood. Welch's success opened the door for many competitors, including the Vineland Grape Juice Company, which operated on the Railroad Boulevard in Vineland. In 1903, the factory site was purchased by the Limpert Brothers. Today, it still produces Marshmallow Fluff, syrups, and dessert toppings made famous by the company in the early 20th century.

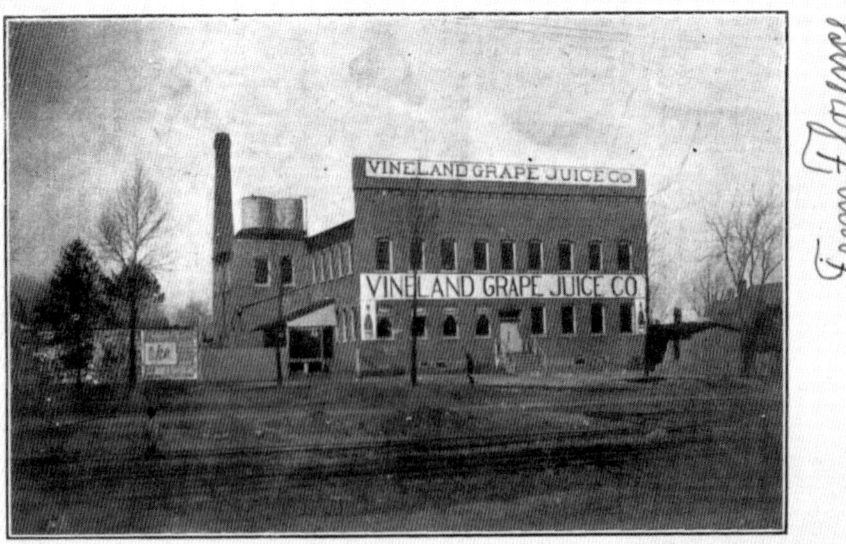

10 A VIEW OF ONE OF VINELAND'S GRAPE JUICE FACTORIES

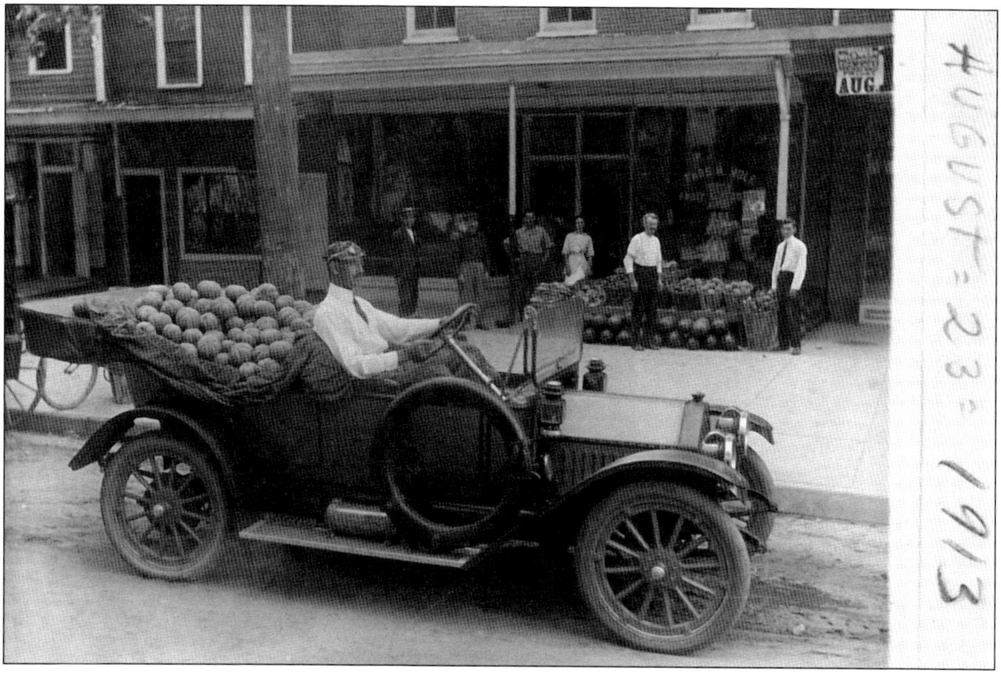

While the automobile was still a novelty in 1913, the Vineland residents watching it pass were probably more surprised to see that it was filled with fresh-picked melons. Charles Landis was not wrong when he predicted that fruit would be the most important product produced in town. In addition to melons, Vineland peaches, strawberries, and cranberries were shipped weekly by train to markets in Philadelphia and New York.

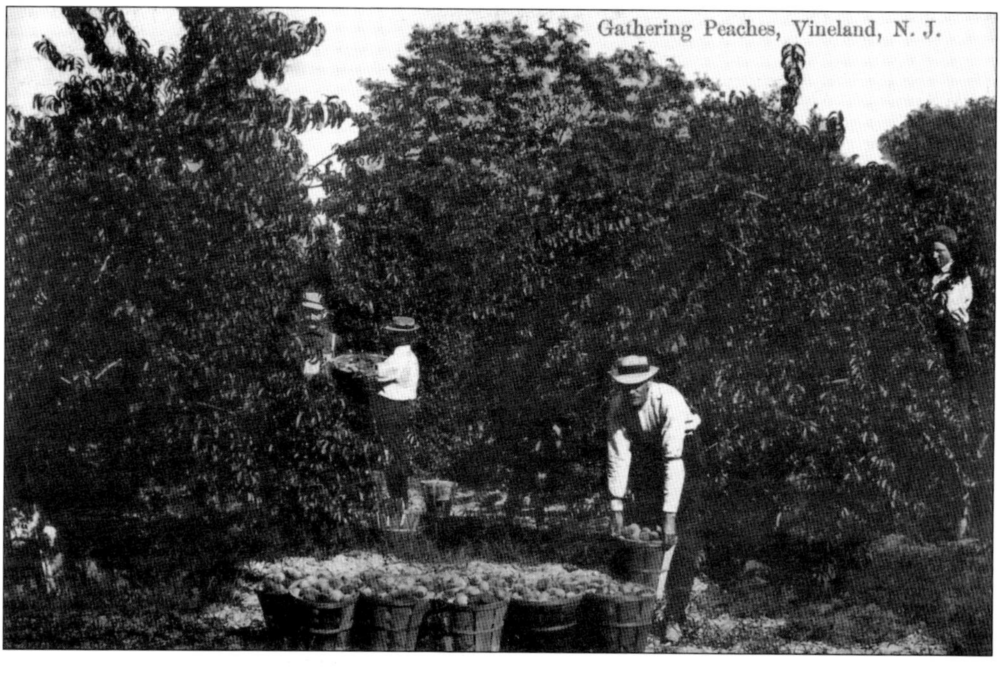

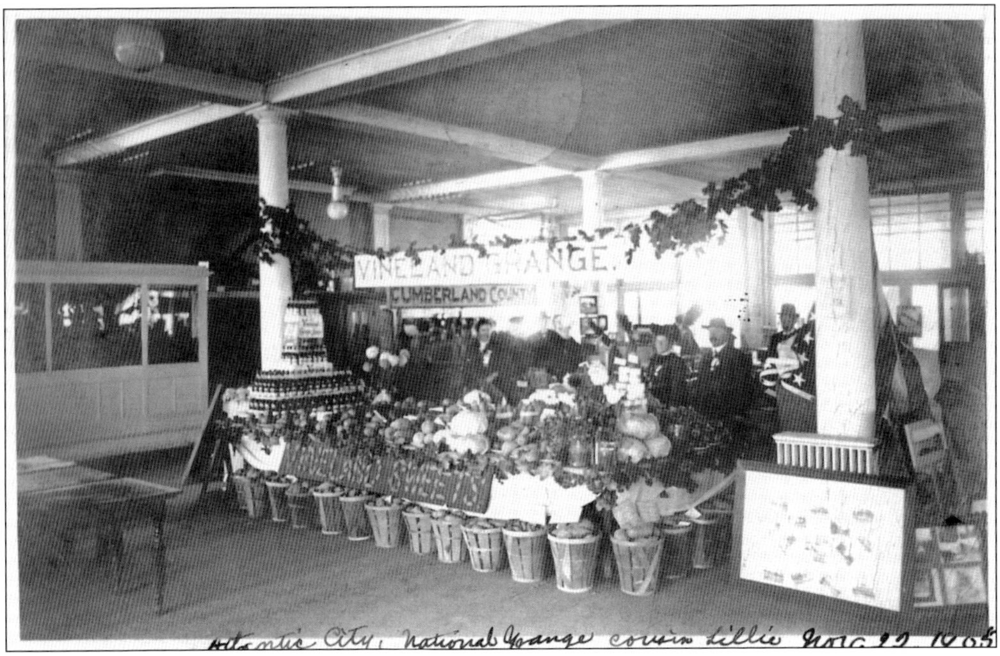

On November 22, 1905, the Vineland Grange set up a booth in Atlantic City at a Grange exhibition to promote locally grown products, including sweet potatoes, grapes, and more. The Grange was a national organization established in 1867 to promote agriculture throughout the United States. In 2005, it still counted 160,000 members in more than 2,000 towns.

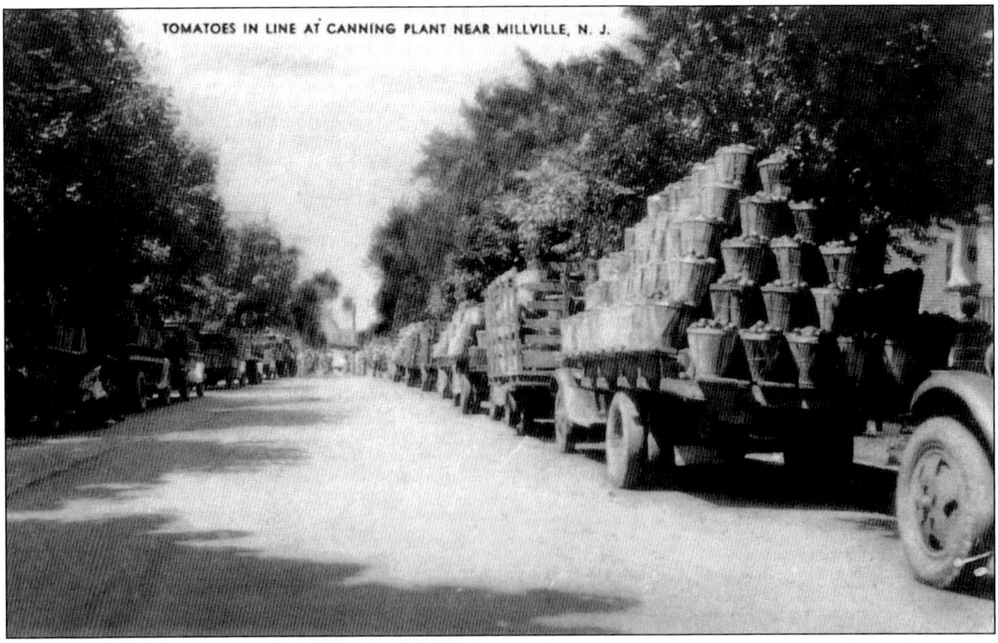

The apparently endless line of trucks carrying locally grown tomatoes to a canning plant near Millville was once a common sight in South Jersey. After immigrants from southern Italy arrived in Vineland in the late 19th and early 20th centuries, many of them produced this crop, which had been a staple in their homeland.

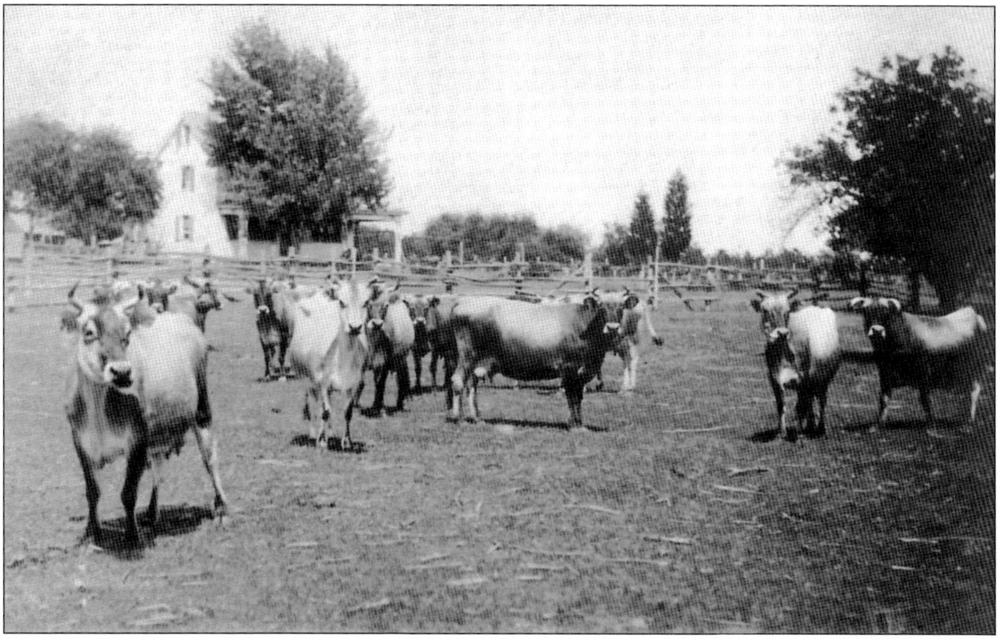

The "Bovine War" was fought in Vineland in 1864 after too many cattle destroyed the crops of local farmers. To stop them, a group of area residents formed an association known as the Cattle League. After league members argued with the cattle owners, hundreds of dead cattle were discovered in out-of-the-way places around Vineland. However, reason soon prevailed, and the Bovine War stopped almost as quickly as it started.

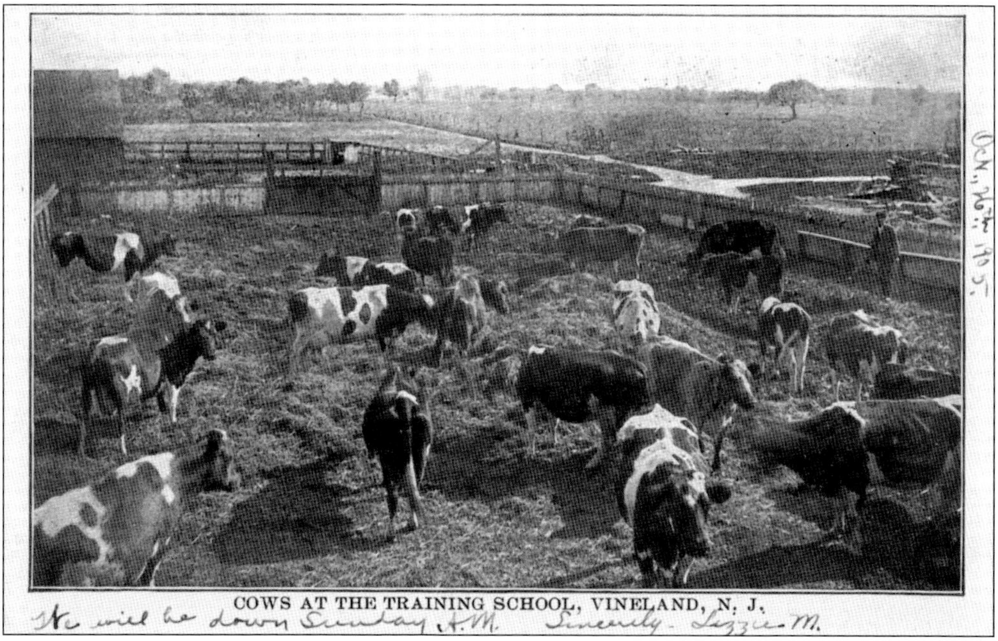

Raising cattle also provided occupational training for the residents of the Vineland Training School, an institution for mentally challenged young men. The facility encouraged its residents to learn different types of trades, including farming, woodcarving, and weaving, which helped the training school to remain self-supporting for many years.

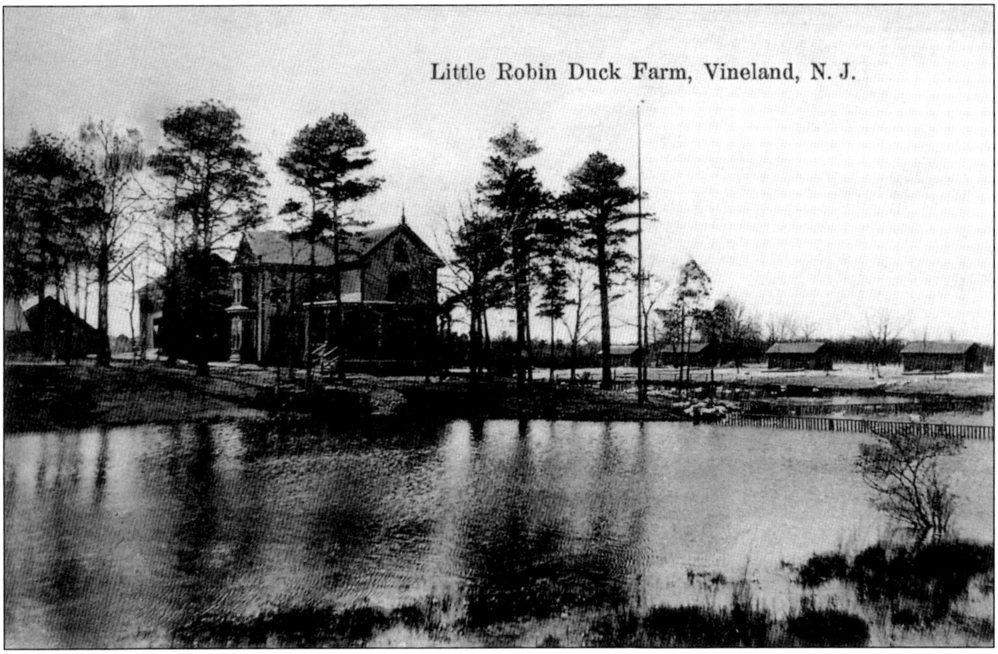

In the early 1900s, Little Robin Duck Farm, on West Landis Avenue, was known statewide for its high quality standards and innovative technology. Situated on 18 acres bordered by a freshwater stream, the farm had room for 7,000 ducks and incubators for the eggs they laid. Horace G. Huey, the owner, ran the farm with the help of five assistants. By 1920, the farm was selling approximately 30,000 ducks each year to hotels.

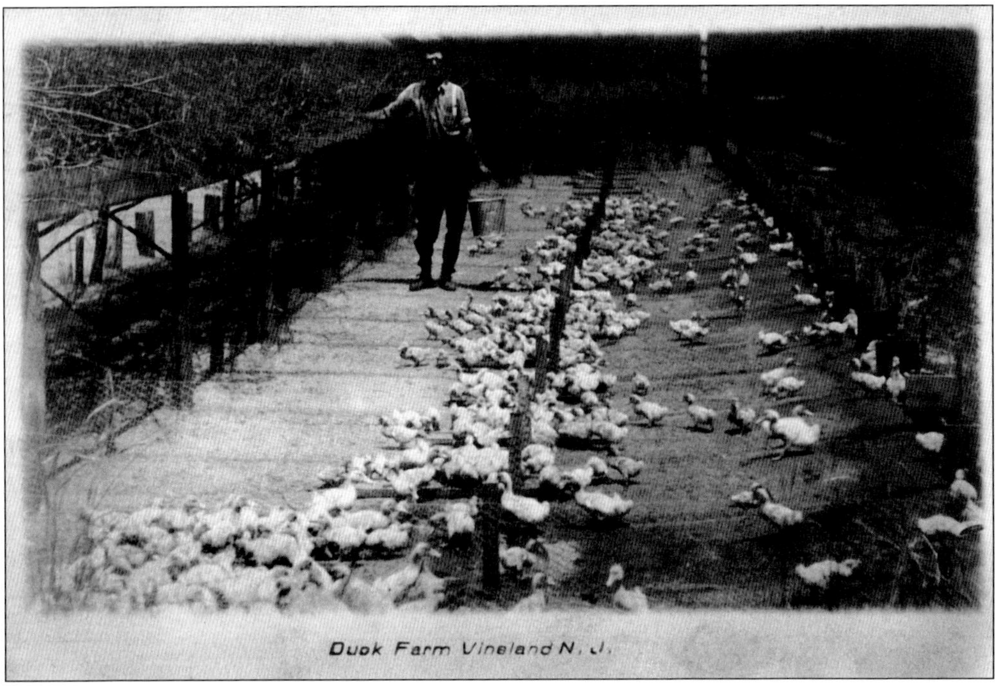

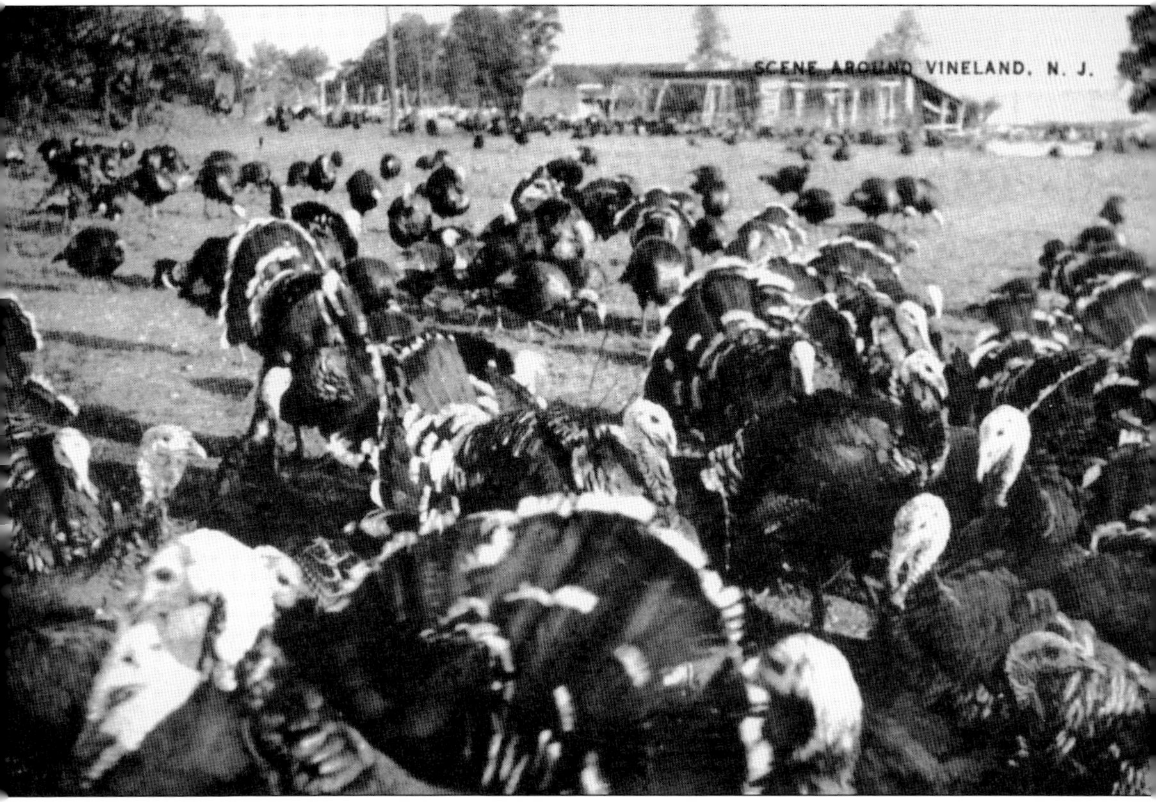

Ducks were not the only delicacy raised in Vineland. In addition to squab, local farmers also raised turkeys to sell to market. Descended from the wild turkeys that still roam South Jersey, the domesticated variety became extremely popular in the early 20th century when it became a staple of most Americans' Thanksgiving dinners.

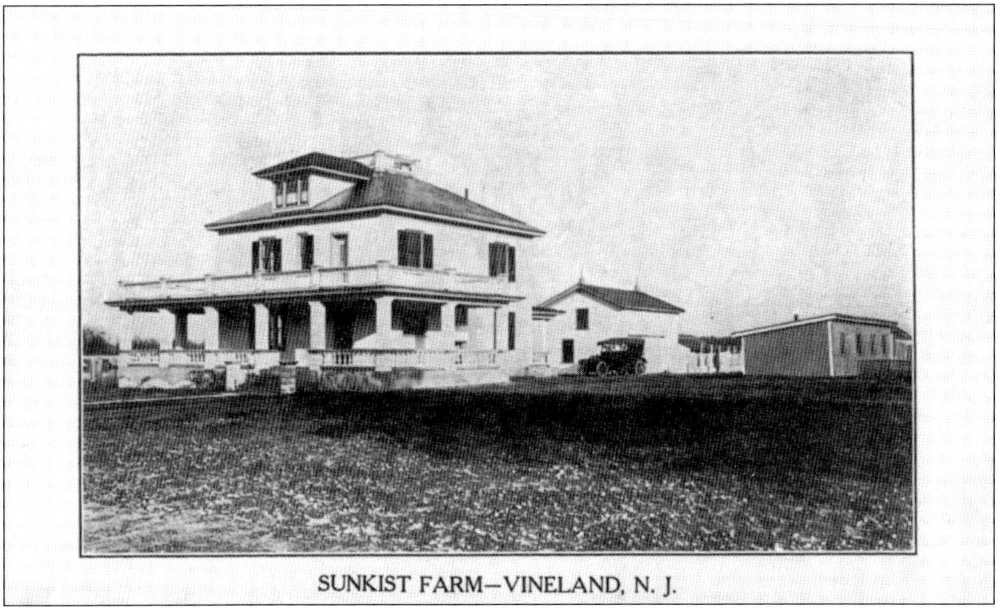

Sunkist Poultry Farm, which won an award for its poultry in 1922 at the Trenton Fair Show, was just one of many farms in Vineland that raised chickens. Part of their success was probably attributable to Vineland veterinarian Dr. Arthur Goldhaft, who invented a serum to protect the chickens from disease.

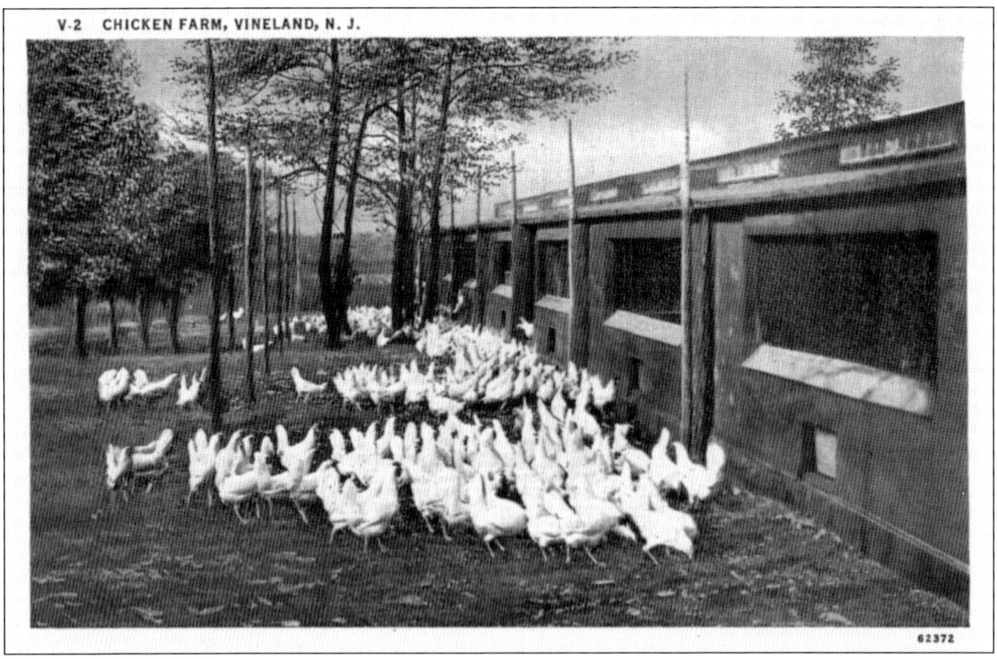

As a result of Dr. Arthur Goldhaft's work at Vineland Poultry Laboratories, the poultry industry flourished. The town eventually became known as the "Egg Capital of the East," shipping eggs for many years to major markets along the East Coast.

Three

Residential

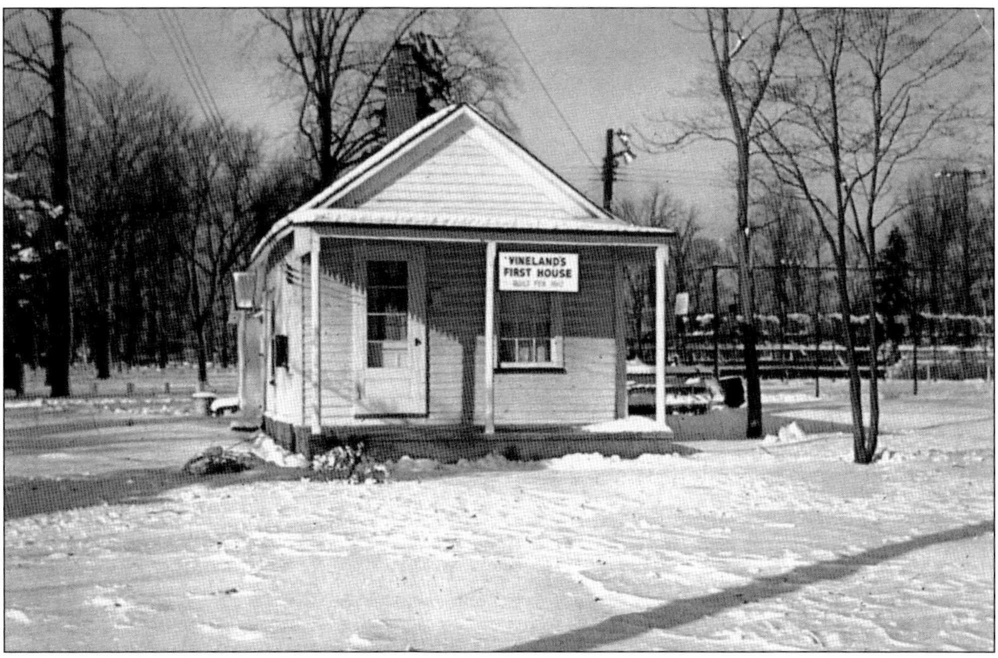

Vineland's first house was built by Chester P. Davis and Lester Richardson on the north corner of Landis Avenue and Railroad Boulevard in 1862, where it may have served for a time as the town's post office. The structure was later moved to the opposite side of the boulevard and eventually relocated to Landis Park. The house was occupied until 1962, when it was moved to the grounds of the Vineland Historical and Antiquarian Society's museum, where it is open to the public for tours.

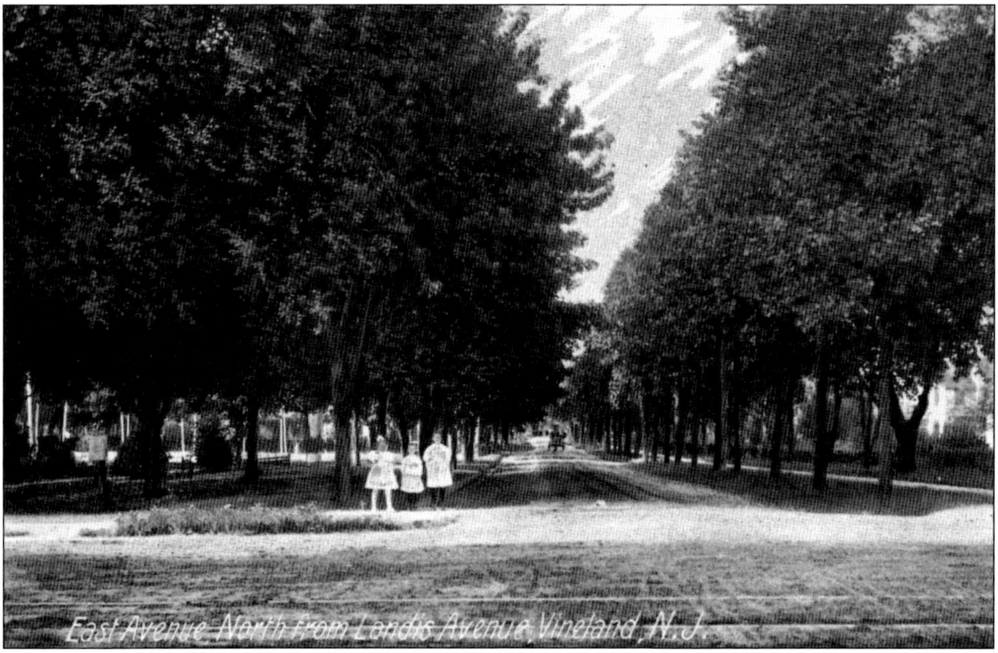

There were many fine residences built in Vineland as the town prospered. Among them was a handsome, large brick house with a mansard roof built on Landis Avenue by H.N. Green. Prof. Marcius Willson, a well-known author who lived on East Landis Avenue about two miles away from the downtown, owned a Gothic home surrounded by piazzas, vines, and shade trees. Opposite Willson's house was a large mansion with a mansard roof owned by George Scarborough.

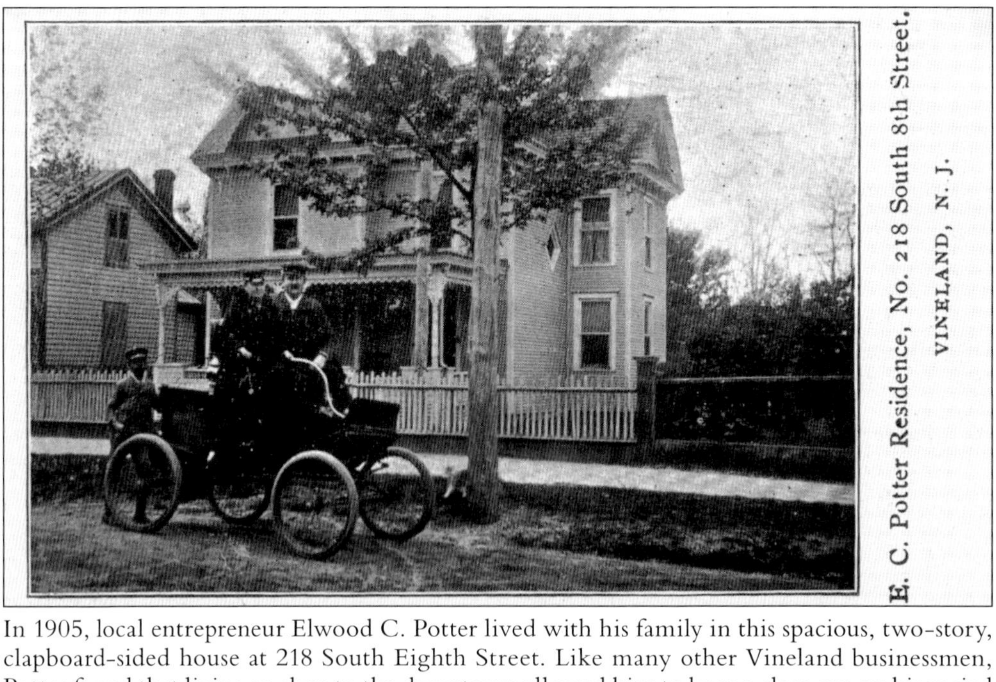

In 1905, local entrepreneur Elwood C. Potter lived with his family in this spacious, two-story, clapboard-sided house at 218 South Eighth Street. Like many other Vineland businessmen, Potter found that living so close to the downtown allowed him to keep a close eye on his varied business interests.

The B.R. Little residence, like so many of Vineland's older homes, no longer stands. But it may have been one of the early homes built by some of the early settlers who arrived in the spring of 1862. James Stewart established the first farm in Landis Township, on Landis Avenue just east of Spring Road. Soon afterward, Augustus Washburn built a house on Landis Avenue west of the railroad. By January 1864, a total of 1,000 acres of land had been sold to different settlers who planned to start small farms.

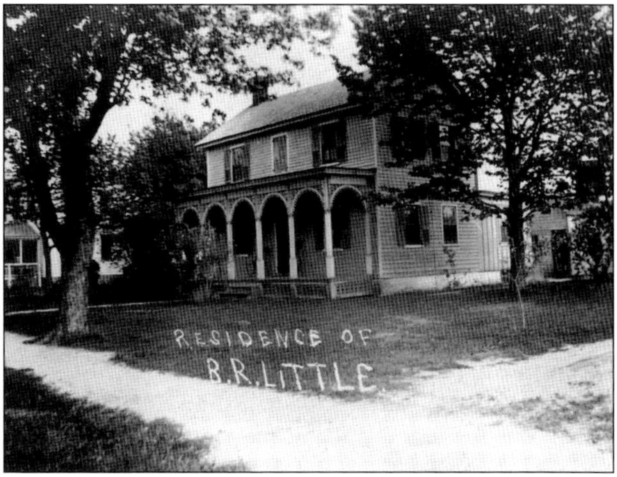

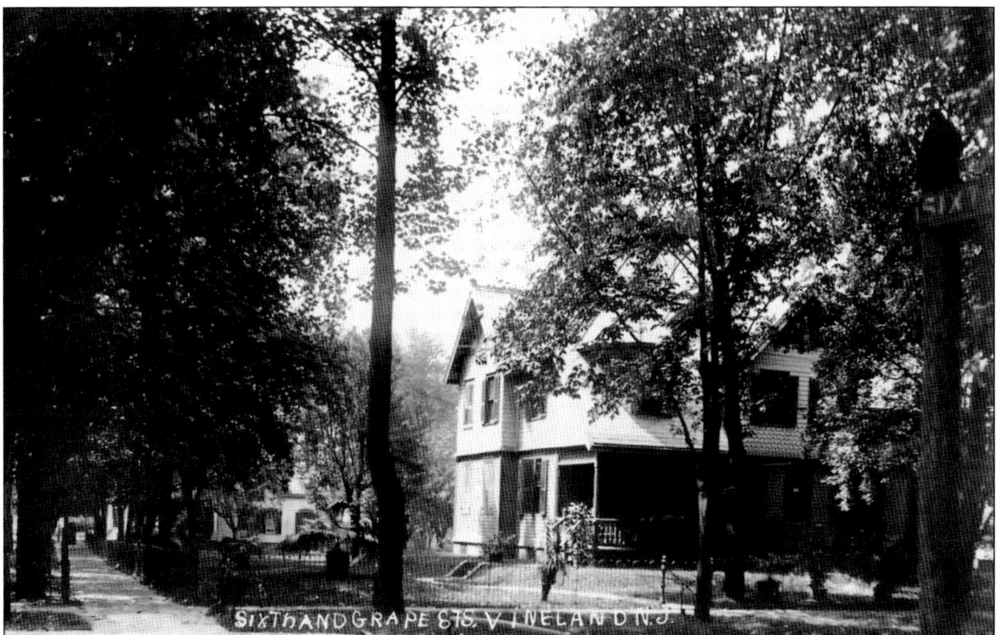

This rambling house that once stood at the intersection of Sixth and Grape Streets was typical of the homes that sprang up in Vineland in the late 19th and early 20th centuries. While styles ranged dramatically from neo–English cottages to grand Gothic houses, most of them were large enough to accommodate the average family, which often included grandparents or other relatives, as well as a servant or two.

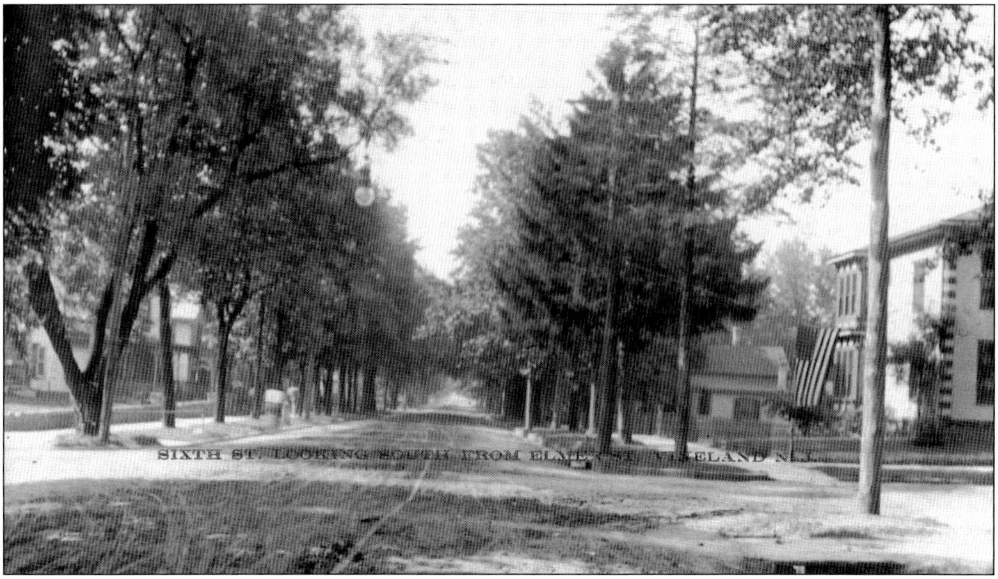

While lots located within the one square mile of the town were often about an acre in size, home prices, like properties in the surrounding township, could range from $1,000 to $5,500 depending on the size of the lots and the number of structures they contained. A number of people tried to infiltrate the real estate market in Vineland in the early years, but Charles K. Landis retained a tight rein on his holdings.

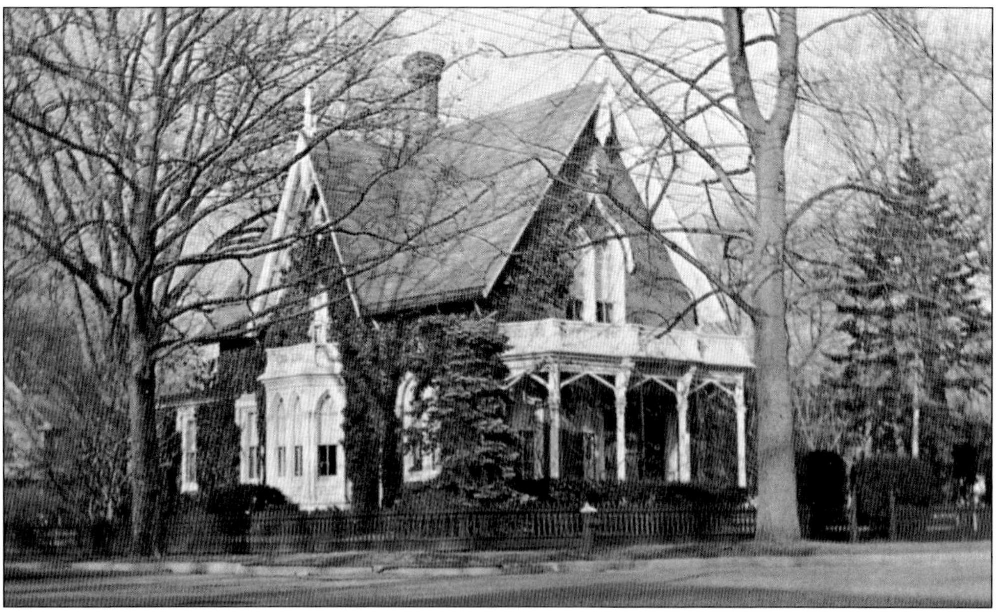

Henry Hartson built a brick residence on the northeast corner of Seventh and Wood Streets, a structure that has changed little since it was first constructed in the mid-19th century. His neighbors included S.G. Sylvester and A.W. Thorndike, who also built imposing brick and stone homes with modern conveniences and elegant flower gardens. The Hartson house was later occupied by Thelma Parkinson Sharp, the president of New Jersey's Civil Service Commission for almost 20 years and a delegate-at-large for New Jersey to the Democratic National Convention; she attended each one between 1924 and 1976.

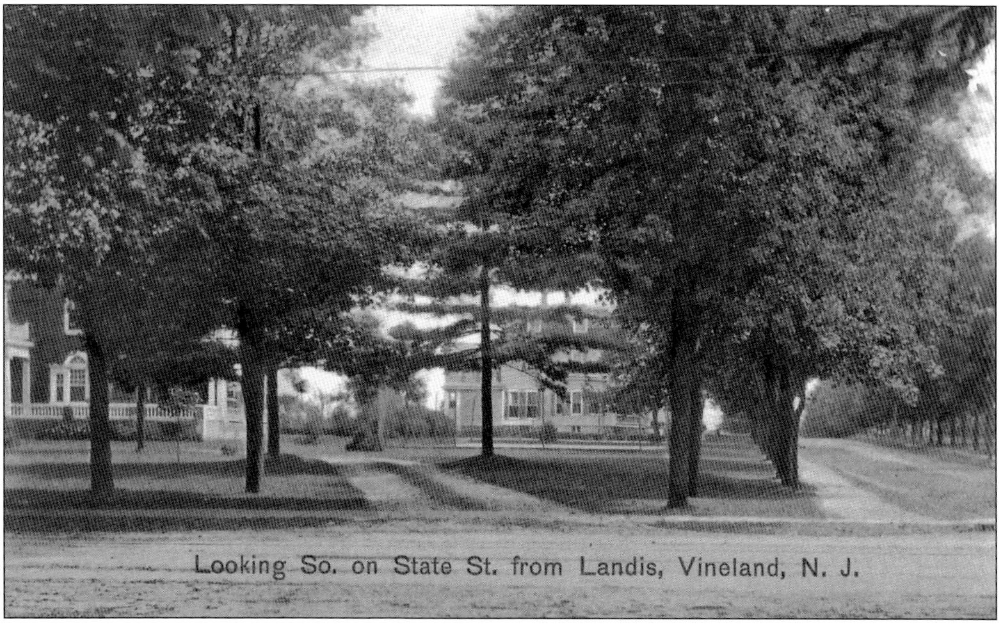

Although not on Charles K. Landis's original plans, State Street was considered a highly desirable neighborhood almost immediately after it was opened. As Vineland's reputation as a "cultural mecca" attracted more and more new settlers, Landis found it necessary to survey and open new streets to accommodate the growing population.

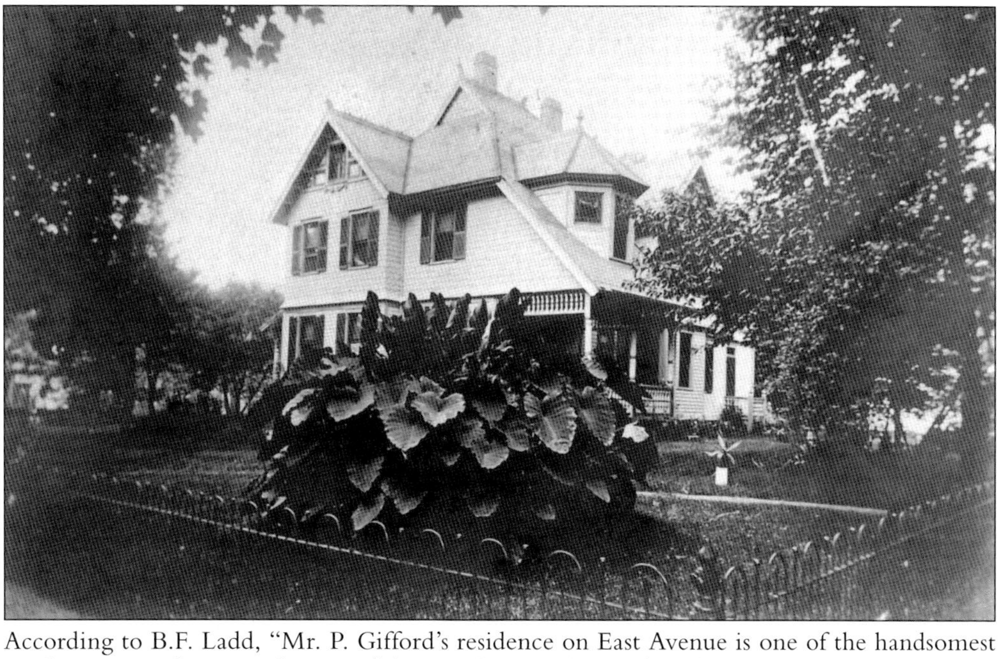

According to B.F. Ladd, "Mr. P. Gifford's residence on East Avenue is one of the handsomest on that street. The grounds are well kept and covered with fine shade trees. Mr. D.F. Morrell and Judge Doughty each have elegant brick residences nearly opposite. Mr. Isaac Hoag's large mansard roof mansion is situated on Pear Street, corner of Sixth." Wheaton Berault's attractive home on Elmer Street west of Railroad Boulevard was three stories tall with piazzas on the east and south sides.

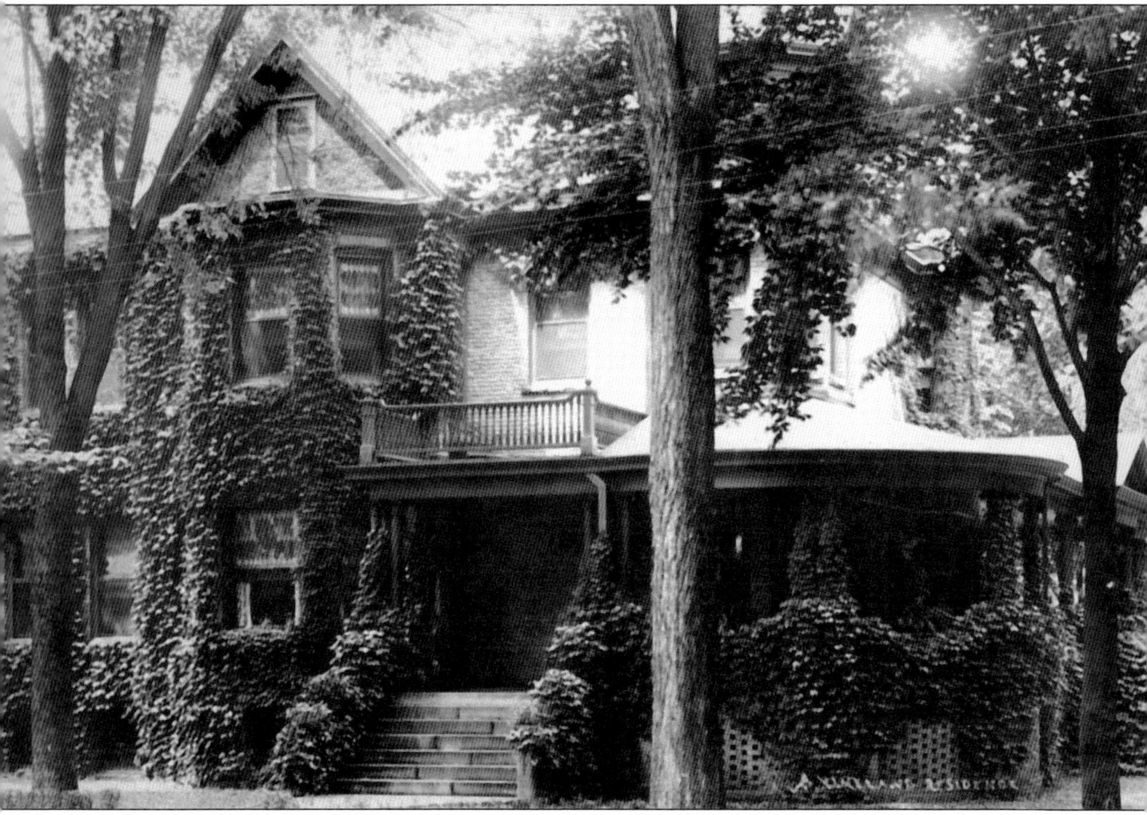

Elegant homes like the one shown here were a common site in Vineland by the early 1900s. Families who had started life in a tiny stipulation house often worked hard enough to build a larger home within a few years of moving to the town. A property like the one pictured here would on average for anywhere from $300 to $500.

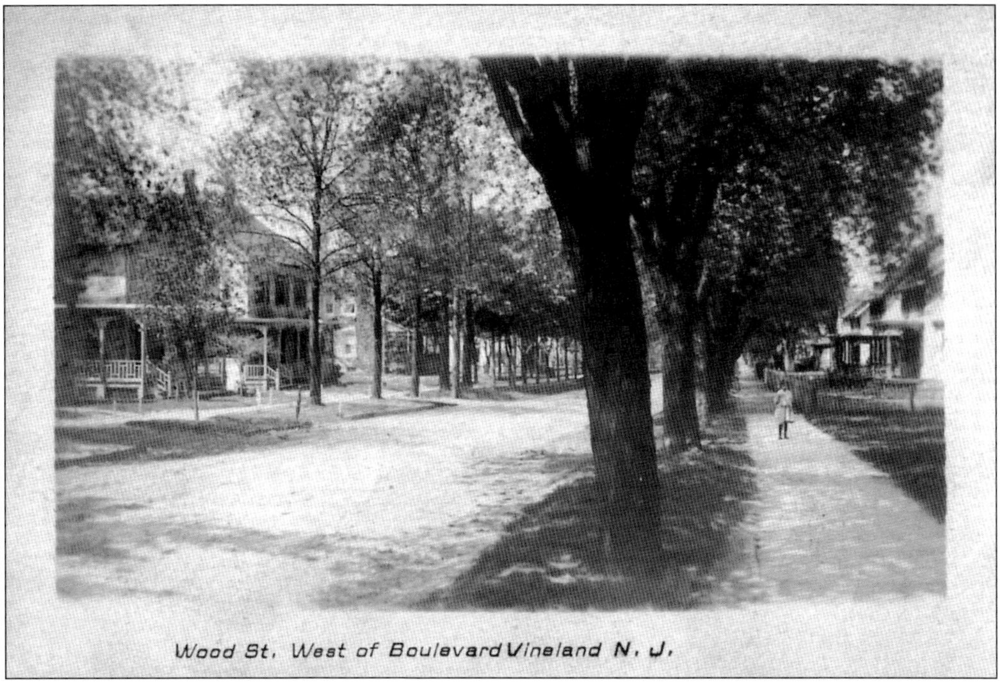

Wood St, West of Boulevard Vineland N. J.

Although Landis did his best to control the real estate market in Vineland, he was occasionally confronted by real estate speculators like Tom Grigg, who was given a property by S.K. Foster to sell. When Landis realized that Grigg had not followed all of the stipulations that Foster was supposed to follow to improve the property, he penalized the speculator, who had demanded a contract in his own name, for violating the terms of the original contract.

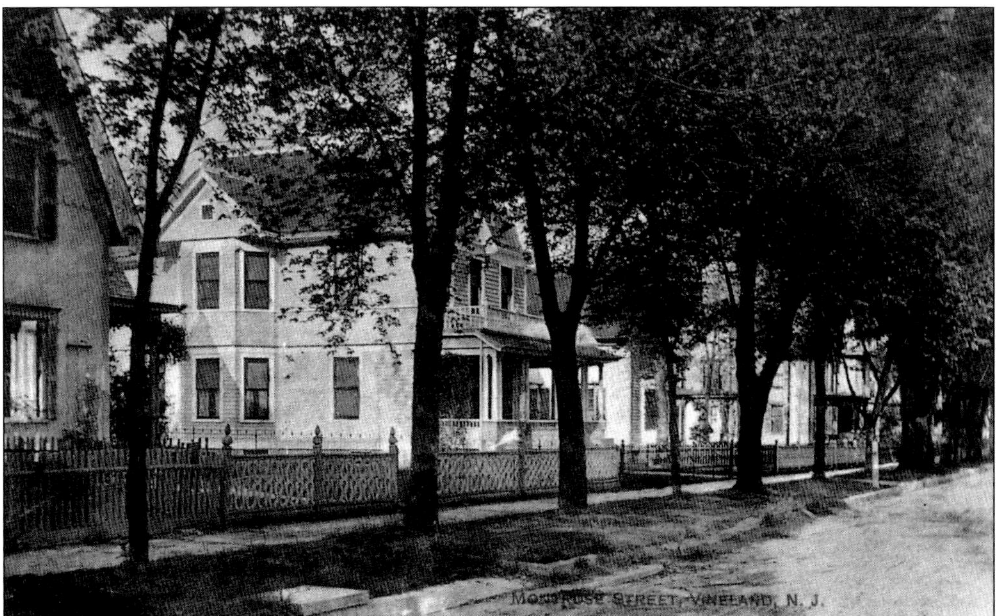

MONTROSE STREET, VINELAND, N. J.
HANDCOLORED

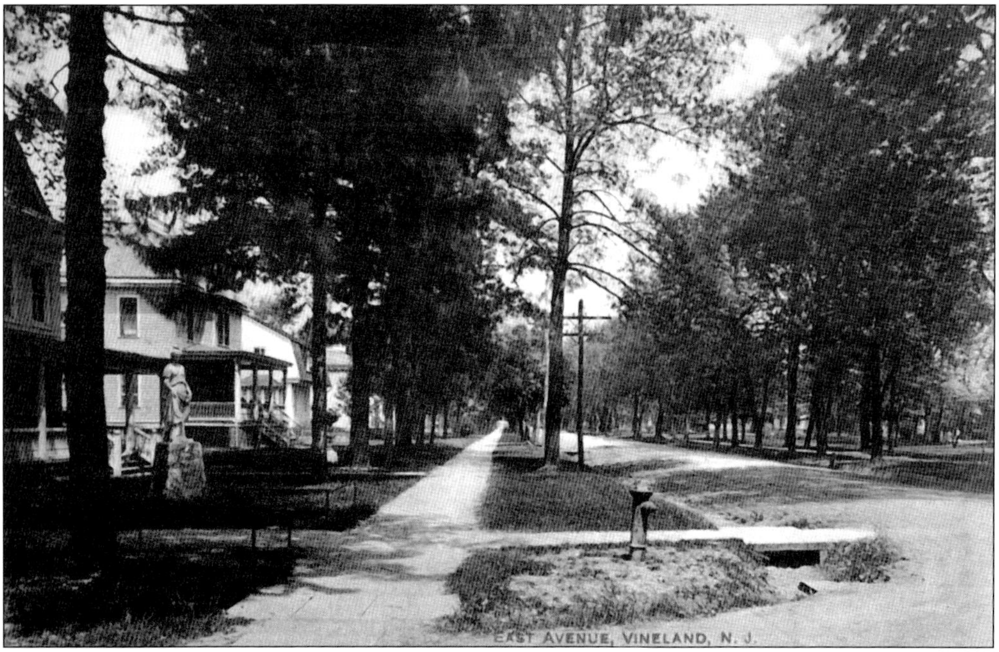

Houses sprang up quickly as new roads were opened on the outskirts of Vineland. While many of them were simple two- and three-story structures, like those shown above, some, like the Kimble mansion, pictured below, were a lot more distinctive in their design. The elegant house, which still stands on East Landis Avenue, was an example of Tudor Revival style, which began in the late 19th century. It was built by Col. Evan Kimble, who owned and operated one of Vineland's largest glassworks from 1902 to 1965 and was a pioneer in the mass production of glassware.

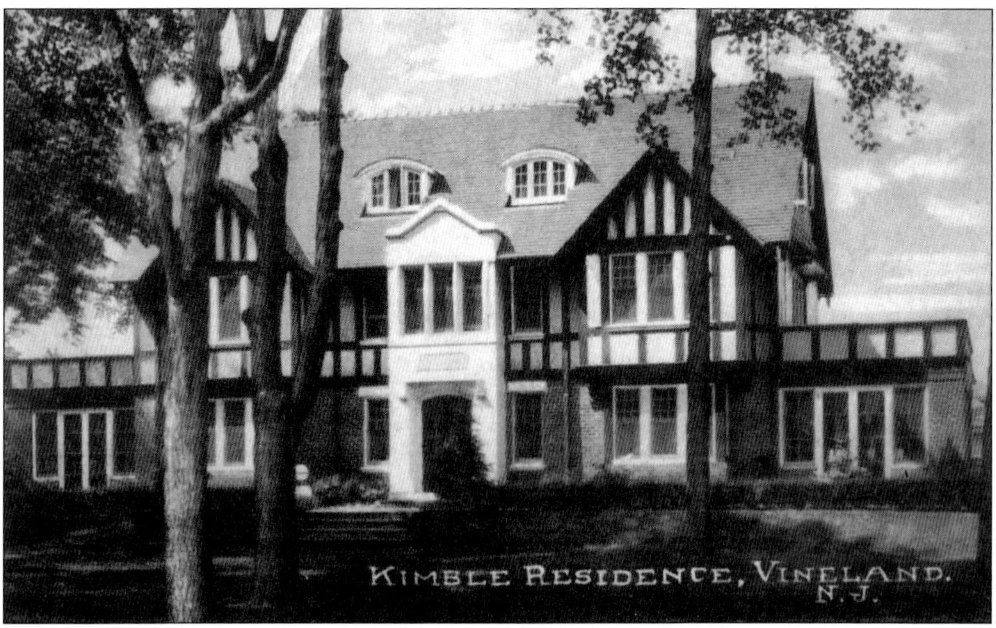

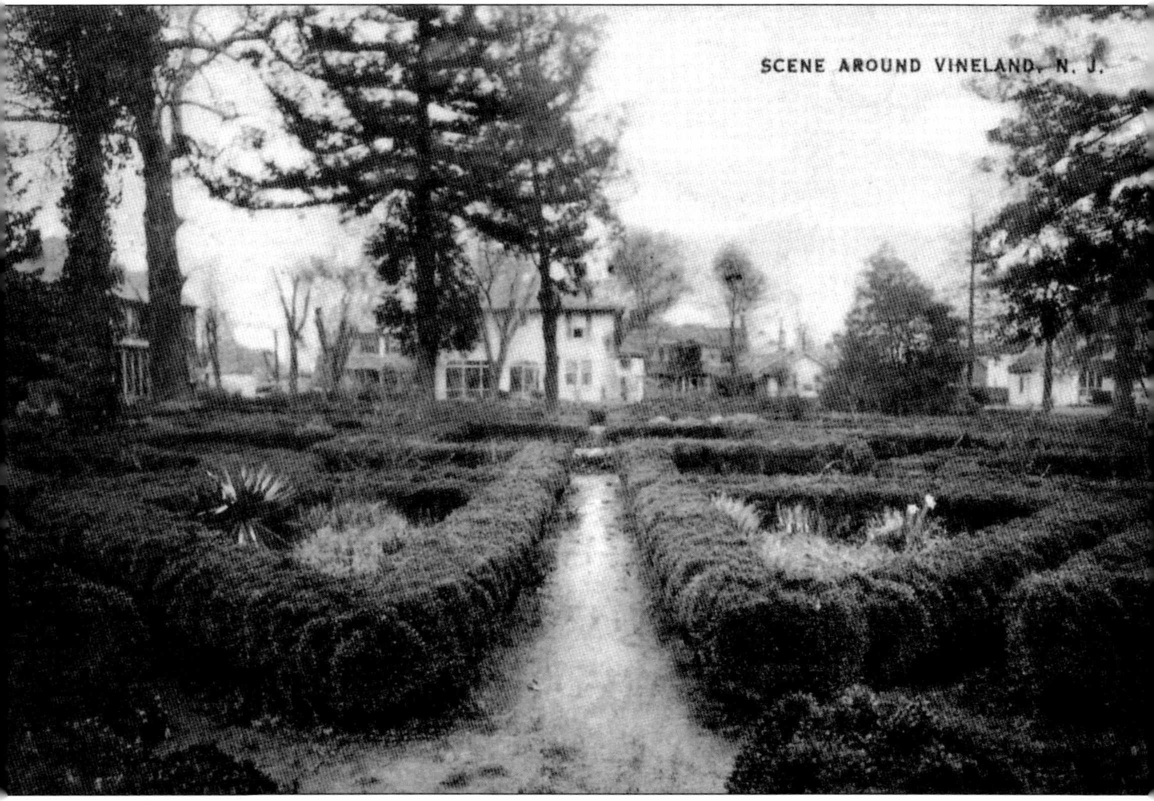

When plumber George Arbuckel purchased a rambling clapboard house on South Main Road in Vineland, he decided that it needed a makeover that, even today, makes it stand out from its neighbors. To find it, just look for the gray, concrete-covered, two-story house that has a yard filled with cast lions, fountains, and a 30-foot replica of the Statue of Liberty. That was not enough for Arbuckel, however, so he created a five-acre hedge maze at the rear of his property.

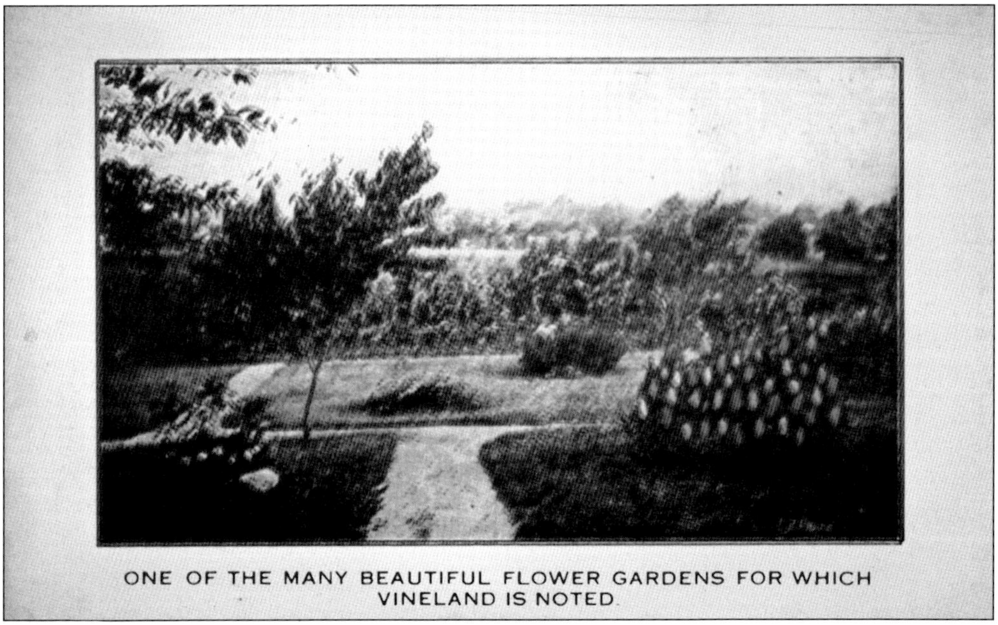

Vineland's Agricultural and Philological Society was another local organization that also encouraged the planting of decorative flowers, in addition to the development of fruits and vegetables for market. Before long, elaborately designed gardens could be found in front and backyards throughout the town. Neighbors vied with neighbors to see whose yard would win first prize in annual competitions.

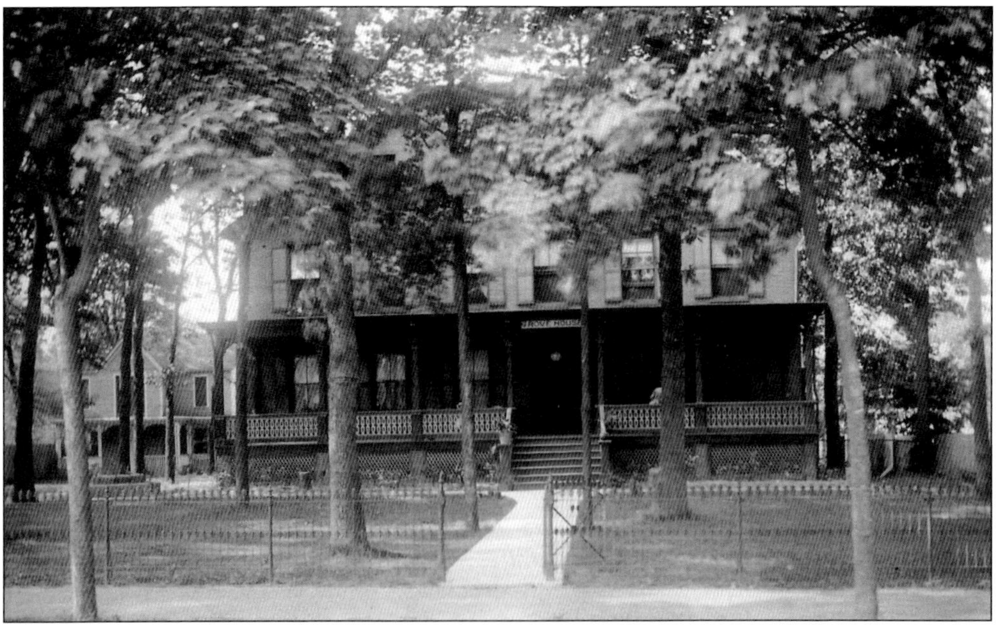

Prof. Marcius Willson was a nationally known author whose textbooks for schoolchildren were published by Harper Brothers of New York. In 1866, Willson used some of his significant royalties to move with his family to Vineland, where he built a luxurious home on East Landis Avenue. The Willsons quickly became socially prominent and active in the community. Willson later moved to Grove House, a local boardinghouse that was run by his daughter.

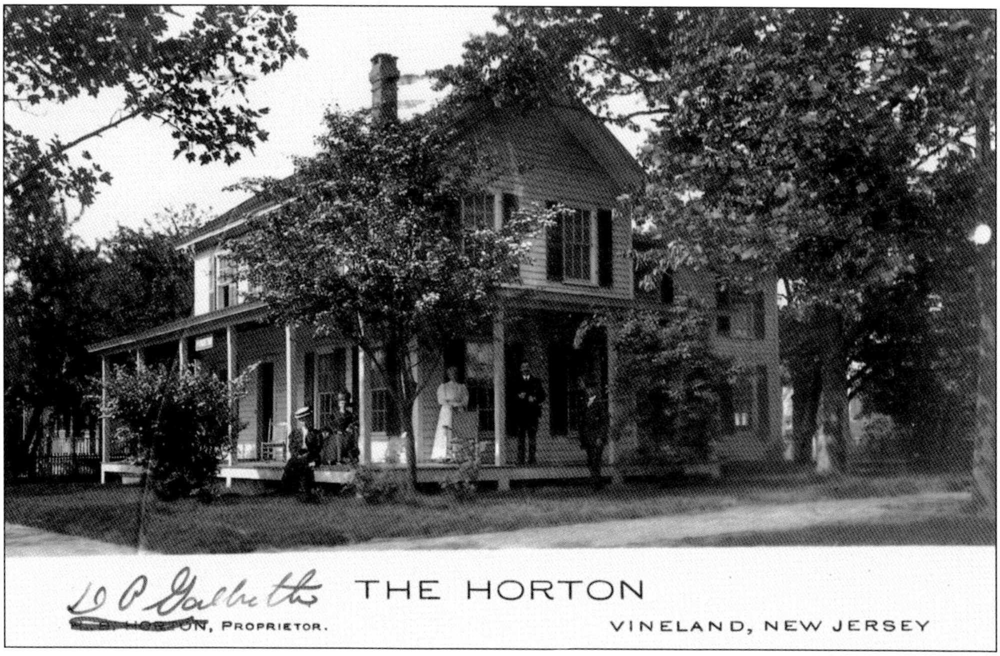

Other boardinghouses included the Horton (above) and Creamer's Cottage (below), which were established to accommodate the population boom in the 19th century. Since many people who flocked to Vineland could not afford the steep price of a hotel room, which cost about $1 a night, the boardinghouses were a great success. Such residences were often run by local widows, whose children assisted with daily operations.

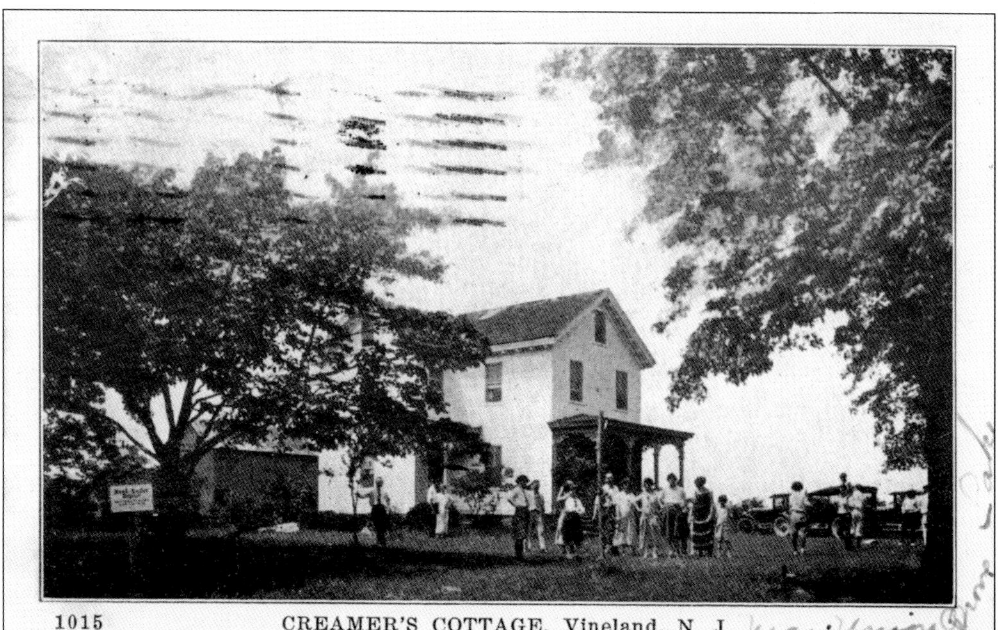

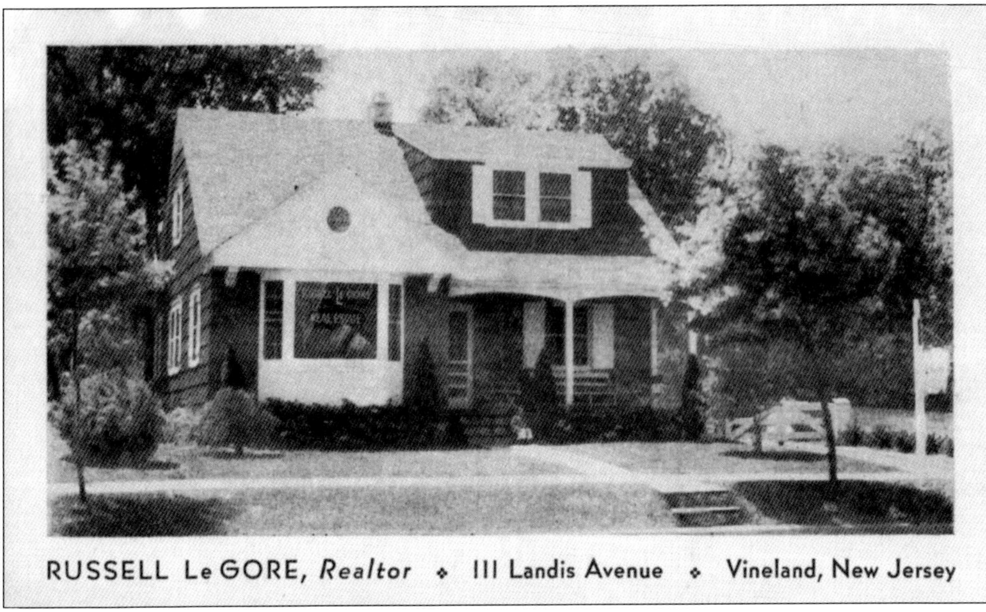

Russell LeGore was one of many Vineland realtors who were kept busy selling houses well into the 1950s as new housing developments were built in the town and the surrounding Landis Township. One of his most unusual transactions occurred in 1929, when he sold a junkyard to George and Florence Daynor, who later built the Palace Depression, a nationally recognized tourist attraction, on the site.

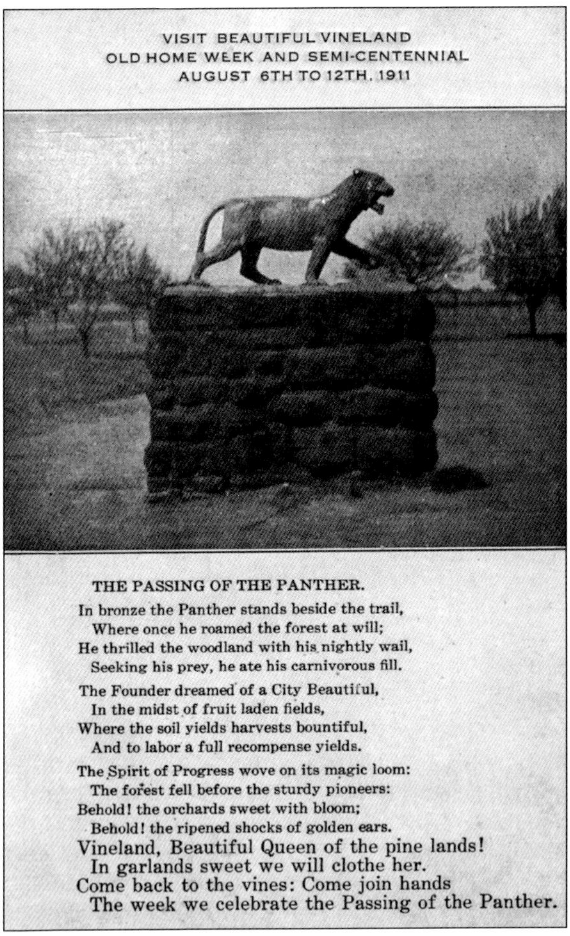

The locally famous panther statue that once guarded Panther Road in East Vineland was a familiar sight to the Italian immigrants who settled there in the 1880s and 1890s. This wave of newcomers who left southern Italy looking for a fresh start helped New Jersey gain its reputation as the "Garden State" by growing fruits and vegetables that were in demand at major East Coast markets.

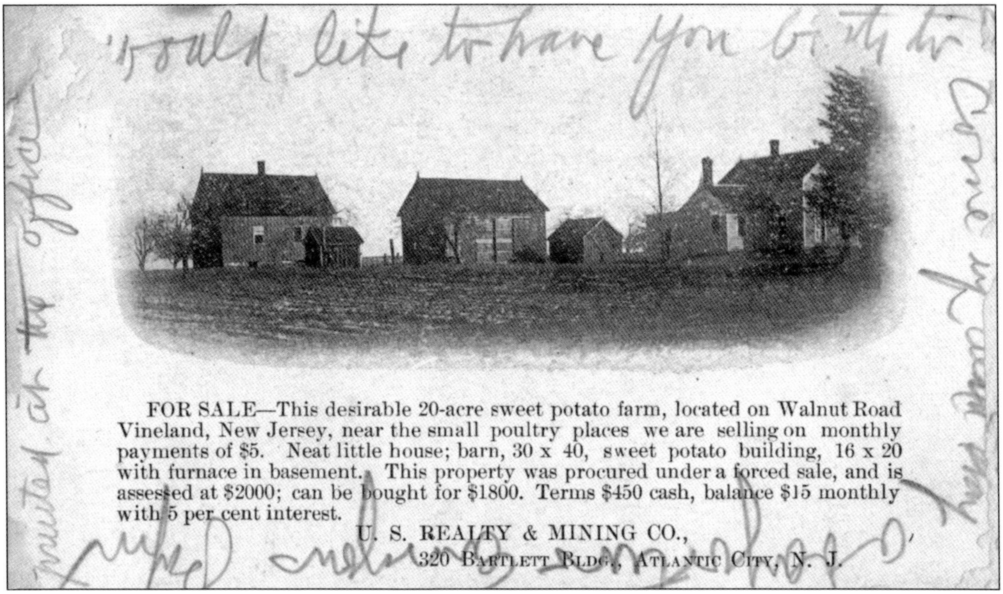

The rapid growth of Vineland might have surprised even its founder. Even though Landis Avenue remained the focal point of the town well into the 1960s, by the early 1900s, companies like the US Realty & Mining Company of Atlantic City were buying and selling foreclosed property in the town and the surrounding township.

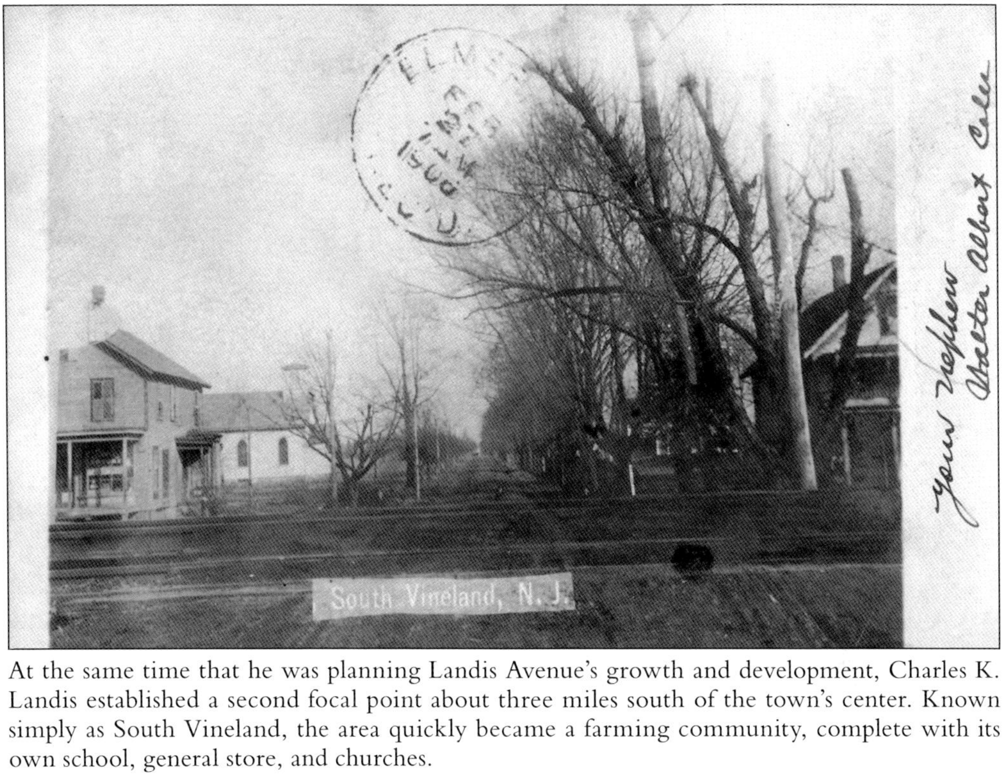

At the same time that he was planning Landis Avenue's growth and development, Charles K. Landis established a second focal point about three miles south of the town's center. Known simply as South Vineland, the area quickly became a farming community, complete with its own school, general store, and churches.

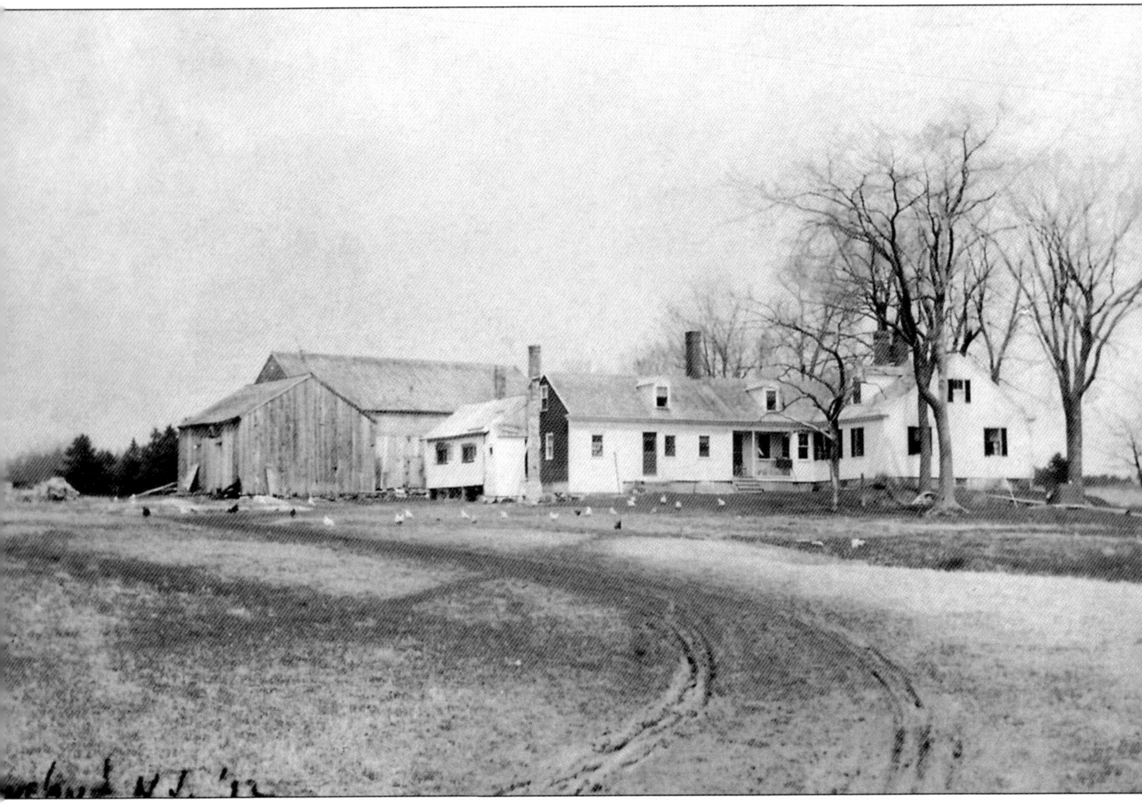

While little evidence remains of the original South Vineland settlement outside of a few homes and a tiny clapboard church, local residents still refer to the area by that name. The area also includes an early-20th-century home originally sold in the Sears catalog.

Four

RECREATION

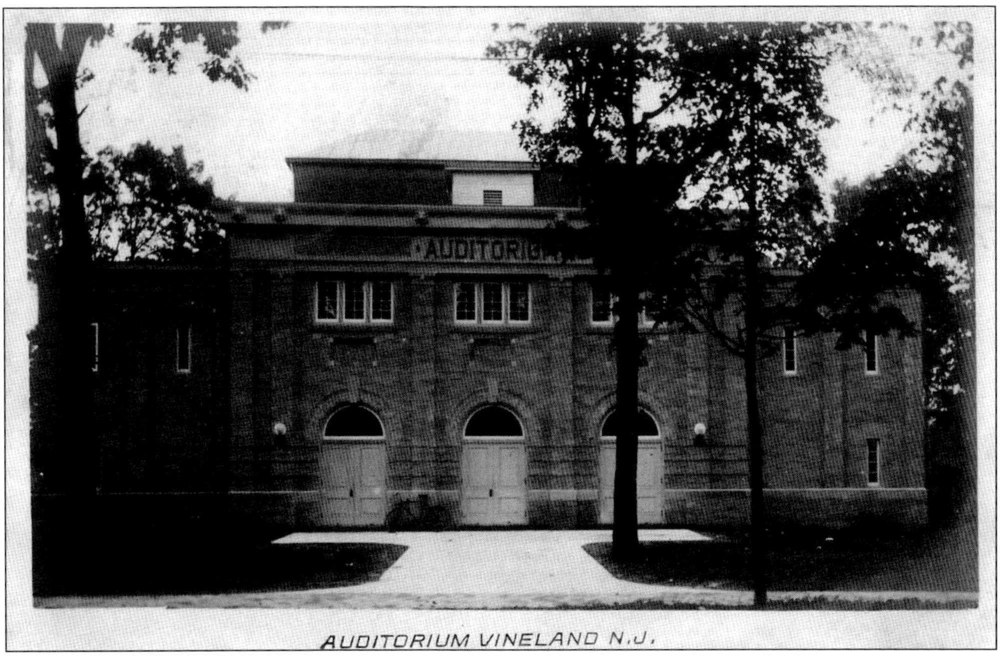

Charles K. Landis was a prolific journal keeper, documenting much of his daily life. On February 14, 1868, he noted in his diary, "Walked out in the afternoon with one of my agents, C.B. Campbell. This gentleman is a man of talent. He has long been the president of the Plum Street Hall Society, composed of spiritualists, atheists and outsiders generally. Campbell is charitable, public-spirited, always doing something to advance the interests of the place." Plum Street Hall is pictured here.

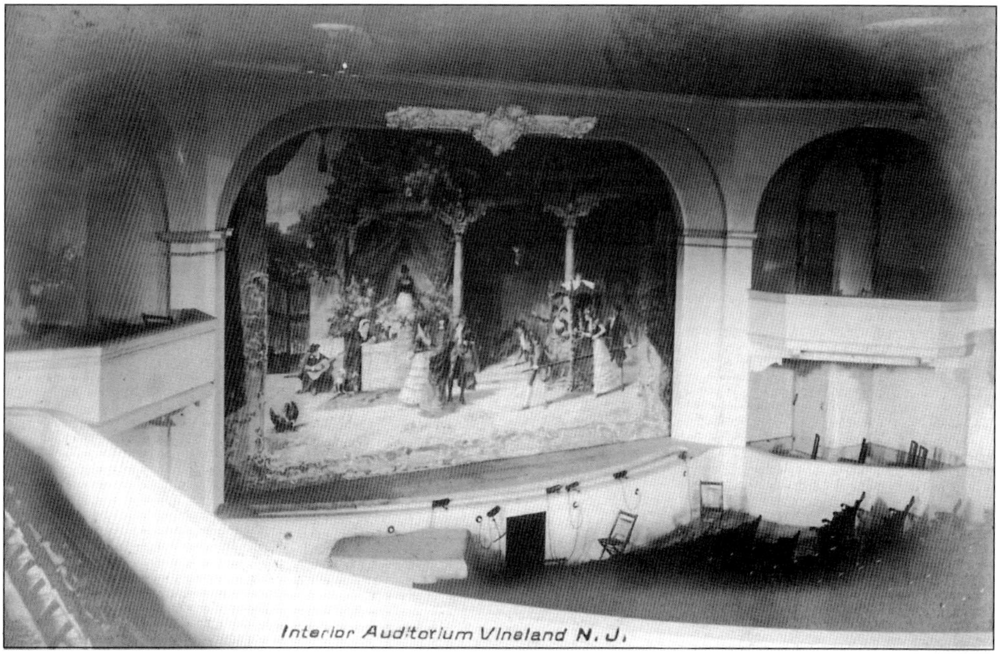

While entertainment ranging from opera to comedy was often performed at the hall, the venue is best remembered as the site where 172 Vineland women symbolically cast their ballots in the 1868 presidential election. Although their votes were not legal, the event inspired women throughout America to stage similar demonstrations to protest their lack of legal rights.

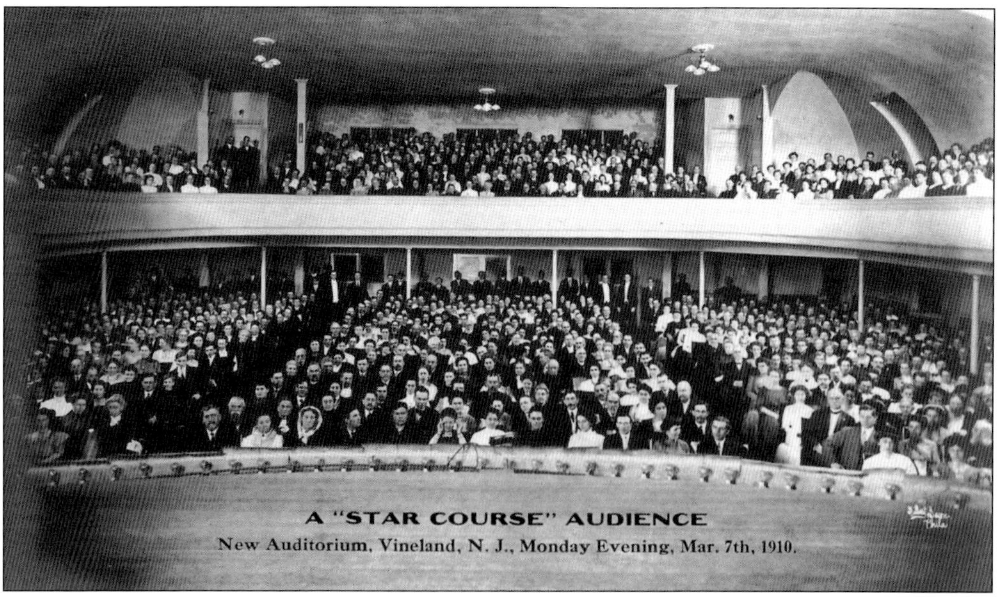

After it was remodeled, Plum Street Hall became known as Cosmopolitan Hall. But when the popular community center began to show its age, local residents banded together to refurbish it into the New Auditorium, which offered local audiences a chance to participate in "Star Course" programs organized by Lyceum Committees that included plays and musical performances. Unfortunately, after serving the town for more than 50 years, the New Auditorium was lost to fire in 1917.

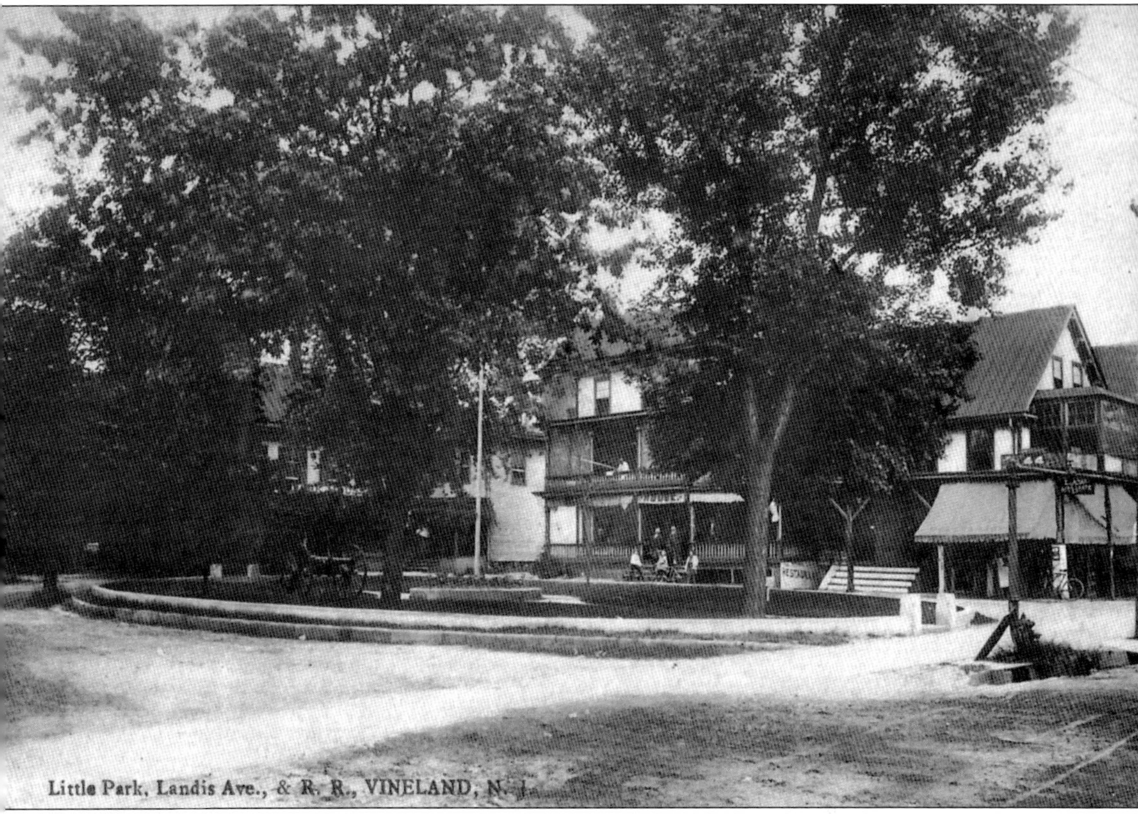

The little parks that mark the four corners of the intersection of Landis Avenue and Railroad Boulevard were one of the first features that founder Charles K. Landis incorporated into the design of his new town. Landis felt that natural elements were a key to the success of the town, and he encouraged local residents to plant flower gardens and fruit trees on their properties.

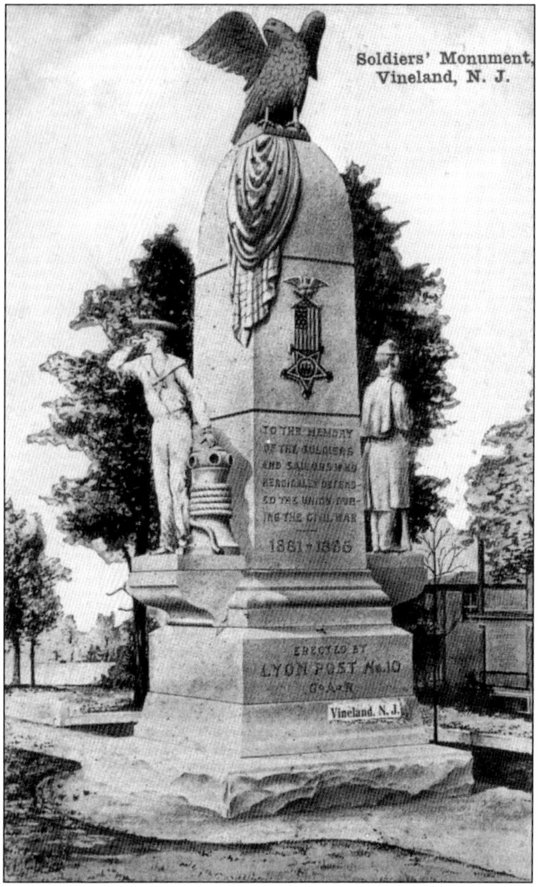

In 1911, the park on the northeast corner of Landis Avenue and Railroad Boulevard became the home of a statue memorializing the servicemen who fought in the Civil War. The statue was erected by Lyons Post 10 of the Grand Army of the Republic (GAR), the first veterans' group founded in America by Union soldiers after the war. In August 1911, Vineland celebrated its 50th anniversary with Old Home Week, which drew thousands of people to the town for the weeklong celebration, which included the unveiling of the statue.

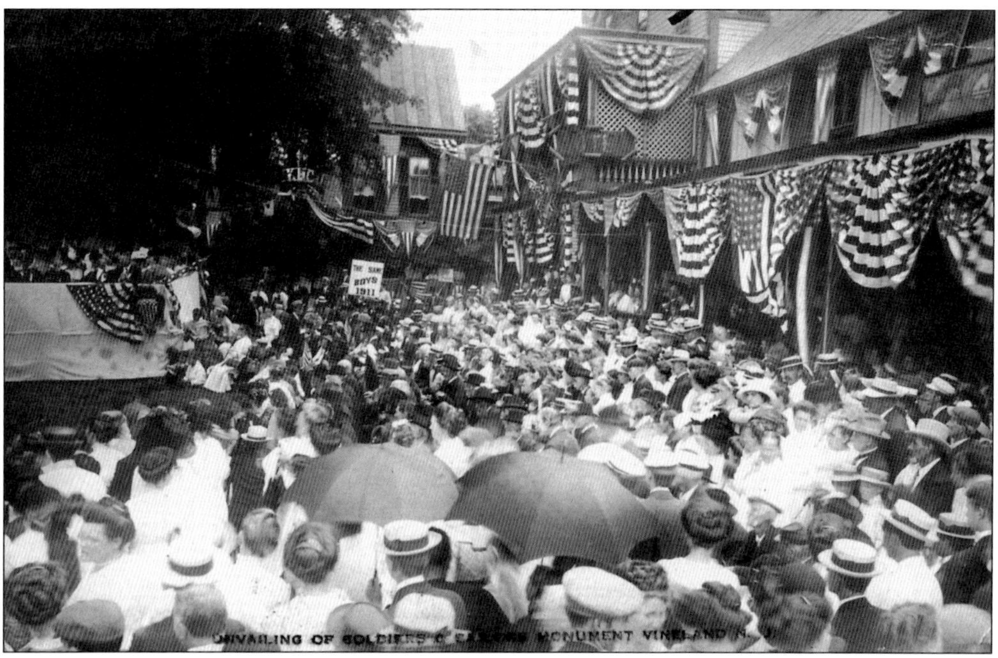

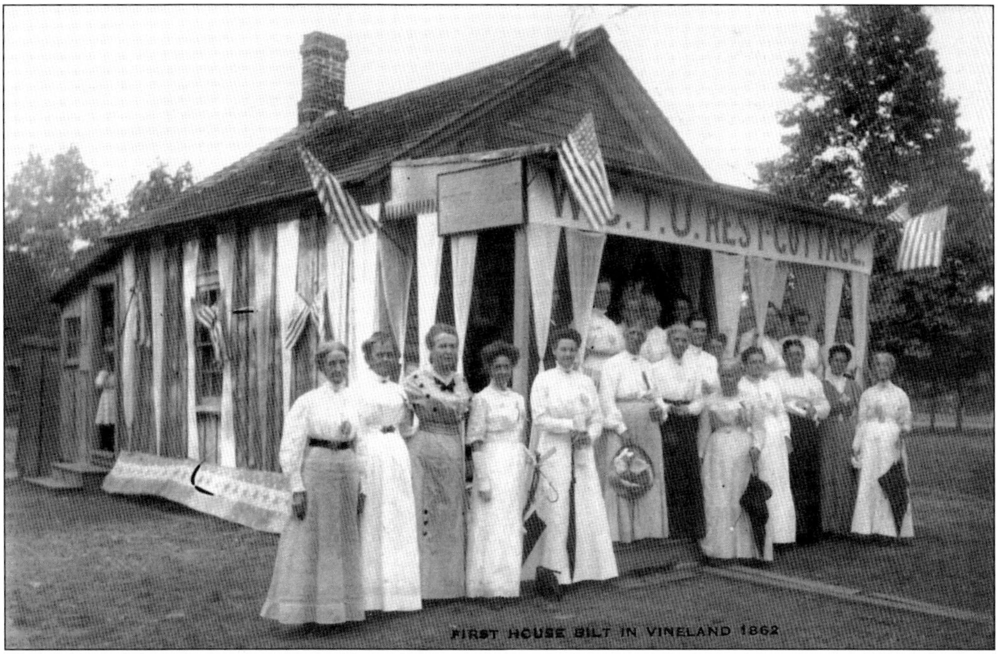

Vineland was founded as a dry town, so it is not surprising that the Women's Christian Temperance Union (WCTU) founded a chapter there in the 1870s. The local chapter hosted frequent meetings and participated in the 1911 celebration by creating a "rest cottage" for revelers at Vineland's First House, which was by then sitting in Landis Park.

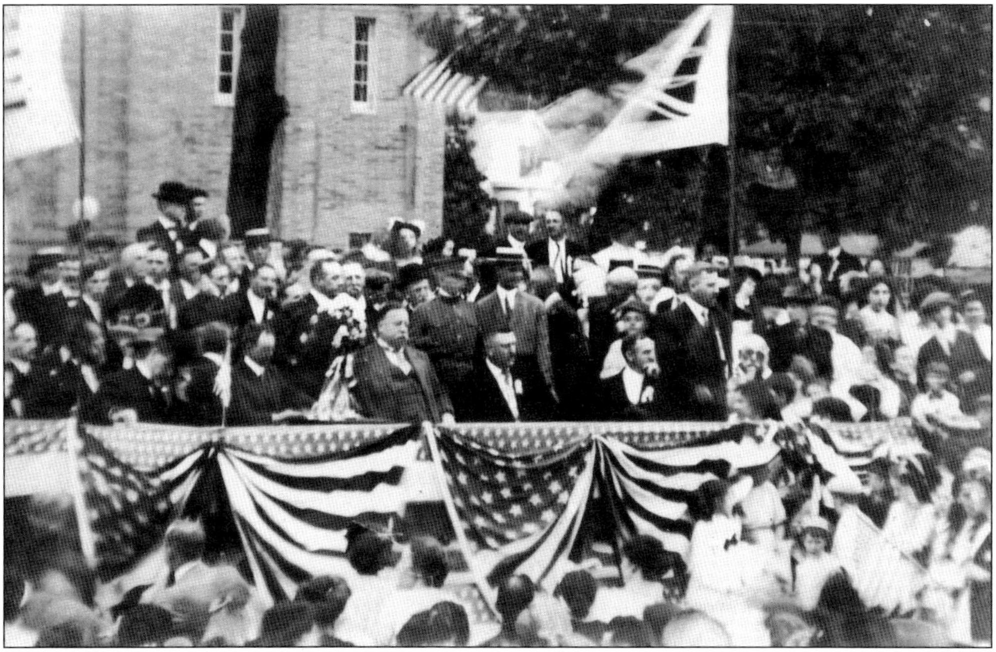

On May 27, 1912, Pres. William Howard Taft visited Vineland to speak to a crowd of about 6,000 people. During his introduction of the president, Mayor Waldo F. Sawyer noted that Taft was speaking from the same location where Pres. Ulysses S. Grant had stood 38 years earlier when he dedicated the town's first high school.

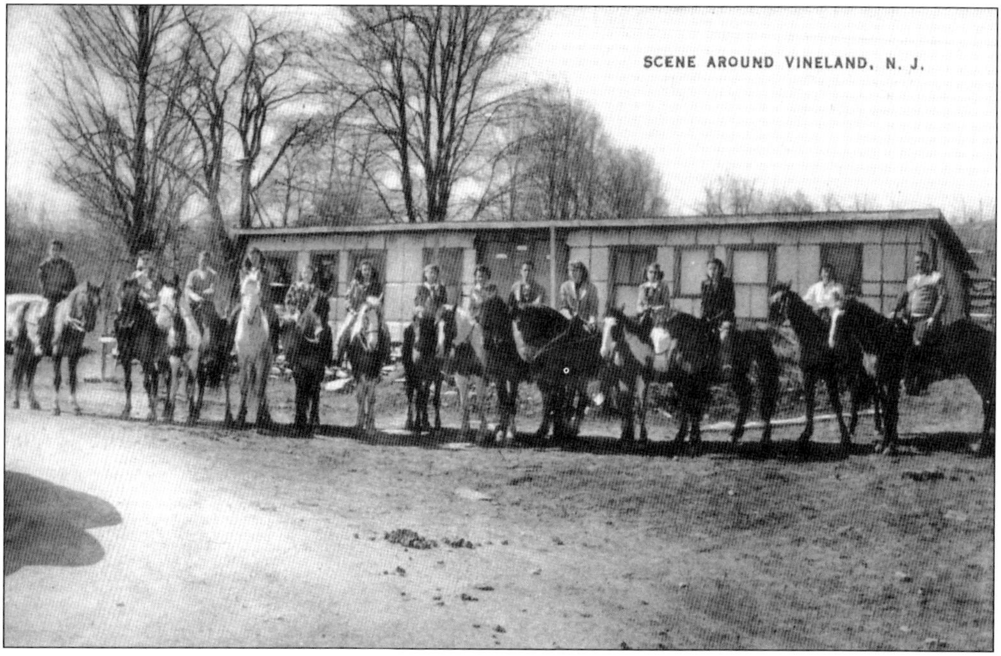

In Vineland's early days, horses were an essential means of transportation for those who could afford them. However, after they were replaced by the automobile, horseback riding became a popular recreational activity for many local young people, who enjoyed scenic jaunts through the surrounding farmland and forests.

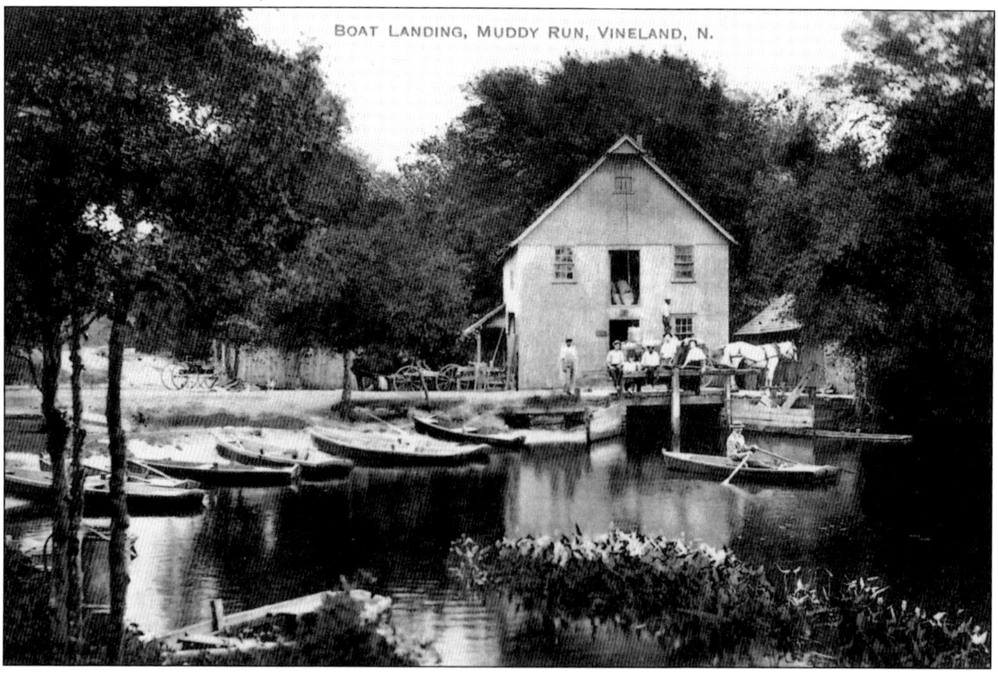

Muddy Run (also known as Muddy River) was a popular freshwater recreational spot just west of Vineland that annually drew new generations of fishermen, swimmers, and sunbathers.The boathouse was probably an early mill that had later been converted for recreational use.

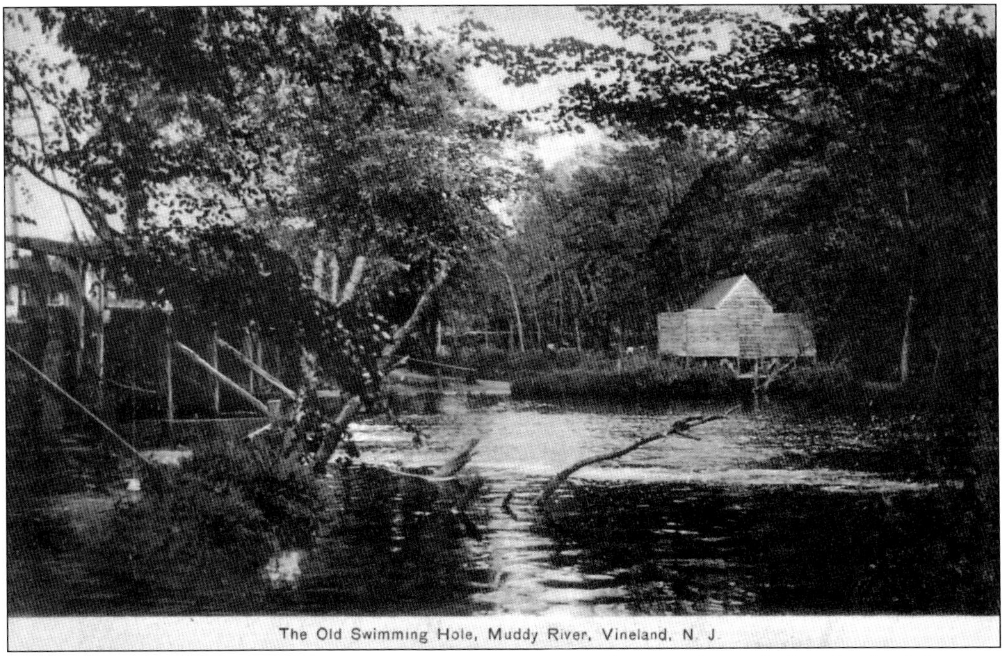

Muddy River was part of the vast network of waterways that run through Cumberland County known as the Maurice River, which increases in size as it moves south into the Delaware Bay. Although no one swims at Muddy Run anymore, a number of similar swimming holes can still be found within the county.

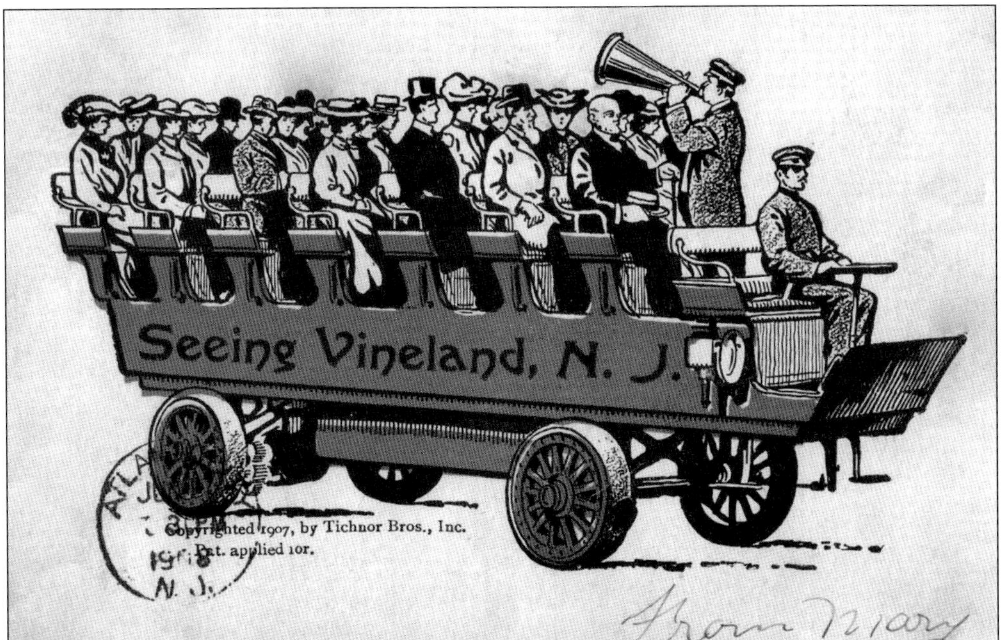

Although busloads of passengers never gawked their way past Vineland attractions, the community continued to draw new settlers and visitors well into the early 20th century. With its numerous social clubs, theatrical performances, and community events, there was always something of interest for both residents and those who were just passing through town.

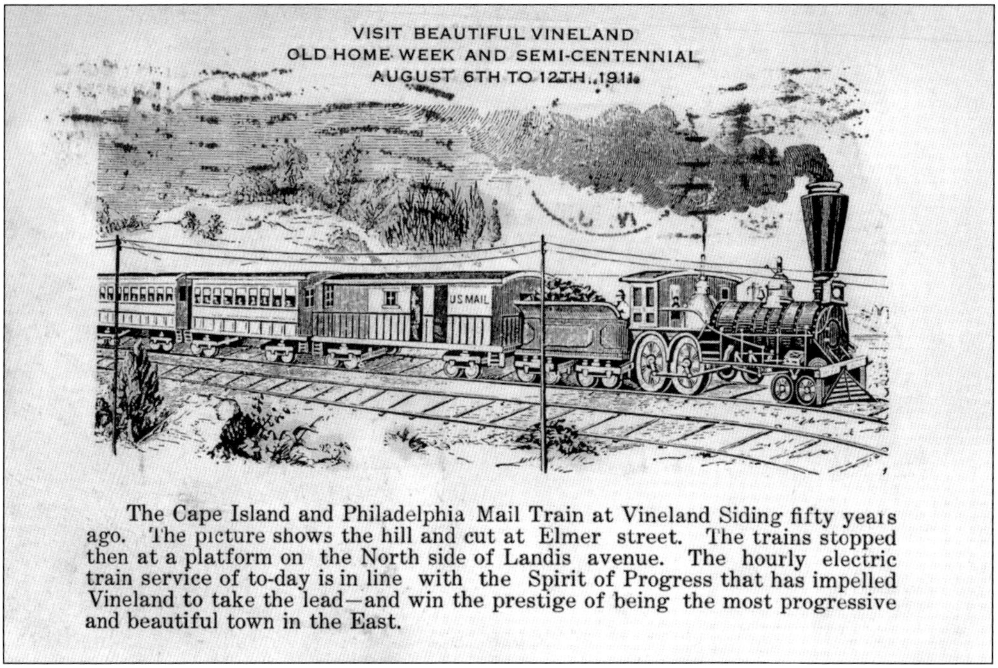

A master at marketing, Charles K. Landis would undoubtedly have been proud of the promotional campaign started in 1911 to celebrate Old Home Week. Vineland's semicentennial included sentimental scenes designed to lure former residents back for the weeklong celebration, which included special events, country fairs, and guest speakers. The trains that had helped Vineland grow and develop brought thousands of visitors to town to participate in the occasion.

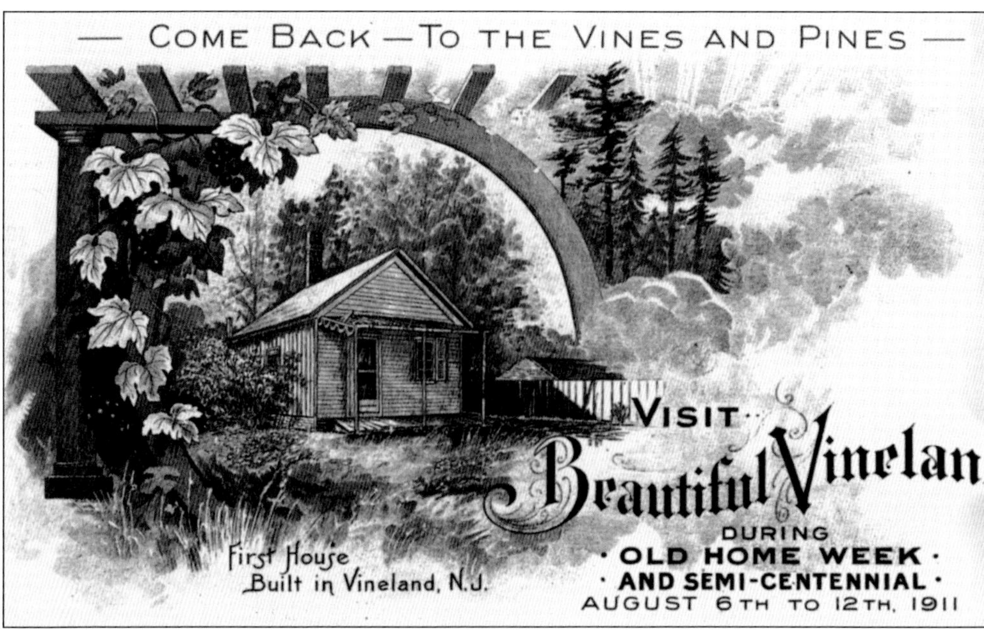

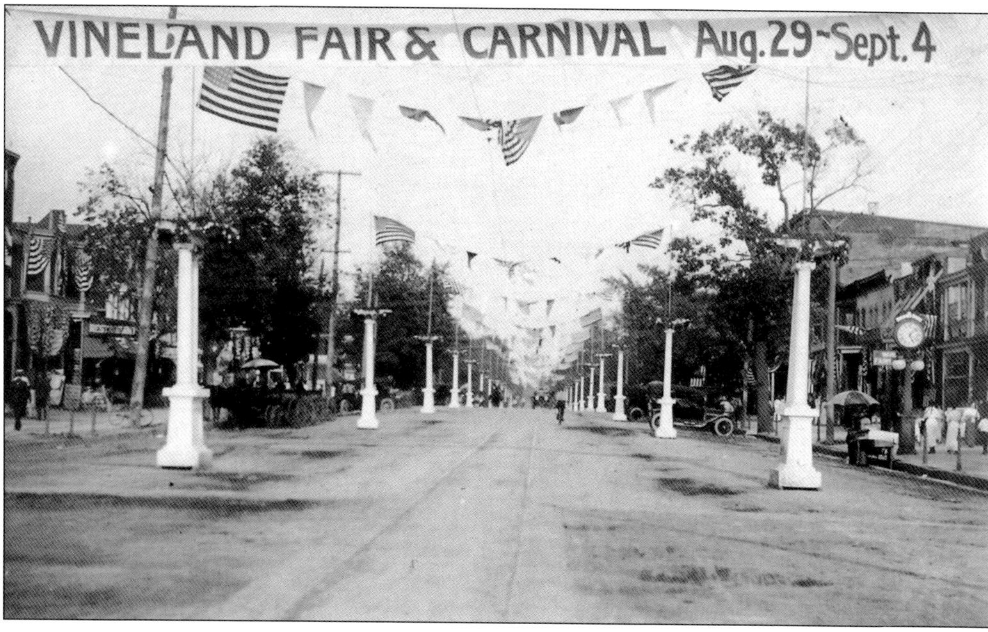

In August 1911, Landis Avenue became the center stage for a constant stream of parades, cheered on by thousands of revelers who participated in Old Home Week. While pedestals lined the broad boulevard, business owners and home owners decorated their stores and homes with flags, bunting, and red-white-and-blue streamers. In addition to the marching bands and club floats, local women also used the event as an opportunity to promote the suffrage movement.

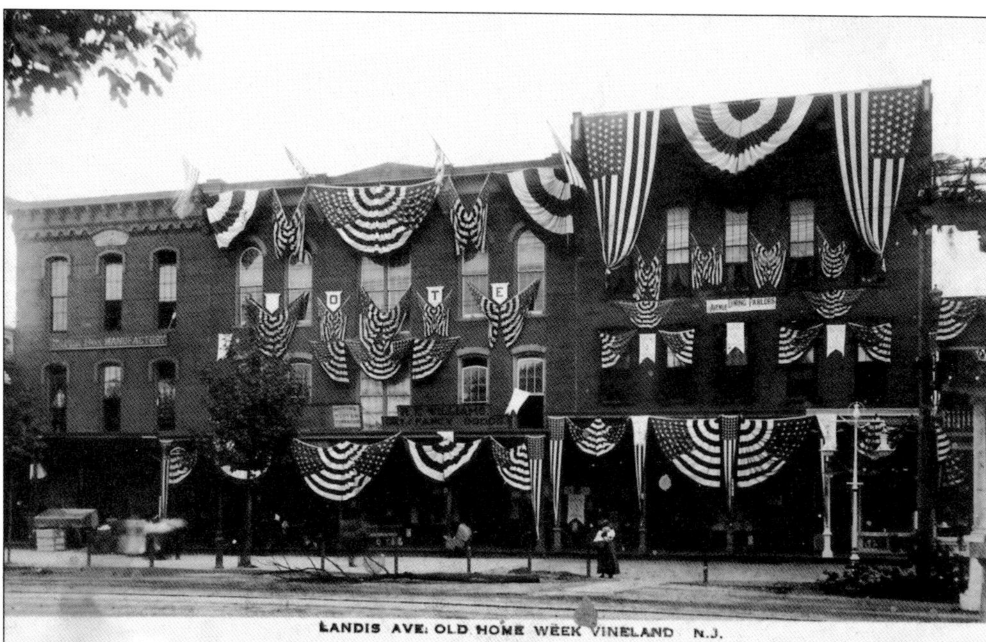

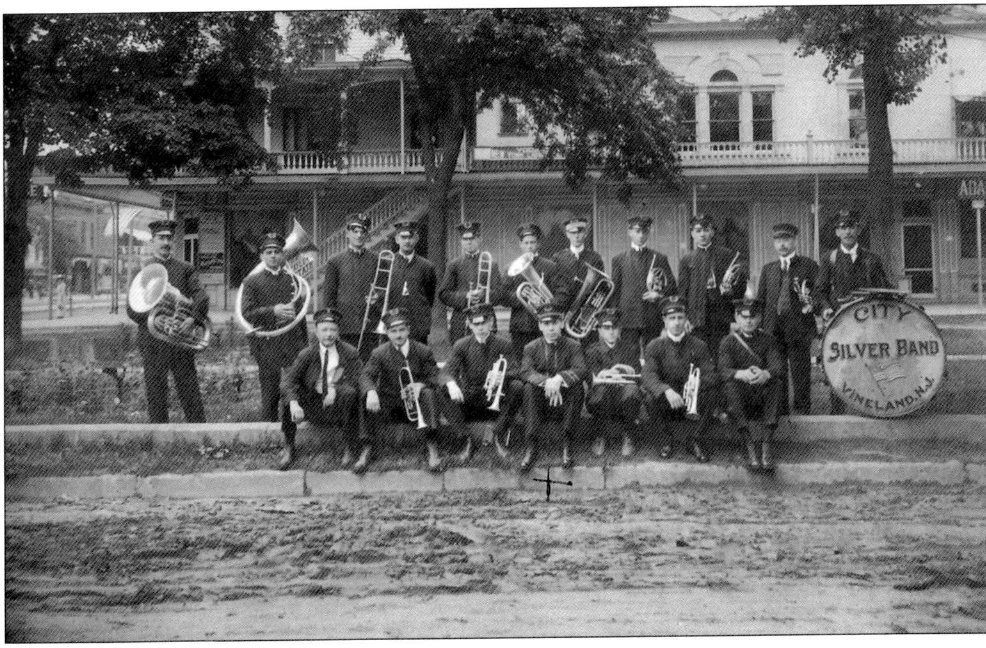

The City Silver Band was Vineland's first municipal band, playing for every special event that took place in town. However, other bands, often organized by immigrants, also displayed their civic pride by marching in parades. By the early 1900s, residents of the Italian Colony formed both the Municipal Band and the Princess Mafalda Band, which often marched in Vineland parades. Music was an integral part of life in Vineland, which produced songwriters such as Henry Clay Work, whose compositions included "Marching Through Georgia" and "My Grandfather's Clock."

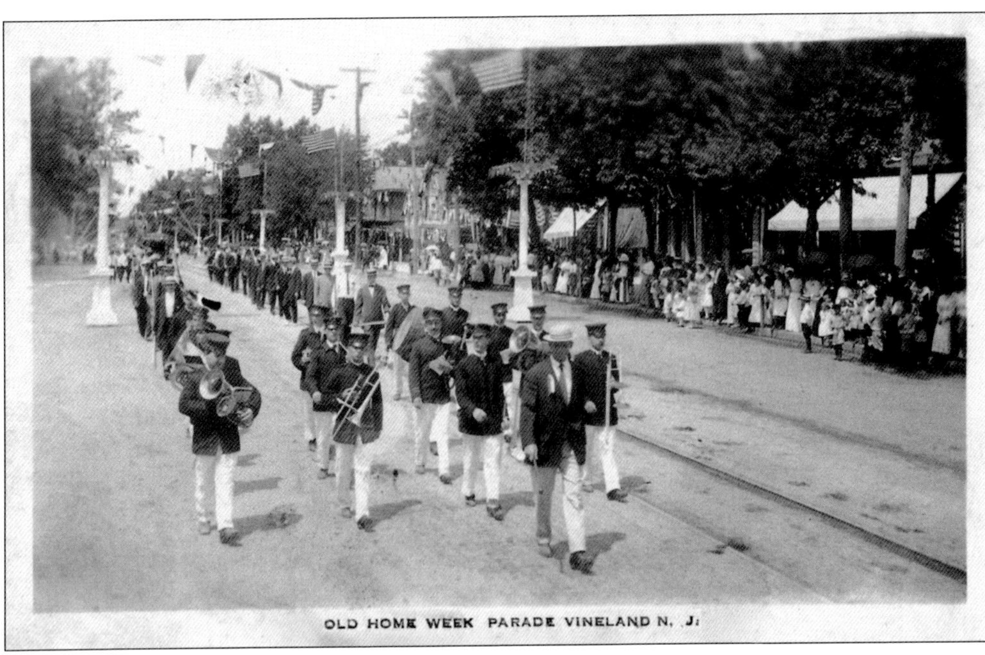

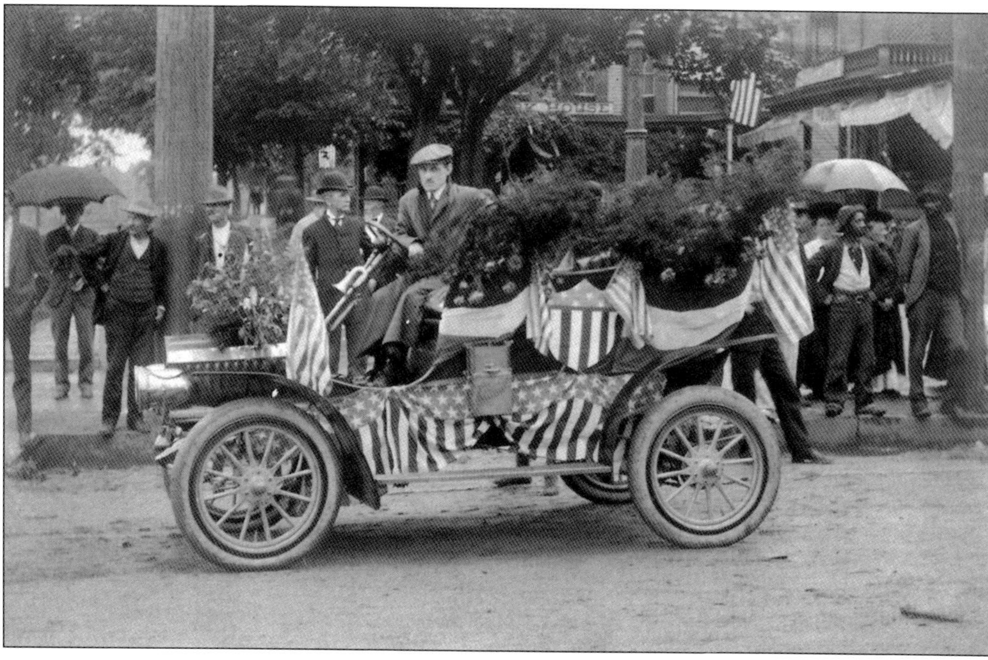

While some area residents used the parade as an excuse to show off their new automobiles, local women turned out in force to participate in the Old Home Week parade as a reminder that the women's suffrage movement started in Vineland, when early settlers organized a protest during the 1868 presidential election. In 1911, they remained undiscouraged even though almost another decade would pass before women were legally allowed to vote.

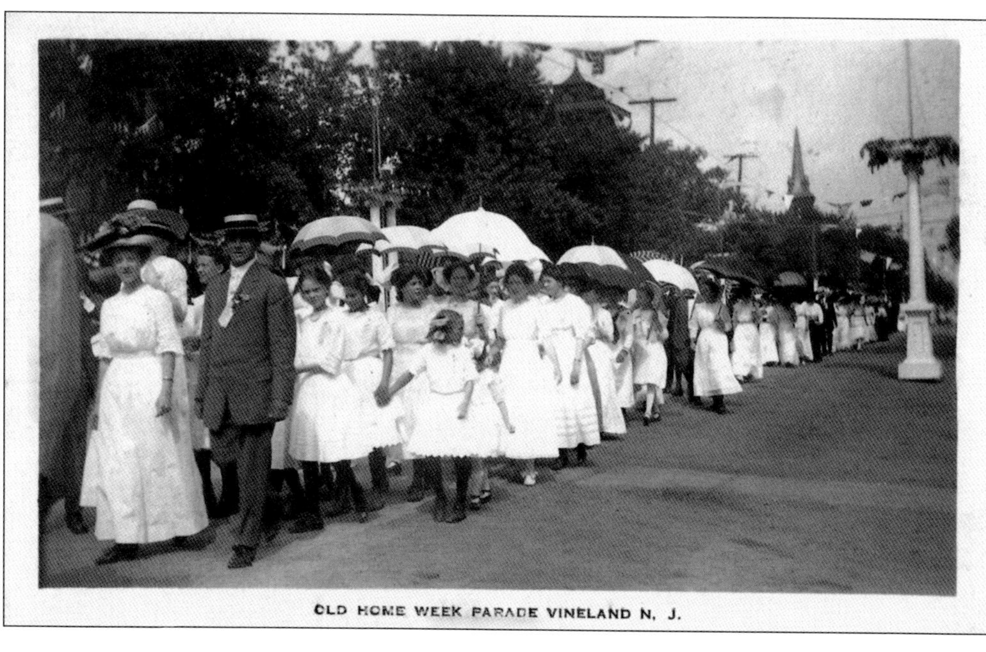

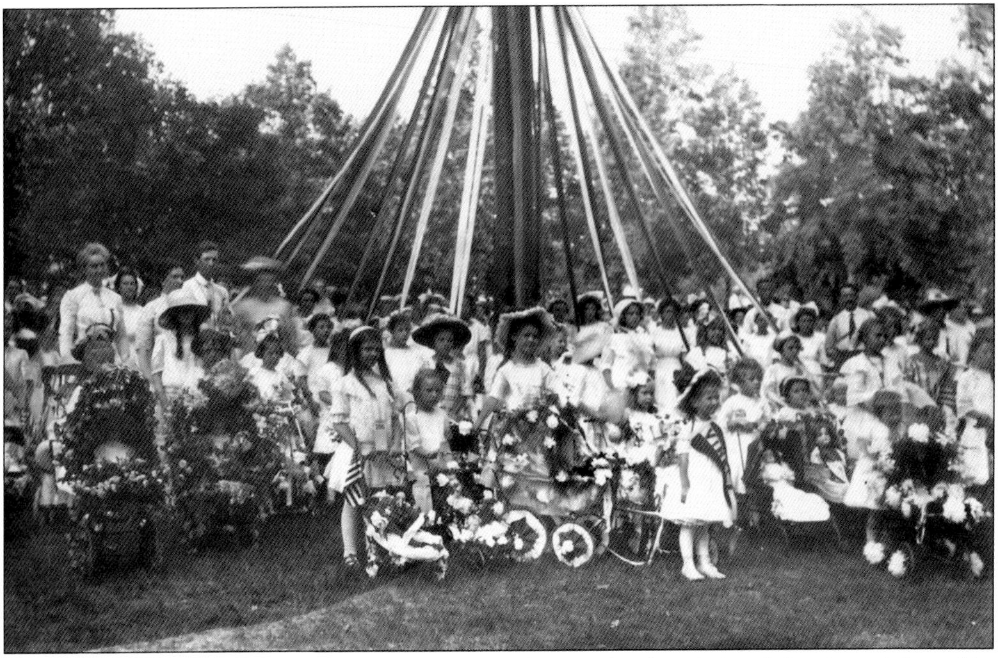

In the early 20th century, children who lived at the Vineland Training School participated in a variety of games and activities year-round to help hone their developmental skills. In 1908, they enjoyed frolicking around the Maypole in addition to camping on the property and trying their hands at creating baskets.

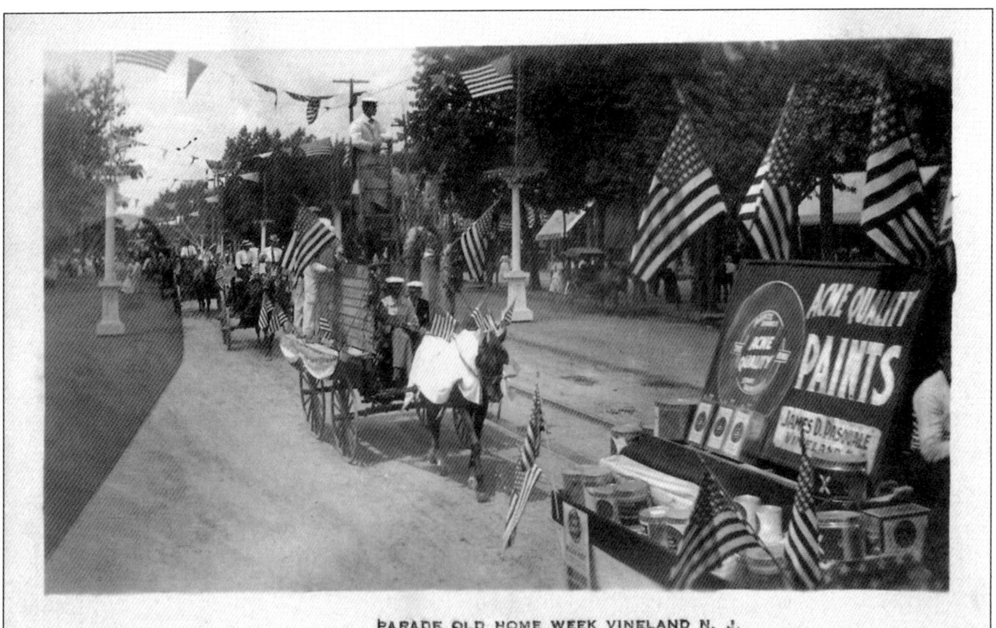

Some local merchants advertised their latest products during parades like the one held in Vineland during Old Home Week. They were often accompanied by the high school marching band, colorful floats designed by local civic groups, and veterans' organizations.

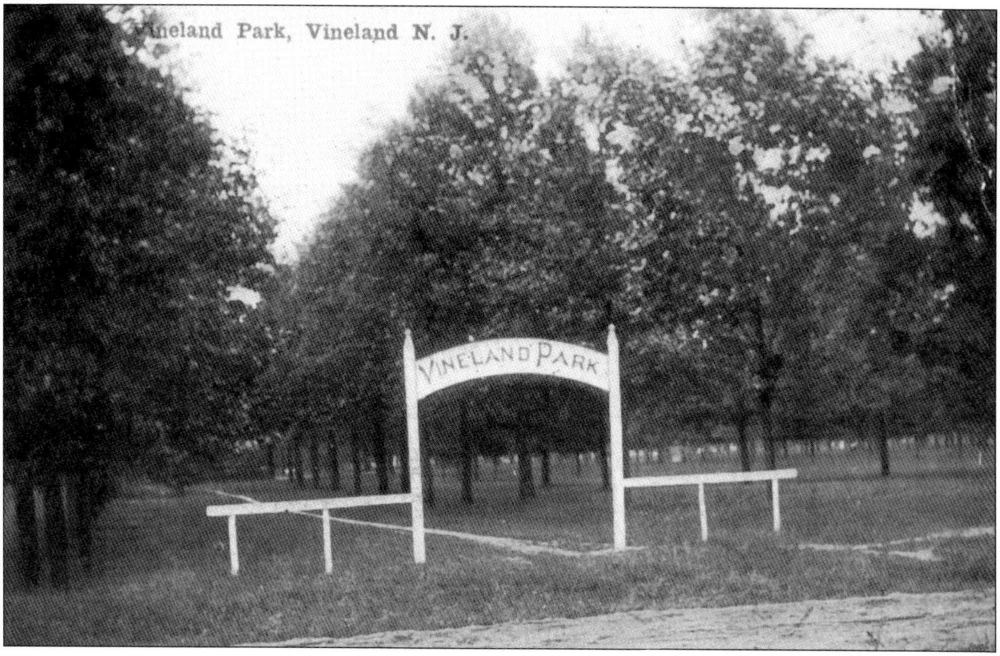

Recognizing the need for a recreational space, Charles K. Landis donated land for the creation of a park almost immediately after the town was founded. Newspaper editor B.F. Ladd noted, "A public park of about forty acres is situated on Park Avenue and East Boulevard, which, when the contemplated improvements are completed, will be one of the handsomest in the State." In June 1865, a grand festival was held at the park to publicize life in Vineland, attracting participants from almost every state.

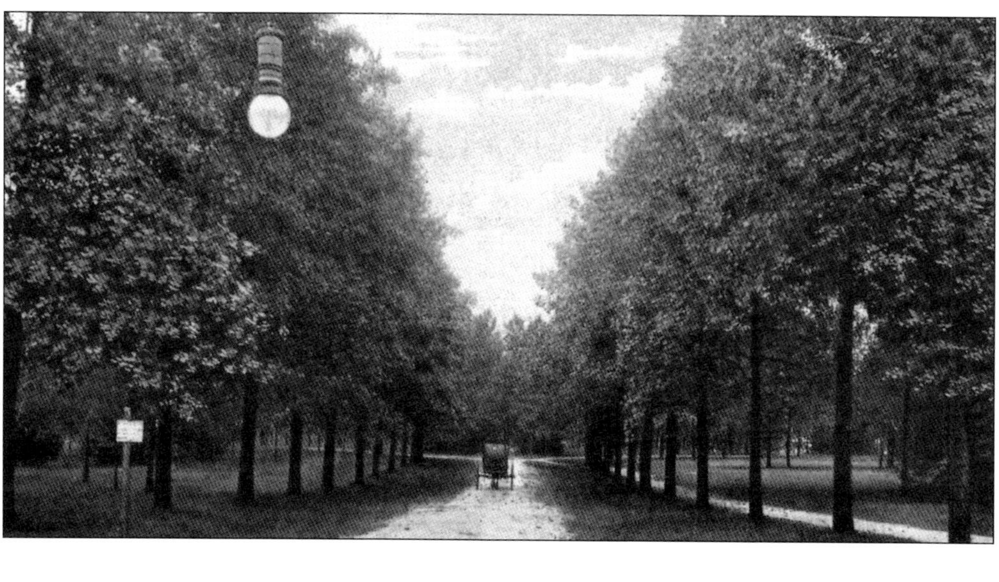

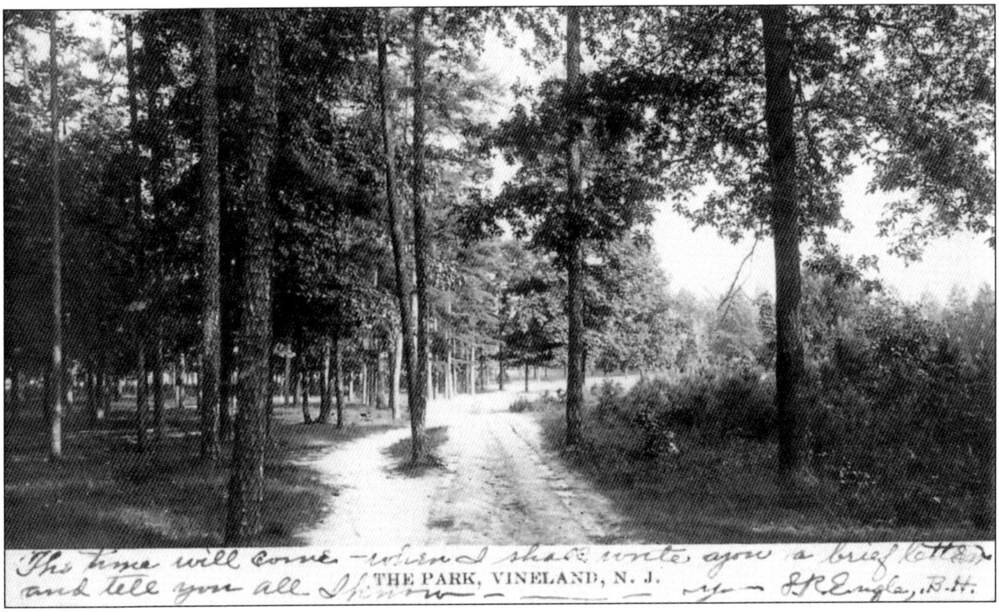

While large sections of the park were left undisturbed for many years, it also featured manicured lawns where visitors could relax beneath tall trees. In 1911, residents and visitors gathered there to await the arrival of, for them, the latest technological marvel that was scheduled to appear: a hot air balloon. Although the balloonist eventually showed, his landing did not quite happen as anticipated. Instead of sailing smoothly down into the park, he managed to set down heavily—after three tries—in a nearby farmer's field.

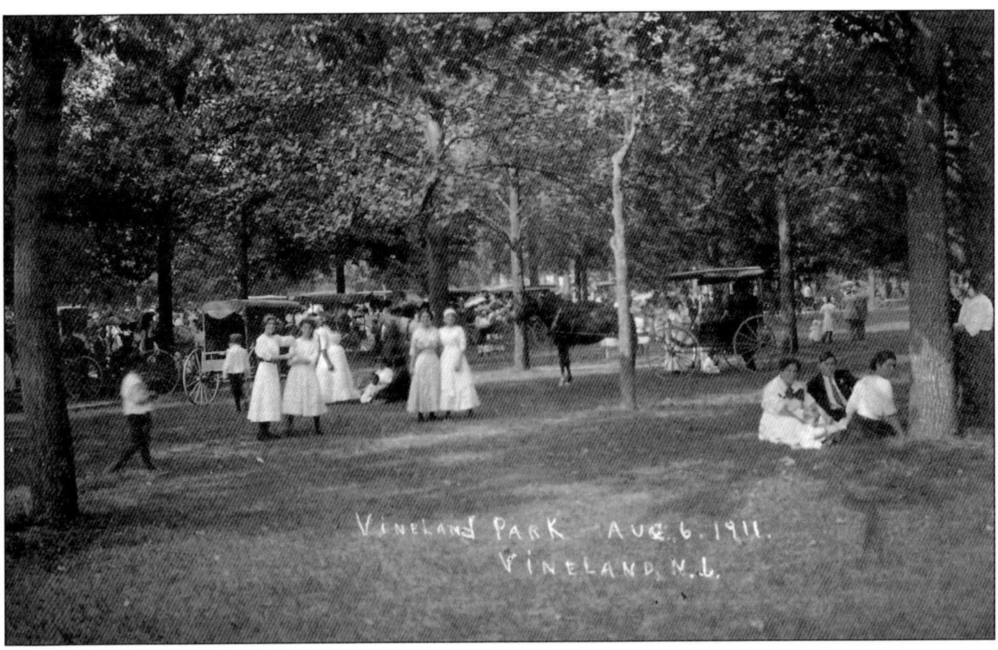

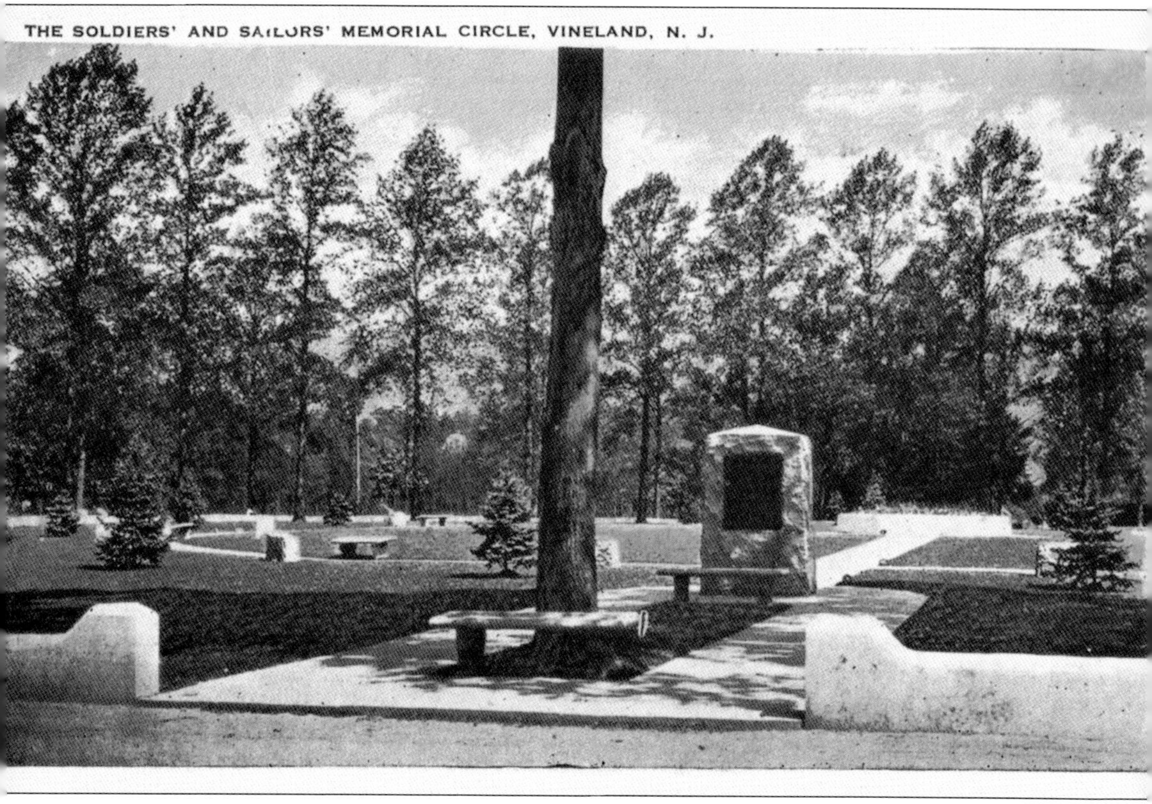

The Veterans Memorial Circle, at the heart of Landis Park, was constructed as a tribute to the soldiers who served in the American military during World War II. The project was organized by the City Beautiful Committee and the Diamond Social Club, and supported by well-known Vineland locals, including Samuel Gassell, Louis Basso, and W.H. Fenton.

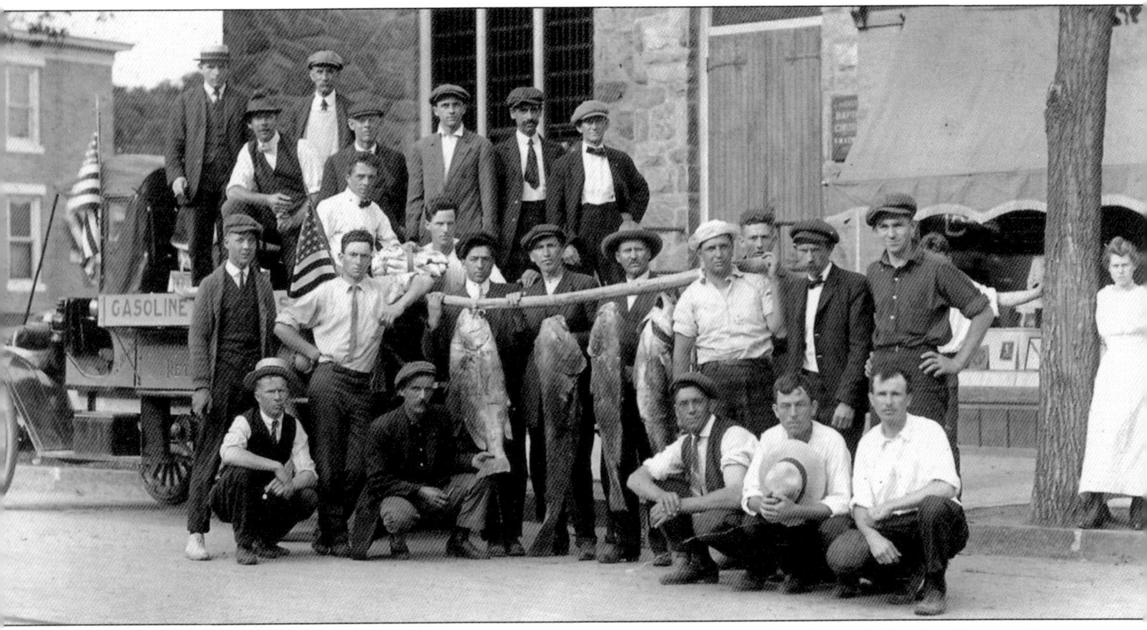

As the area was ringed by waterways and lakes, fishermen in Vineland rarely had to boast about "the one that got away." While commercial fishing has long been a way of life for many South Jersey communities, freshwater fish such as bass, catfish, and weakfish—caught in local waterways using just a bamboo stick and a bobber—were often served at the family dinner table.

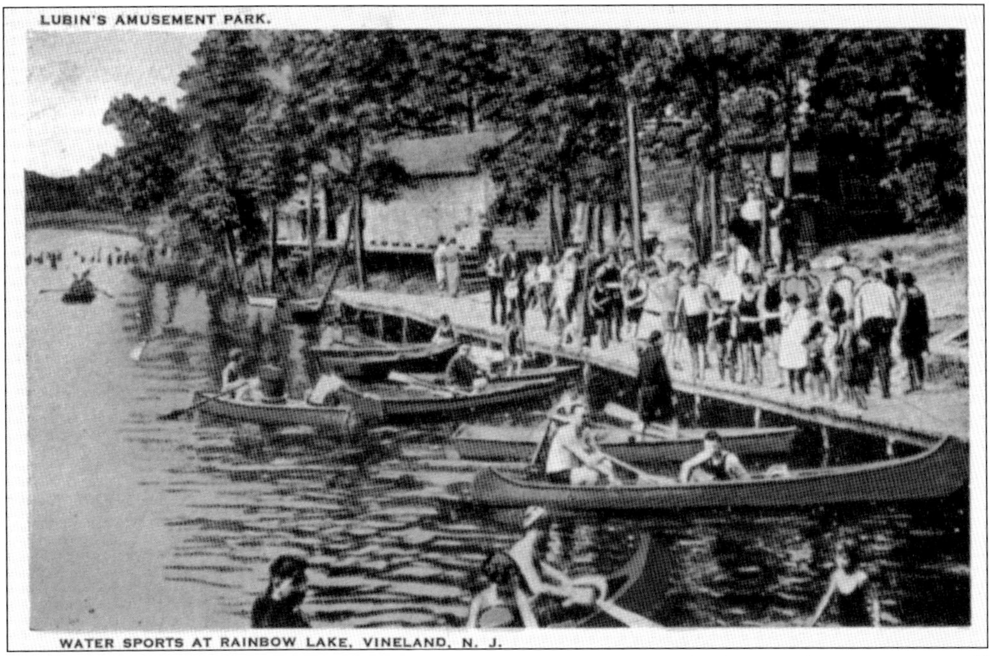

Even today, Rainbow Lake draws thousands of swimmers and sunbathers each summer, as well as fishermen and folks who enjoy a peaceful boat ride. The Lubin family, Russian immigrants who also owned the Grand Theater in Vineland, established an amusement pier at the lake where visitors could enjoy carnival games and rides. Although that area is no longer considered part of Vineland, it was marketed as part of the growing town in the late 19th century.

Older Vineland residents still recall the open field at the west end of Landis Avenue where a traveling carnival would set up each summer in the 1920s. Like many traveling shows, it included a gypsy fortune teller, games, and other attractions that were eagerly anticipated by the townsfolk, who spent the evening ogling sideshow exhibits while eating hot dogs and cotton candy.

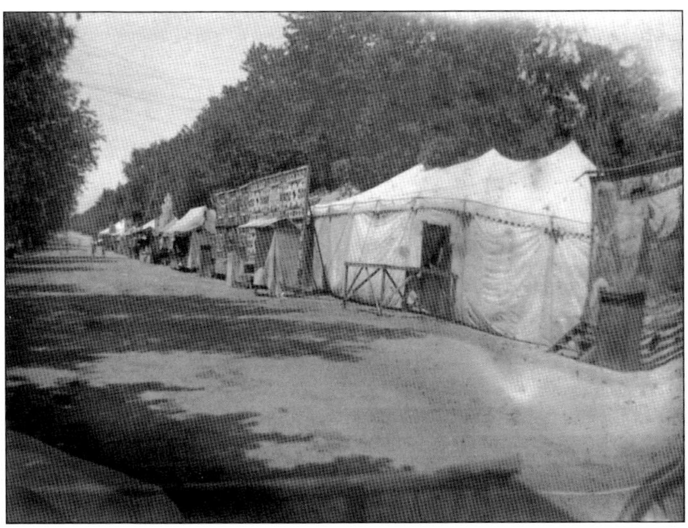

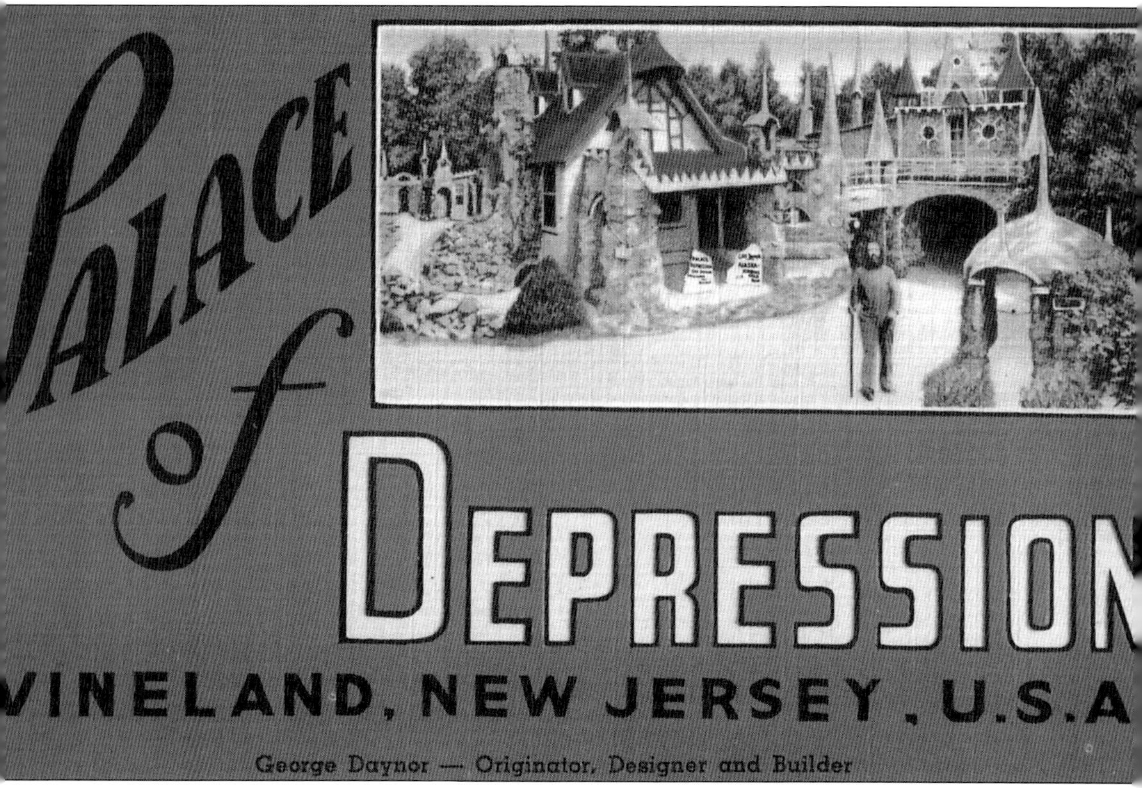

Perhaps the best-known of all Vineland's tourist attractions was the Palace Depression, built by George and Florence Daynor between 1929 and 1931. The "castle of junk" was literally erected from old car parts, broken bottles, and petrified wood, all held together with mud from the bed of a nearby creek. The novel structure attracted more than 200,000 visitors from the 1930s to the 1950s. Although the original was razed in 1964, a re-created Palace Depression is almost complete and will soon be welcoming tourists once again.

Five

Public Buildings

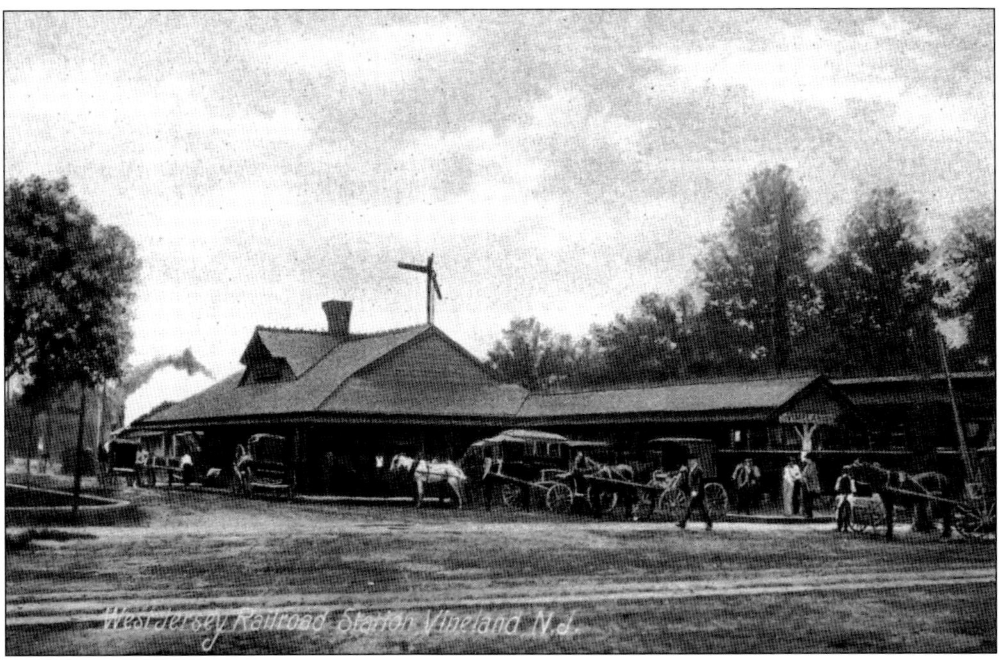

The West Jersey Railroad was just one of a number of train lines that connected Vineland to larger cities, including Philadelphia and New York. The railroad was a vital link for the community in its early years, carrying produce and passengers in and out of the new town. Local Vineland residents invested in their own line in 1867, but, when they were not able to meet the expenses, it was sold in 1873 to Jay Gould for $10,000. The train depots that once dotted the town were later demolished or purchased by private investors.

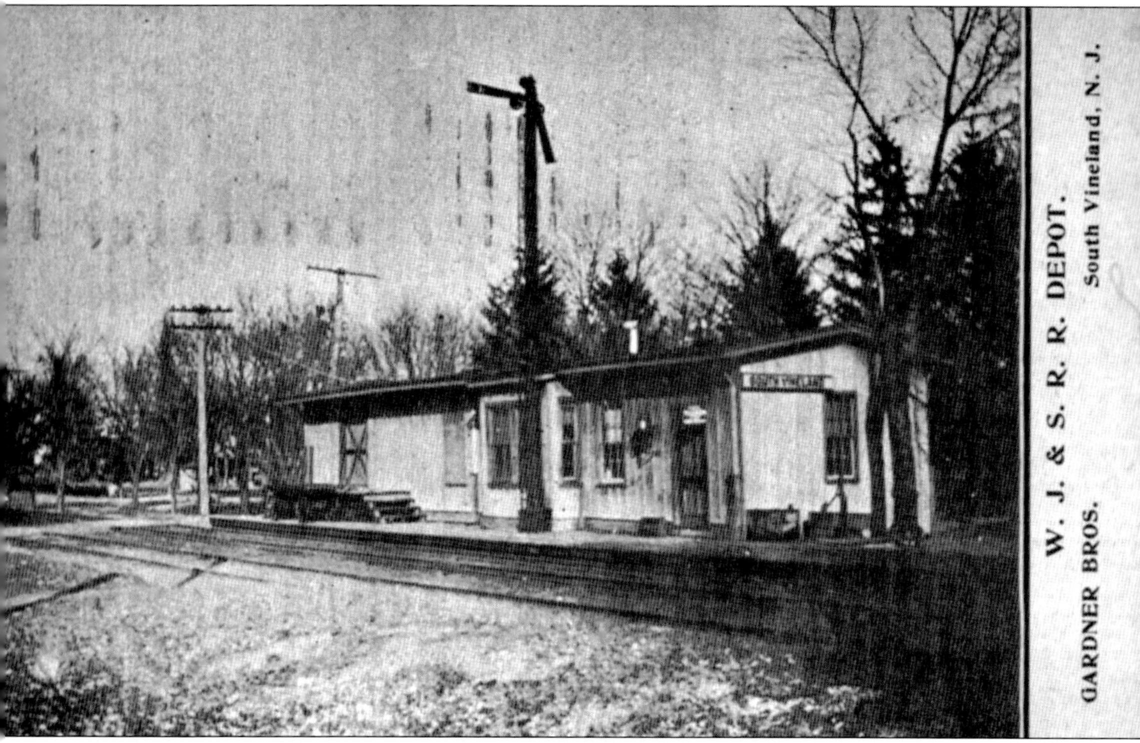

Shown here is the West Jersey & Seashore Railroad depot. In addition to carrying passengers, the trains moved thousands of crates of fresh fruits and vegetables, as well as shoes, cast-iron products, and rugs manufactured in Vineland during the 19th and early 20th centuries.

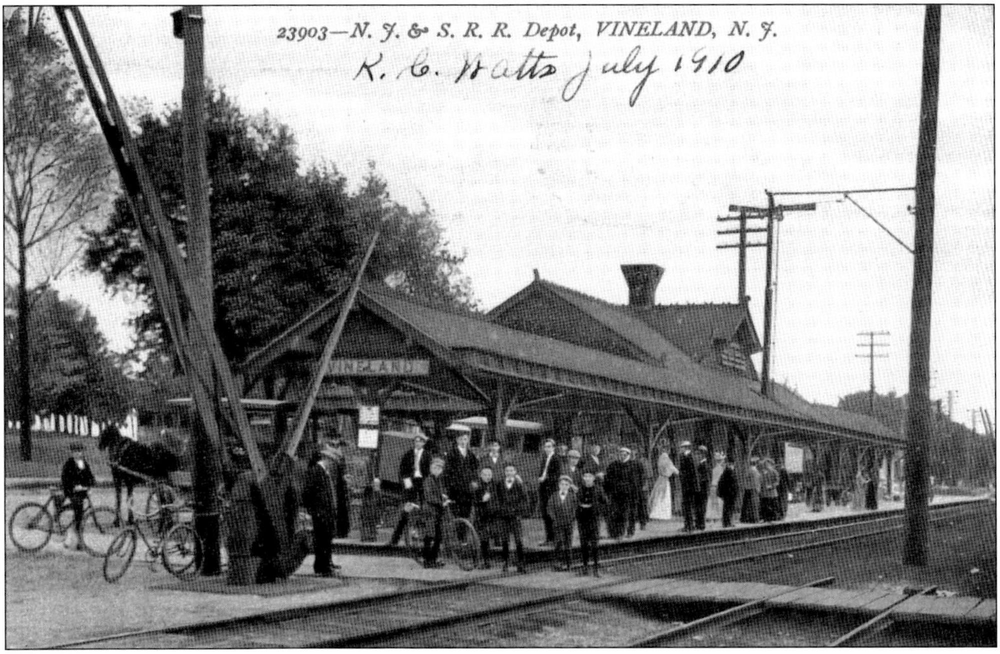

In 1896, a promotional booklet reported that the development of the railroads had encouraged the growth of seaside resorts such as Cape May, Sea Isle City, Ocean City, Stone Harbor, Anglesea, Wildwood, and Holly Beach. With a network of depots spread throughout South Jersey, local residents could easily purchase a round-trip ticket for 50¢ to enjoy a day at the shore, swimming in the ocean or strolling on the boardwalk before it was time to return home.

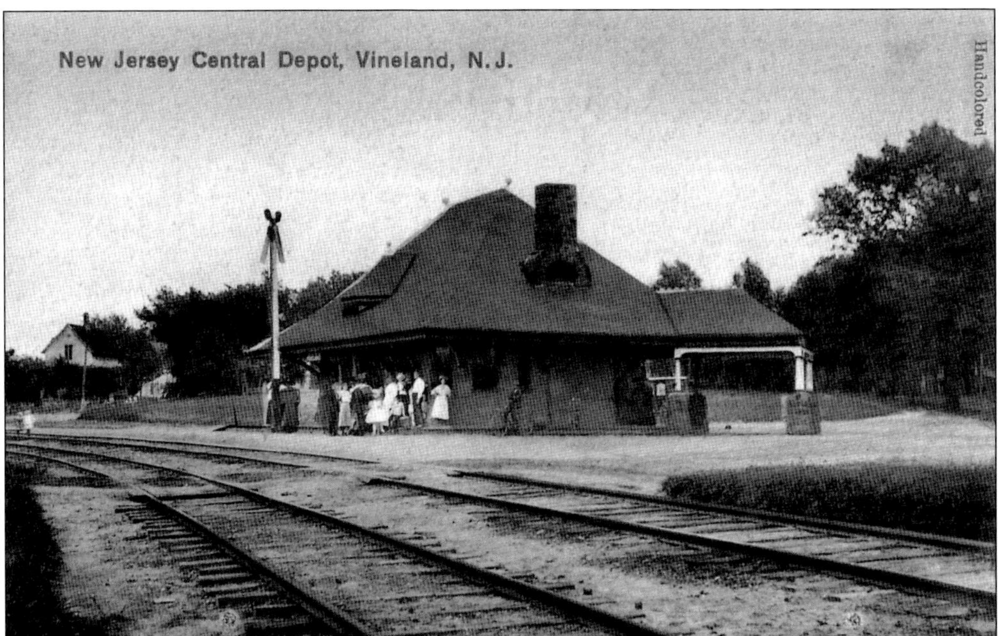

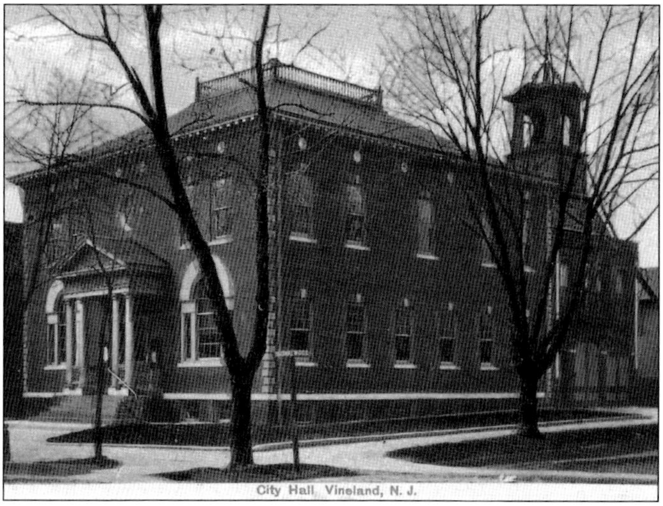

The first city hall, built on the southwest corner of Sixth and Wood Streets, not only served as home to the mayor and the board of commissioners (later known as the city council), but also housed the police department, public works offices, and the City Beautiful Committee. The multipurpose structure served the town until 1970, when a modern, five-story building replaced it at the nearby intersection of Seventh and Wood Streets.

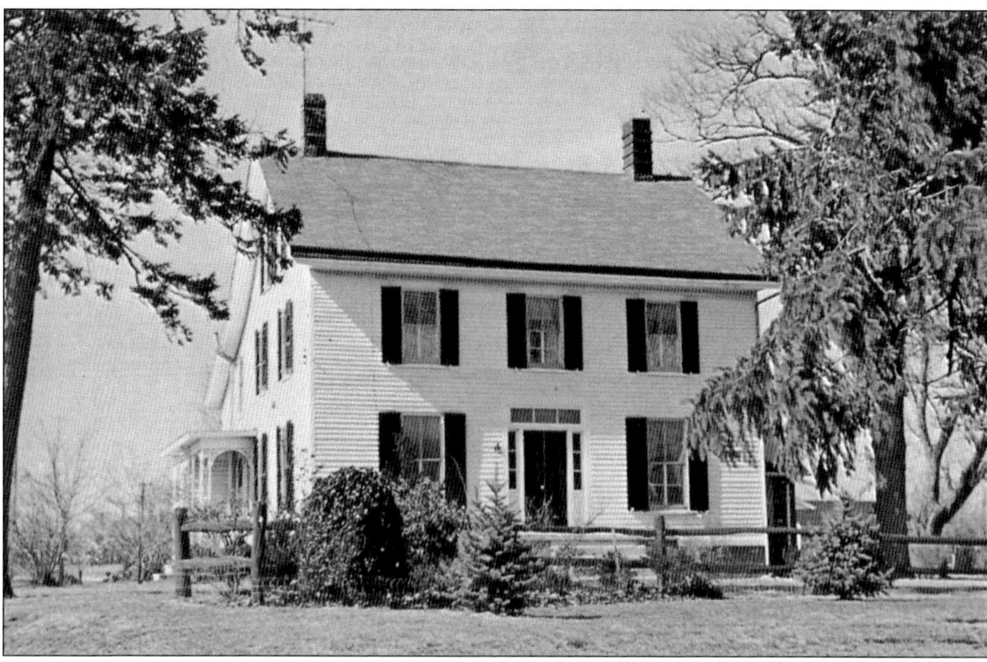

In 1862, Vineland's first post office was located at the Sharp farm and was managed by Charles K. Landis, who was appointed the town's first postmaster. Since Landis quickly became busy with his booming real estate business, he appointed H.M. Holbrook as assistant postmaster, and the post office was removed to the back of Davis's hotel. Holbrook was succeeded as deputy postmaster by C.P. Moorehouse.

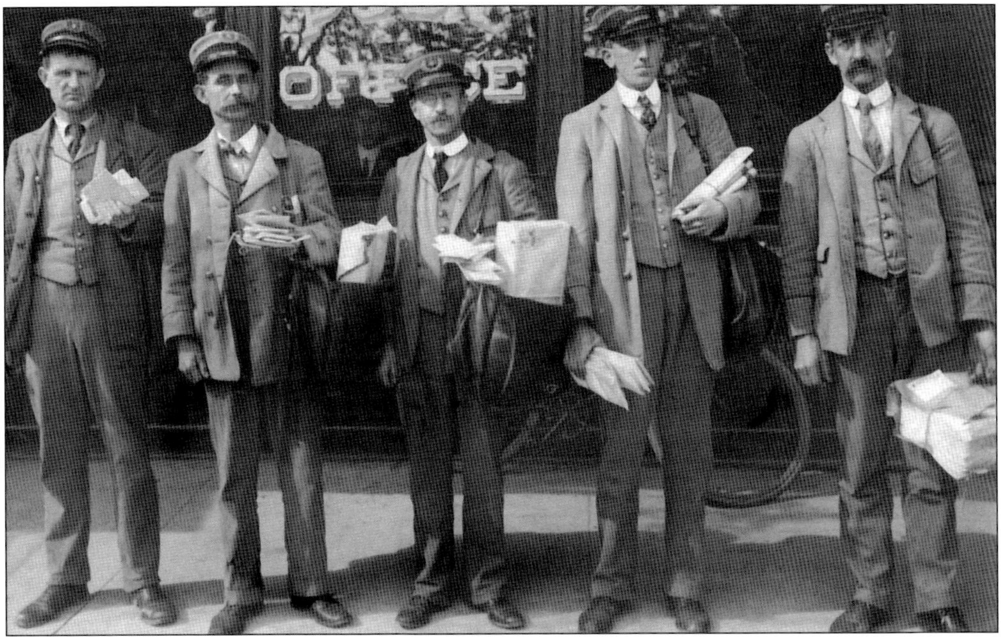

After Landis became too busy with his real estate business, he gave up the job of postmaster. In 1863, the post office was relocated W.F. Bassett's store, at the rear of Davis's hotel. Bassett oversaw operations until the store was purchased by William G. Smith, who then became the town's postmaster. In the late 19th century, mail carriers attached small shaded lanterns to their coats since they often delivered mail well after dark.

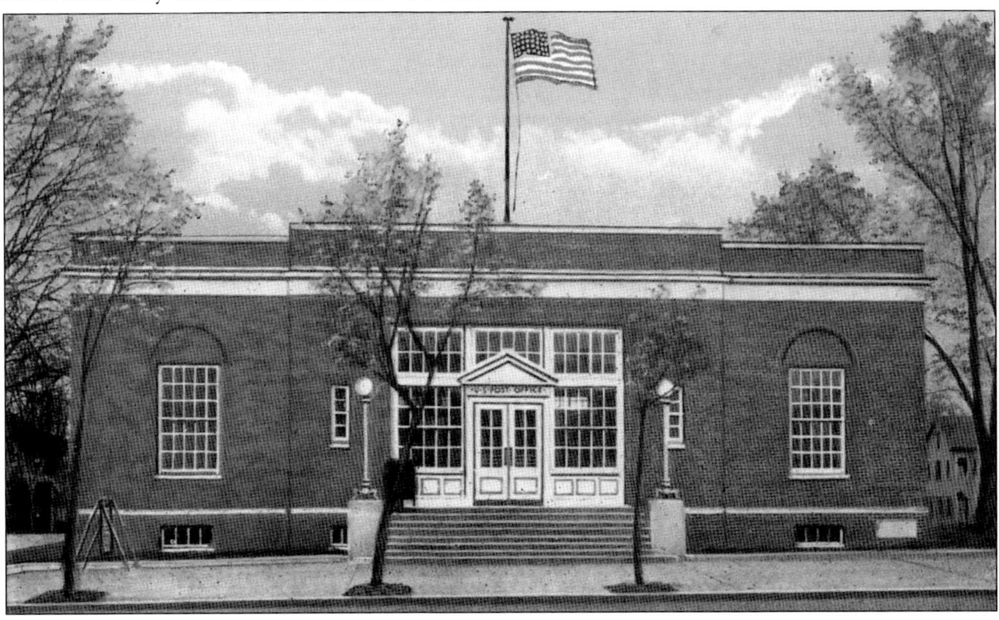

By June 1890, the Vineland Post Office had already done $10,000 worth of business, prompting the post office to offer free delivery to local residents. The post office moved a few more times before finally settling into this handsome brick building on East Landis Avenue. In 2002, the facility was converted into the municipal courthouse and a new post office was built next door, just west of its predecessor.

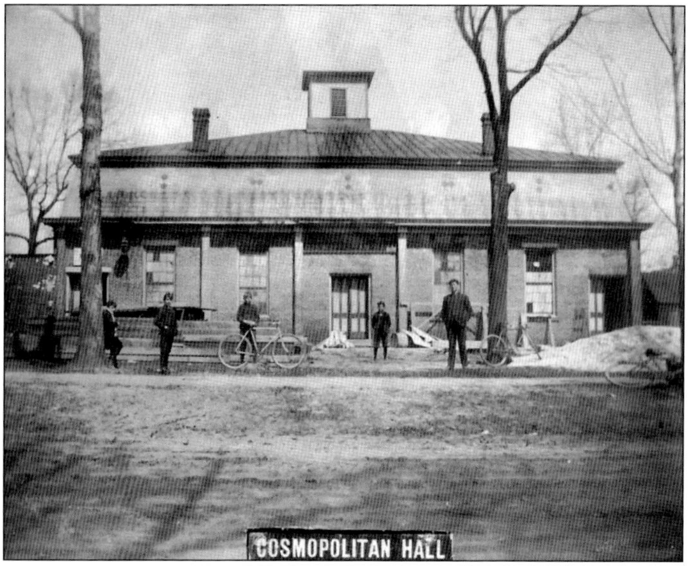

Vineland's civic-minded Spiritualist community was behind the construction of Plum Street Hall in 1875, which was later refurbished and rechristened Cosmopolitan Hall. Generations of local residents enjoyed live performances by traveling acting troupes and musicians, as well as guest speakers who lectured on important topics of the day. The hall continued to serve the townspeople until 1918, when it was destroyed by fire.

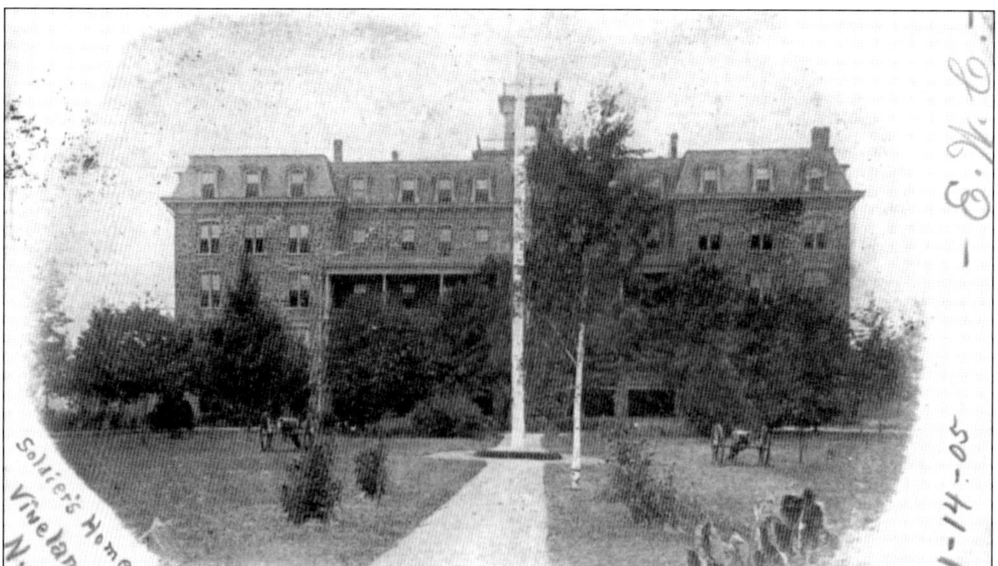

Known simply as the Soldiers Home by most local residents, the New Jersey Veterans Memorial Home was originally constructed in 1868 as a Methodist seminary. When the project proved too costly, it was foreclosed on, and it later served as a preparatory school for men training to become Catholic priests. In 1898, it was purchased by the State of New Jersey and converted into a nursing facility for veterans of the Civil War. Although the original structure was torn down in 1990, an expanded facility is still in operation there, serving veterans from throughout the state.

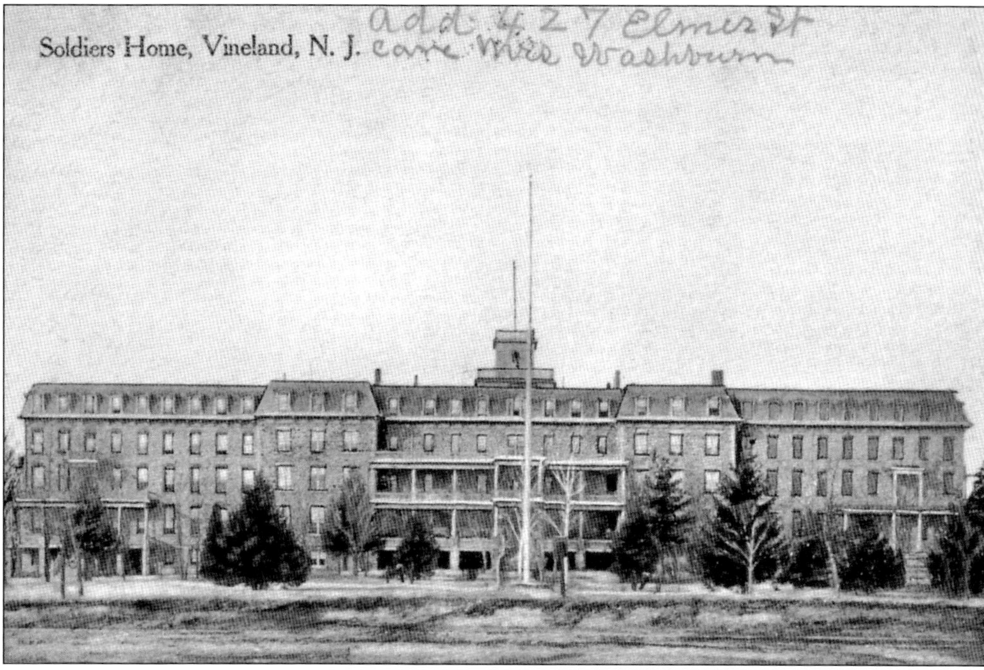

The first residents of the Soldiers Home enjoyed round-the-clock care from a dedicated staff—ranging from medical treatment to domestic care. The facility, which offered 150 rooms and its own hospital set on spacious grounds, was open to men from all branches of military service, as well as their wives and widows. In the years that followed and after continued military conflicts, the home was repeatedly renovated to accommodate a growing number of residents.

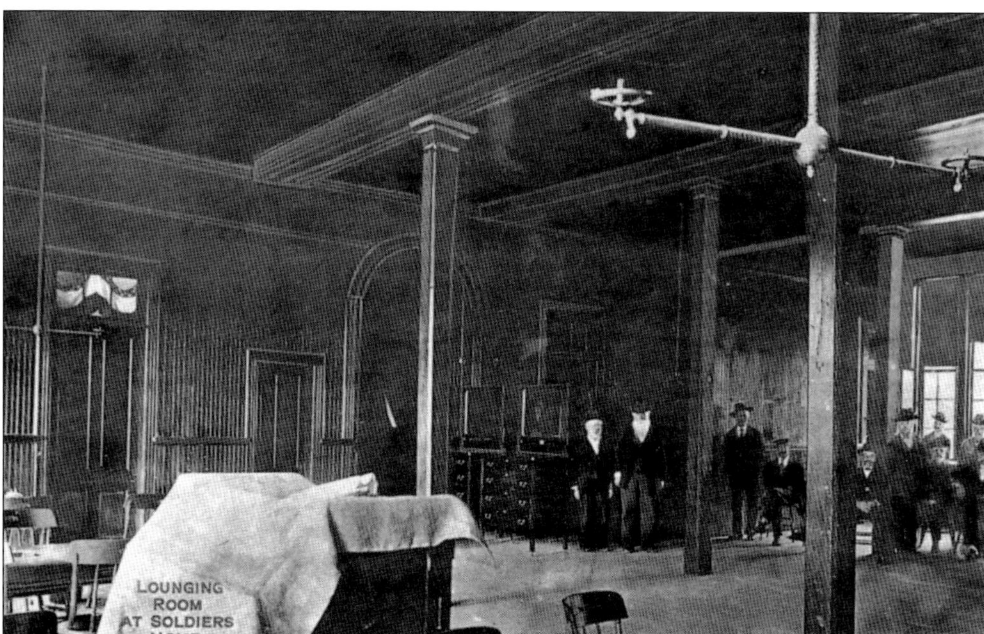

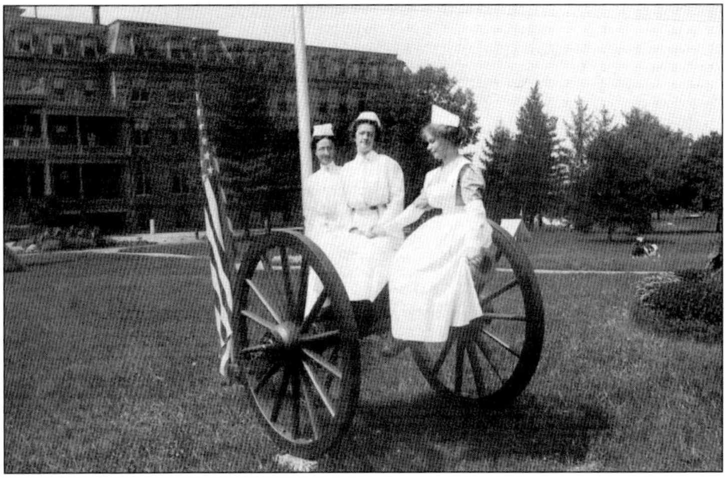

The nursing profession was still in its infancy in the years following the Civil War. Although initially derided as being in an "inappropriate" profession for women, the growing corps of women who became nurses soon filled a real need at institutions like the soldiers homes that sprang up in different states.

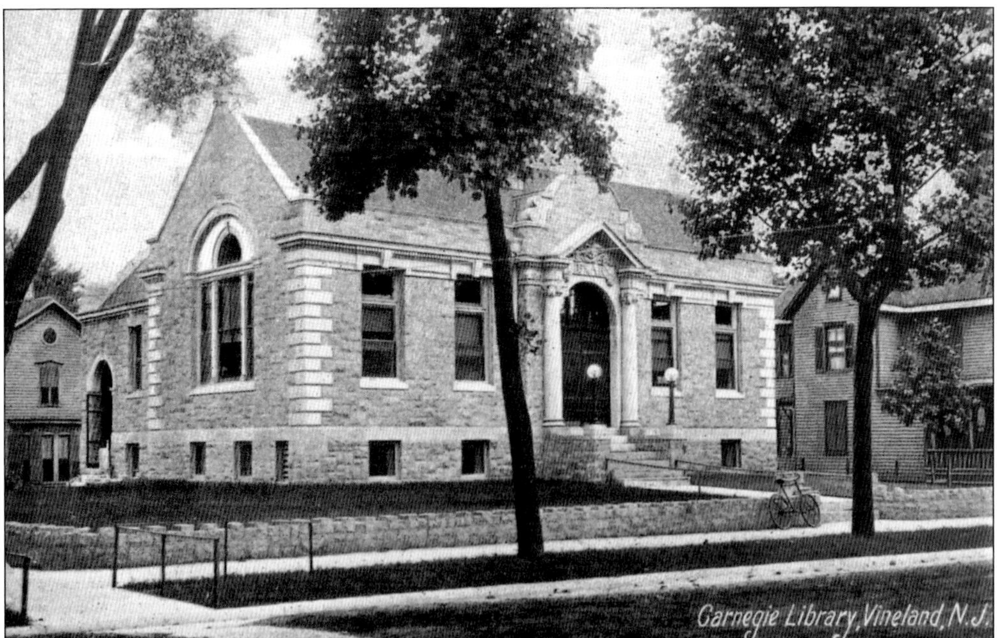

In the late 1860s, the early settlers established a library association, which unfortunately was not successful long term. However, in the early 20th century, the town received funds from philanthropist Andrew Carnegie of Pittsburgh and built the gray stone library at the intersection of Sixth and Elmer Streets in 1906. After a new library was built on East Landis Avenue in the 1970s, the old library was repurposed as a senior center for area residents, and it remains in use today.

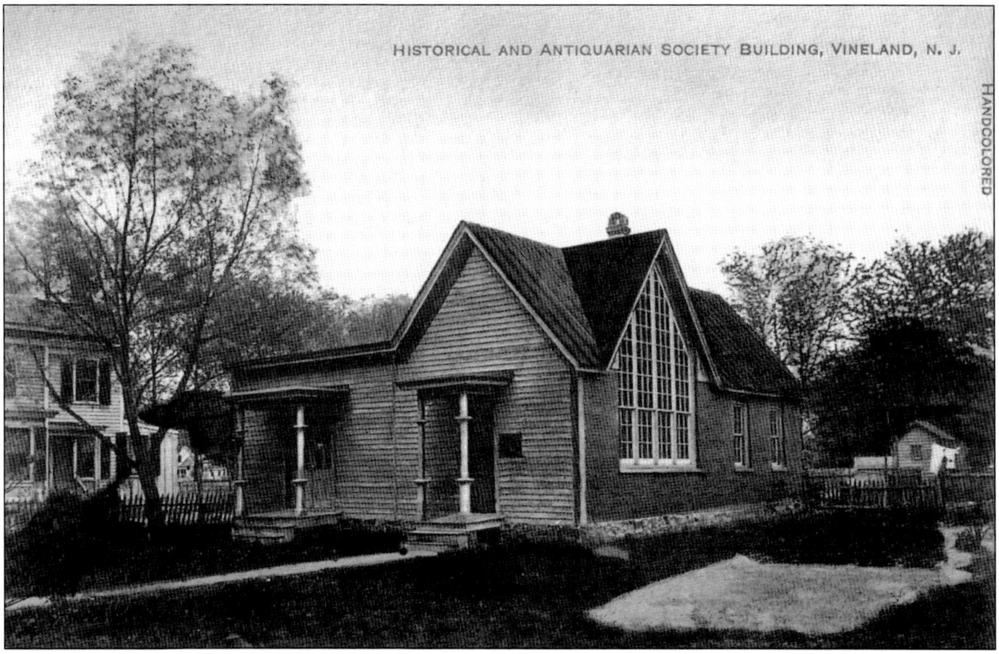

The Vineland Historical and Antiquarian Society was formed in 1864, just three years after the town of Vineland was founded by Charles K. Landis. About 20 years later, the members started a fundraising drive to build a small museum on the grounds where the current museum has stood since 1910. In 2014, the society celebrated its 150th anniversary as the oldest local historical society in New Jersey, headquartered in the oldest purpose-built museum in the state.

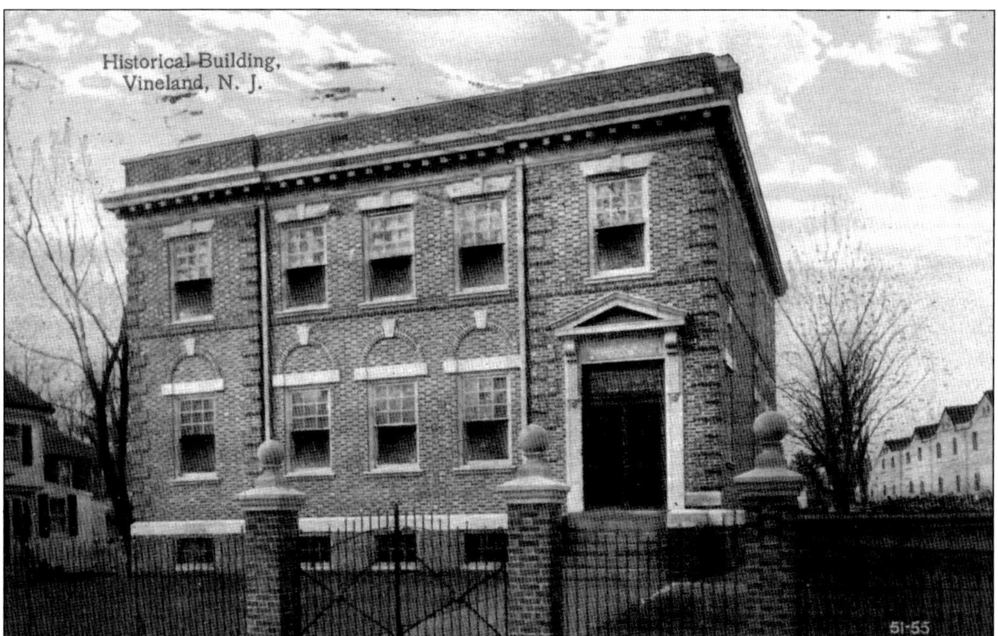

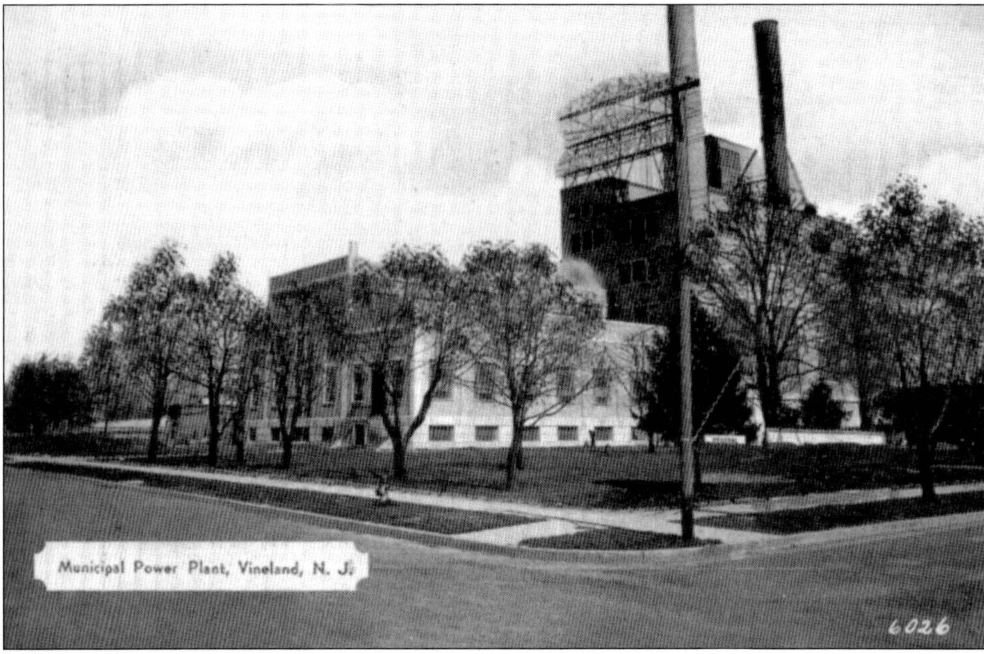

Vineland is one of the few towns in New Jersey to own and operate its own electric utility. Although the original plant was small, it provided electricity to about 2,000 homes and streetlights by 1920. The current power plant, located on the corner of North West Avenue and Plum Street, is one of the largest in the northeastern United States.

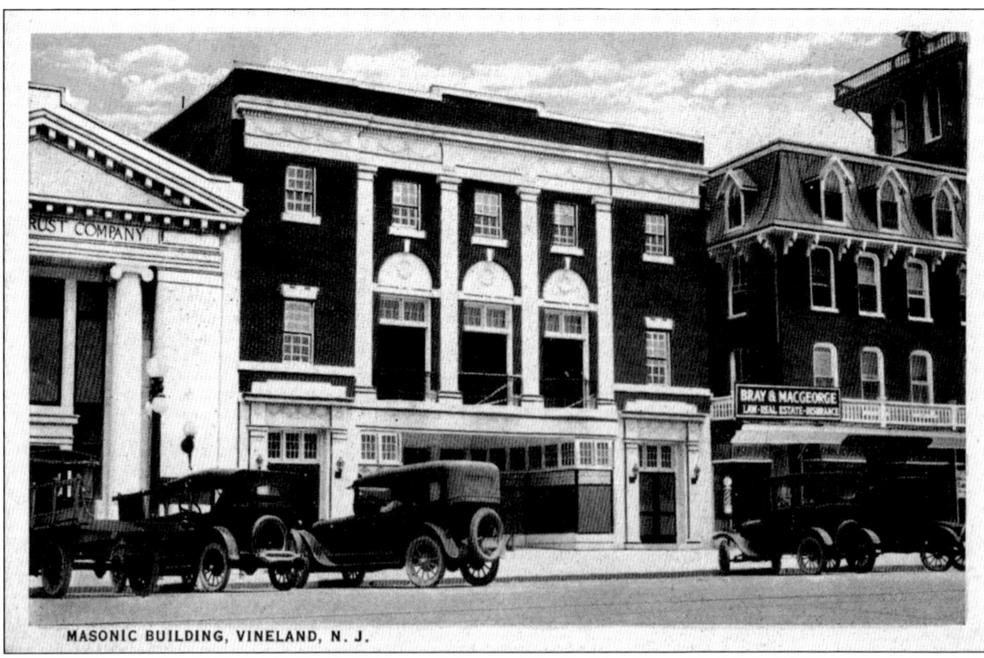

This brick building, once neighbors with the prestigious Baker House Hotel, still stands at the heart of Landis Avenue, proudly bearing the words "Masonic Building" across the stone trim at the top. The original home to Vineland's Masonic Lodge No. 69, the building was later converted into a site for a succession of small businesses.

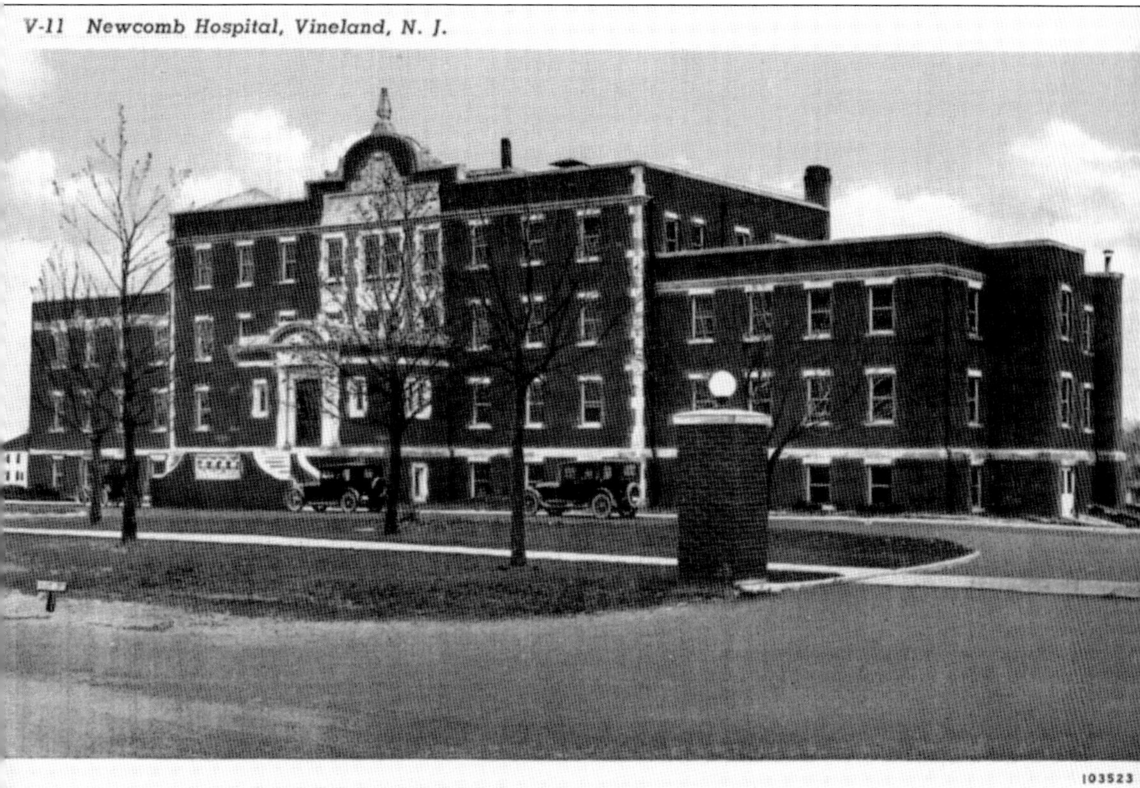

Vineland's early residents were served by private hospitals like the Hatch Sanitarium and the Turner Hospital, often run by doctors at their individual homes. In 1924, local businessman Leverett Newcomb donated land on South State Street, where Newcomb Hospital was constructed. The redbrick building was added onto several times in the years that followed to accommodate the growth of Vineland's population. By the 1970s, the fully accredited hospital had 230 beds for patients, 50 doctors, and 400 employees.

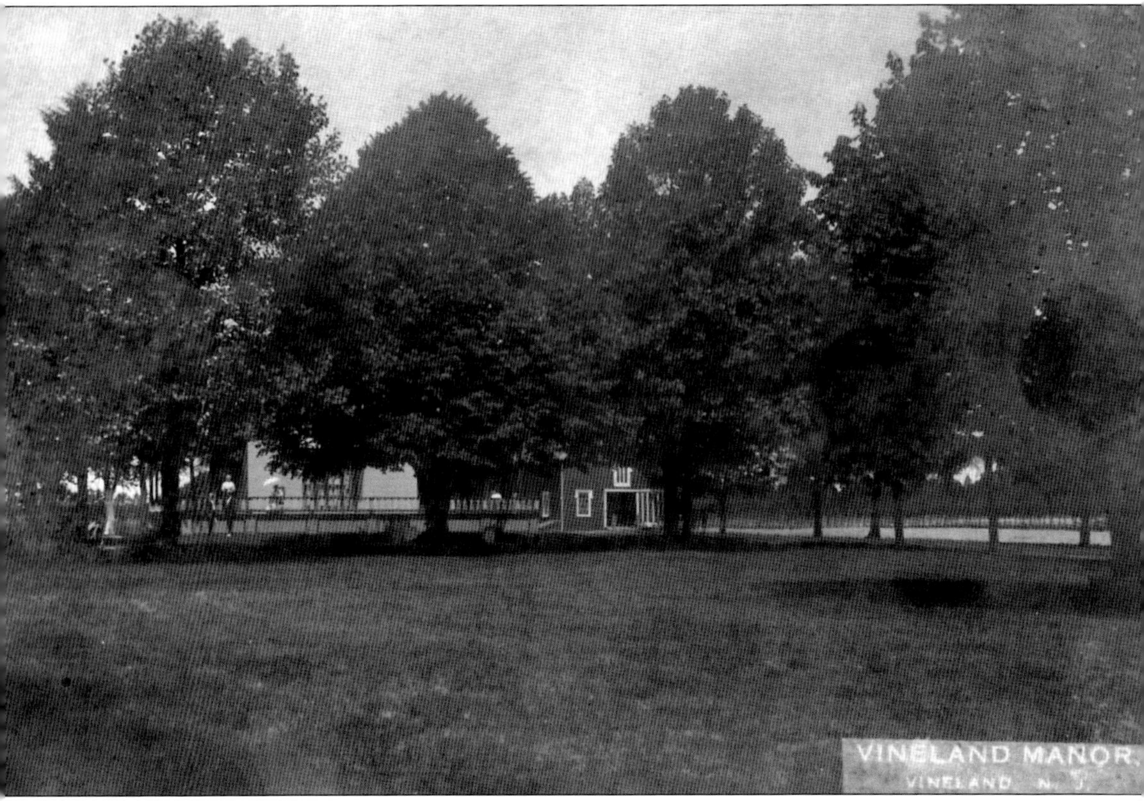

American communities often established residences where indigent locals could live and work. Around the turn of the 20th century, Vineland residents created the Vineland Manor, a self-sufficient agriculture facility that housed older residents who could no longer afford to live on their own.

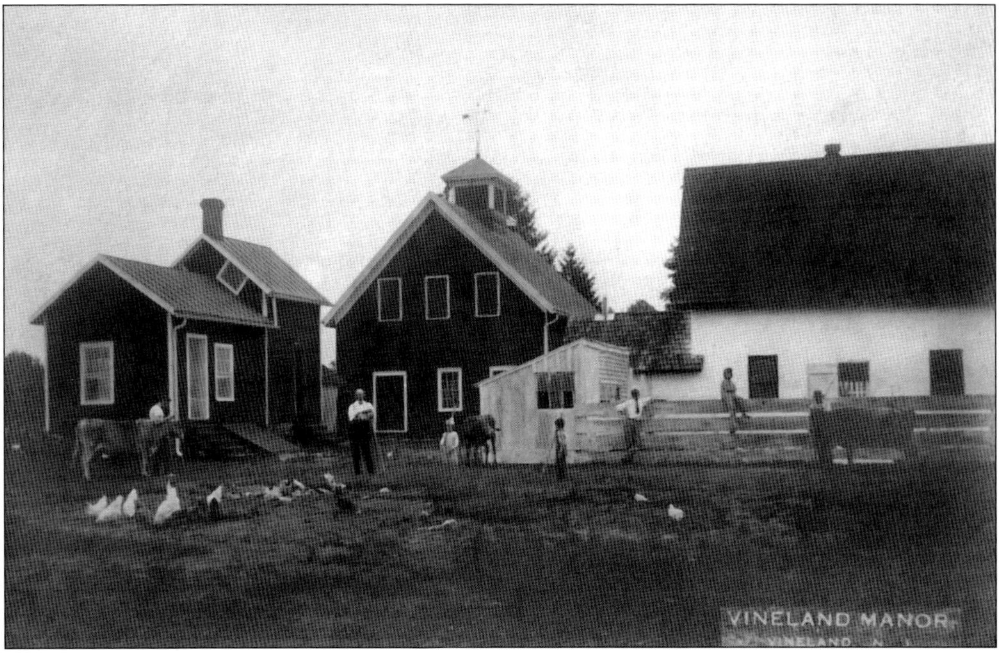

Although Cumberland County had established an almshouse in the early 1800s for the poor and sick in neighboring Hopewell Township, outside of Bridgeton, the county seat, Vineland created its own home for poor residents so that they could continue living in their hometown.

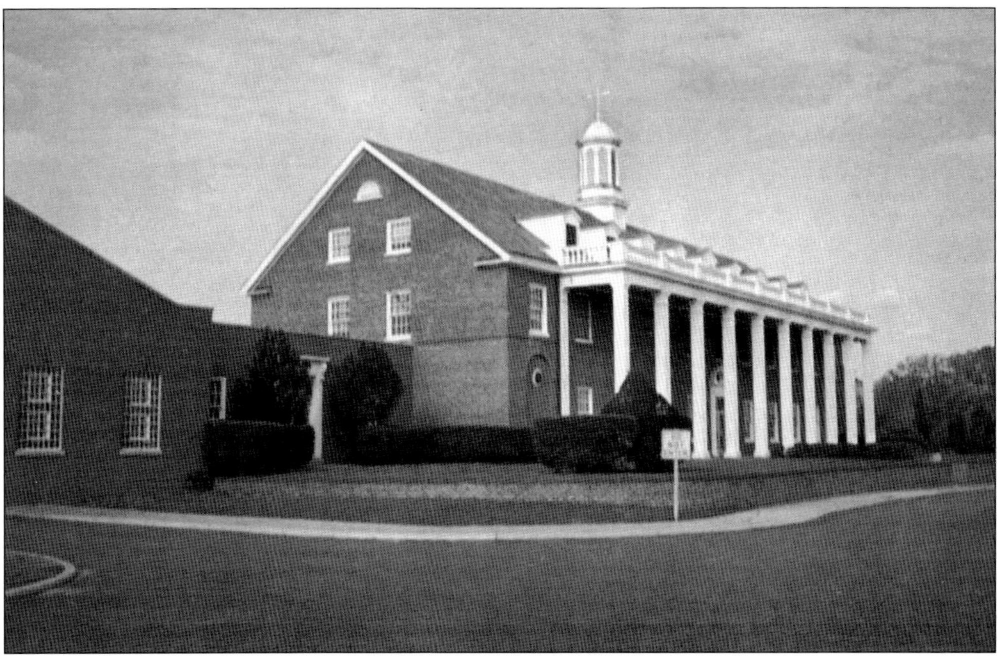

The residents of Vineland, who sold more war bonds than any town in America during World War II, also showed their patriotism in 1940 by building a National Guard armory on South Delsea Drive. The armory remains in use today as the headquarters of the 1st Battalion, 50th Armor New Jersey Army National Guard.

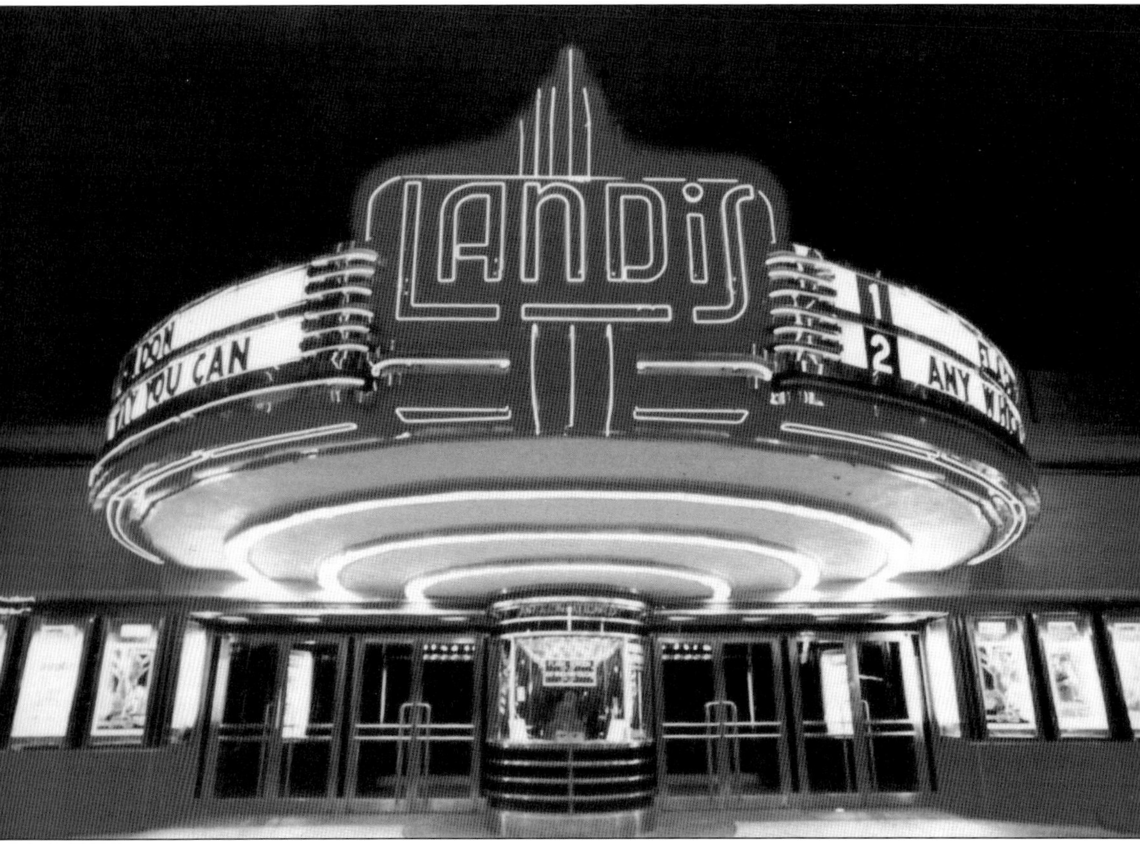

For generations, the Landis Theater drew thousands of local residents, who attended Saturday matinees as children and, later, evening features as adults. Opened in 1939, the movie theater was almost demolished in the 1980s, when the downtown was undergoing a renaissance. A dedicated group of local residents banded together to save the theater, which unfortunately was closed just a few short years after it reopened.

Six

Education

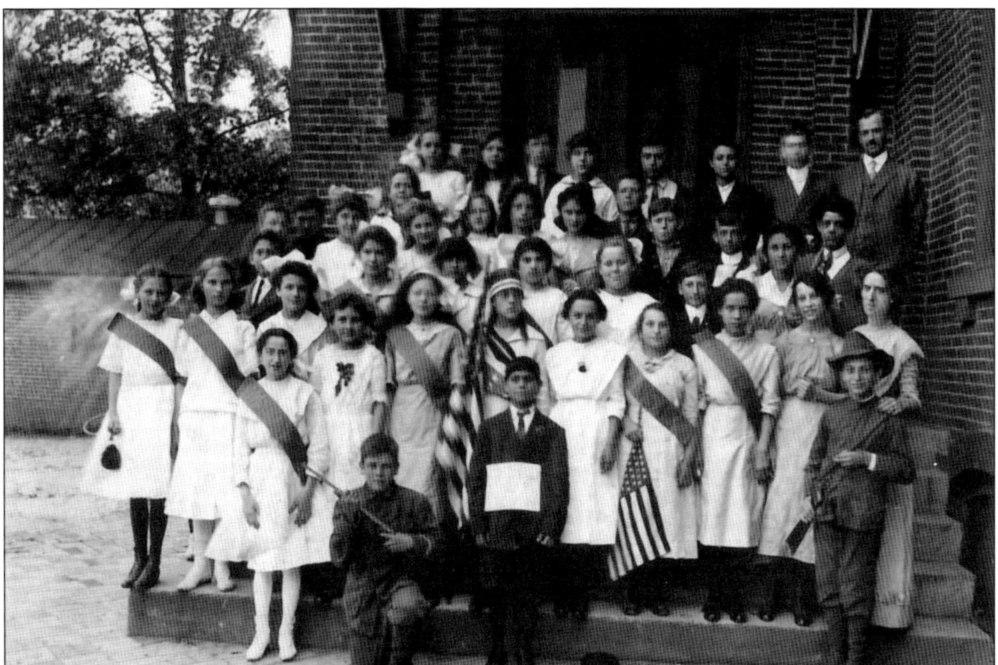

In every elementary school, students eagerly looked forward to the annual pageants that were presented to parents and friends. While larger schools sometimes had an auditorium where such events could be held, smaller schools often had to improvise a space for both the performers and the audience.

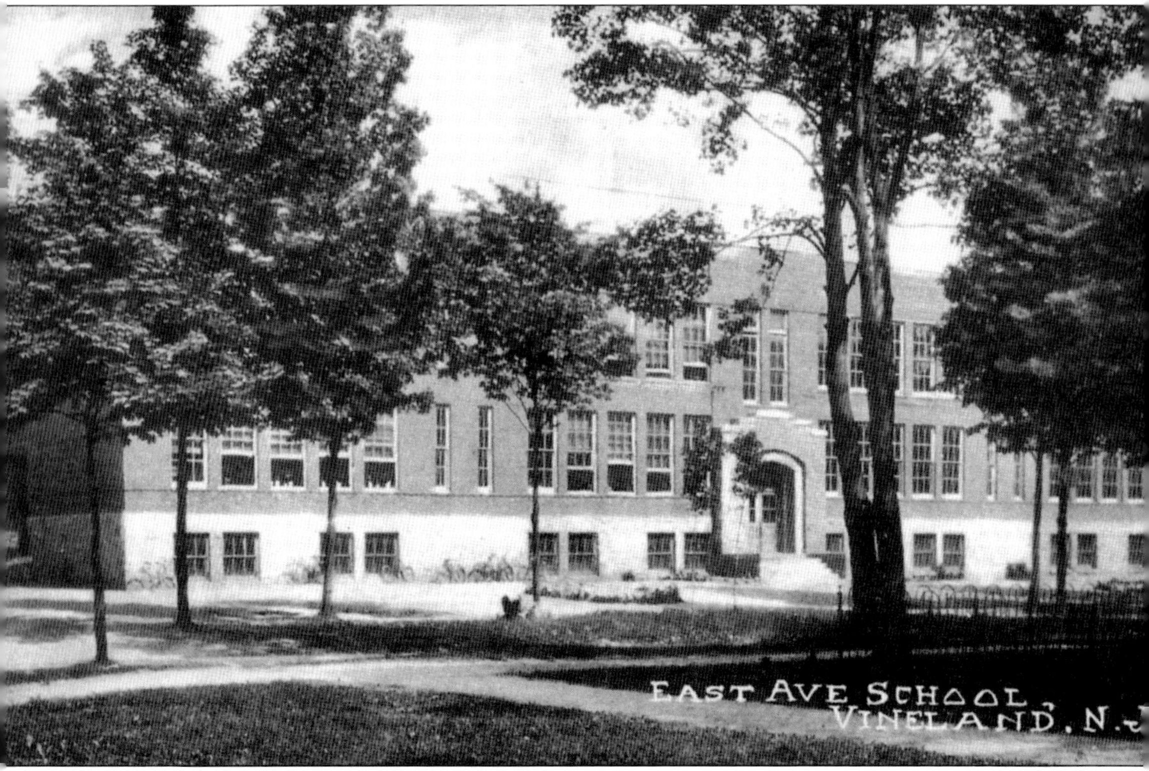

East Avenue School was built in 1918 at a cost of more than $600,000 on three acres of land on South East Avenue. The redbrick building, which remains in use today, was later renamed Dr. George Cunningham School, out of respect for a local physician who was very active in the community.

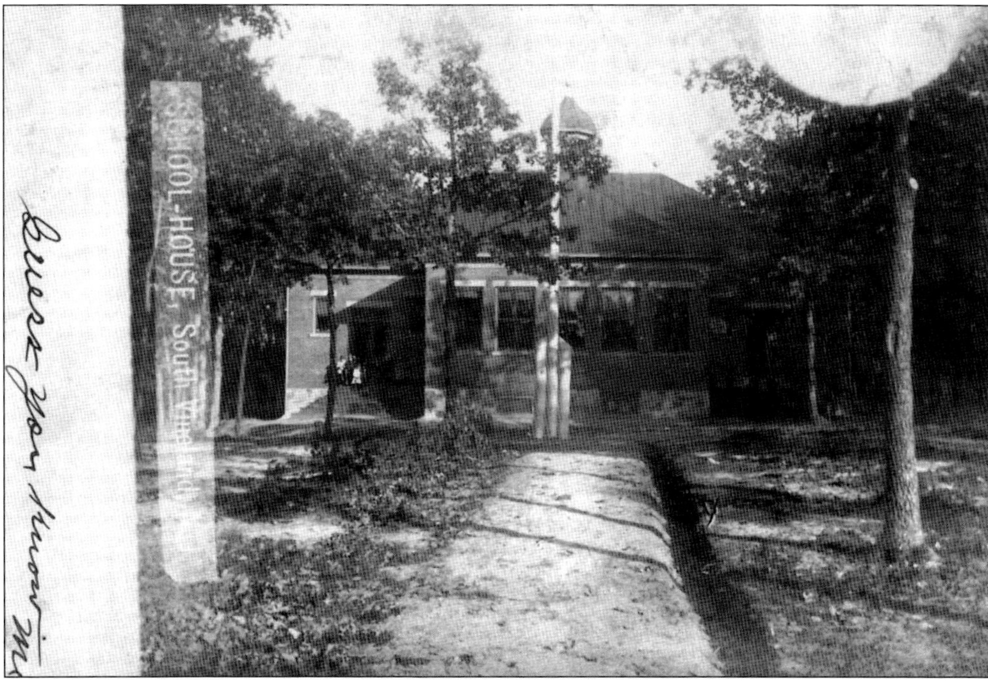

The first one-room schools in South Vineland had disappeared long before the five-room South Vineland School was built in 1903. Generations of farming families sent their children to the redbrick school, which later served as a home for special education classes and then alternative education classes. Although they were sometimes isolated by what was then a considerable distance, the children still had the opportunity to participate in district events. Unfortunately, the school was demolished in 2013.

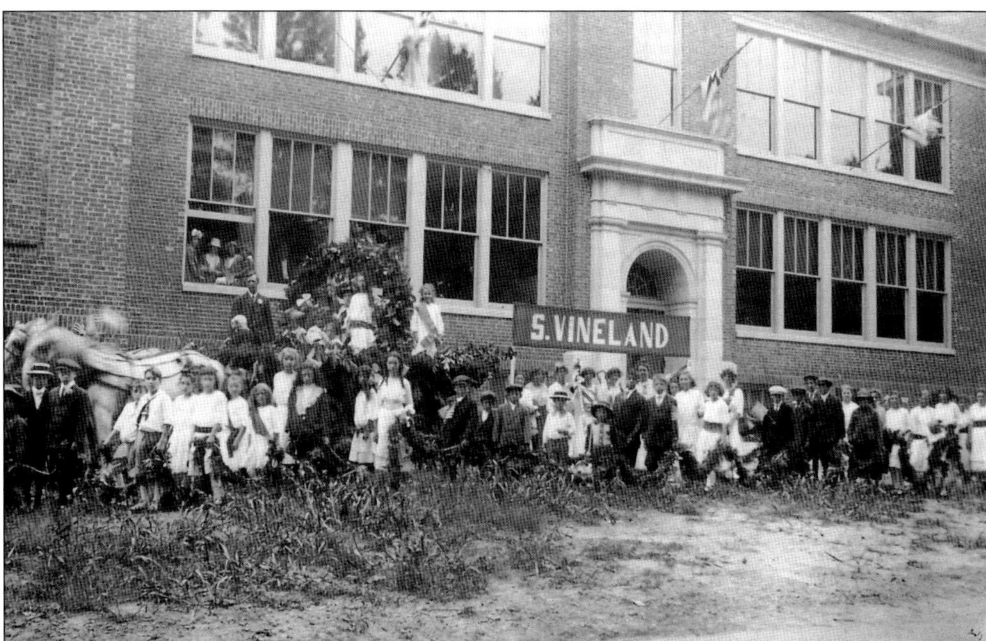

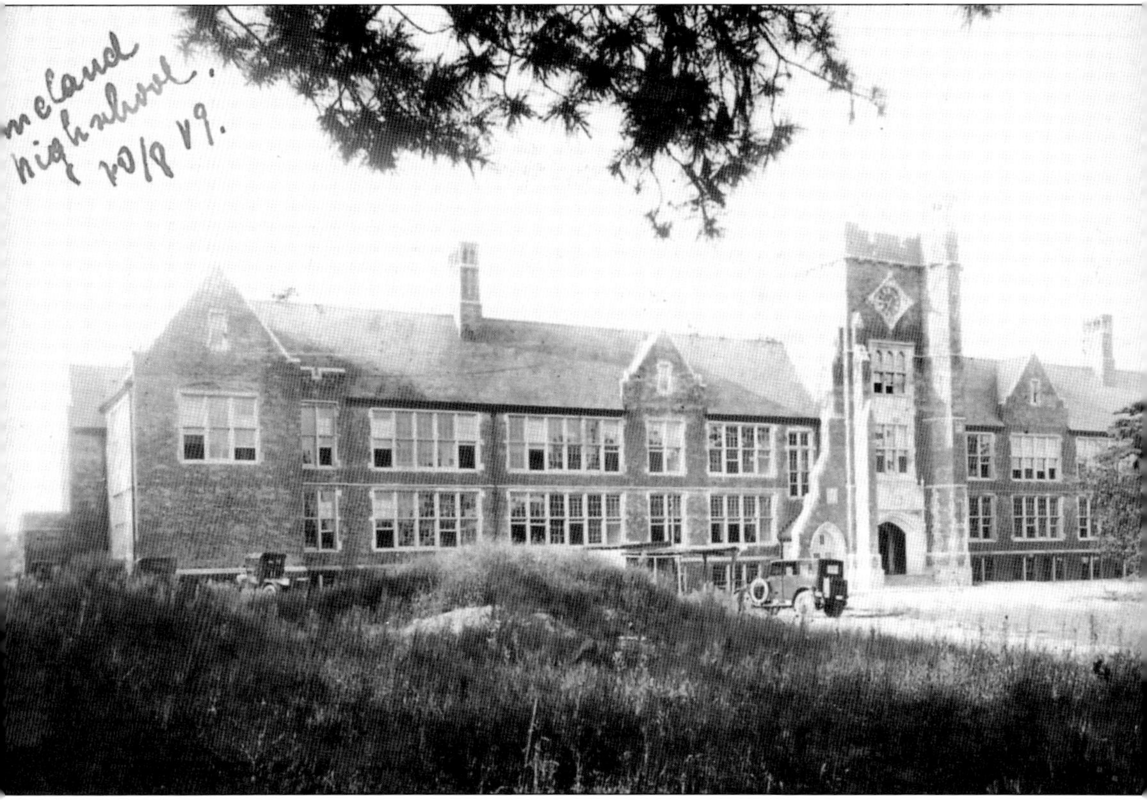

In 1927, Vineland opened a new high school on Landis Avenue that was later replaced by a larger high school in 1963, which is still in use today. The building pictured was rechristened Landis Junior High School and housed the seventh through ninth grades. In the 1980s, it was renamed Landis Middle School and became home to the sixth through eighth grades.

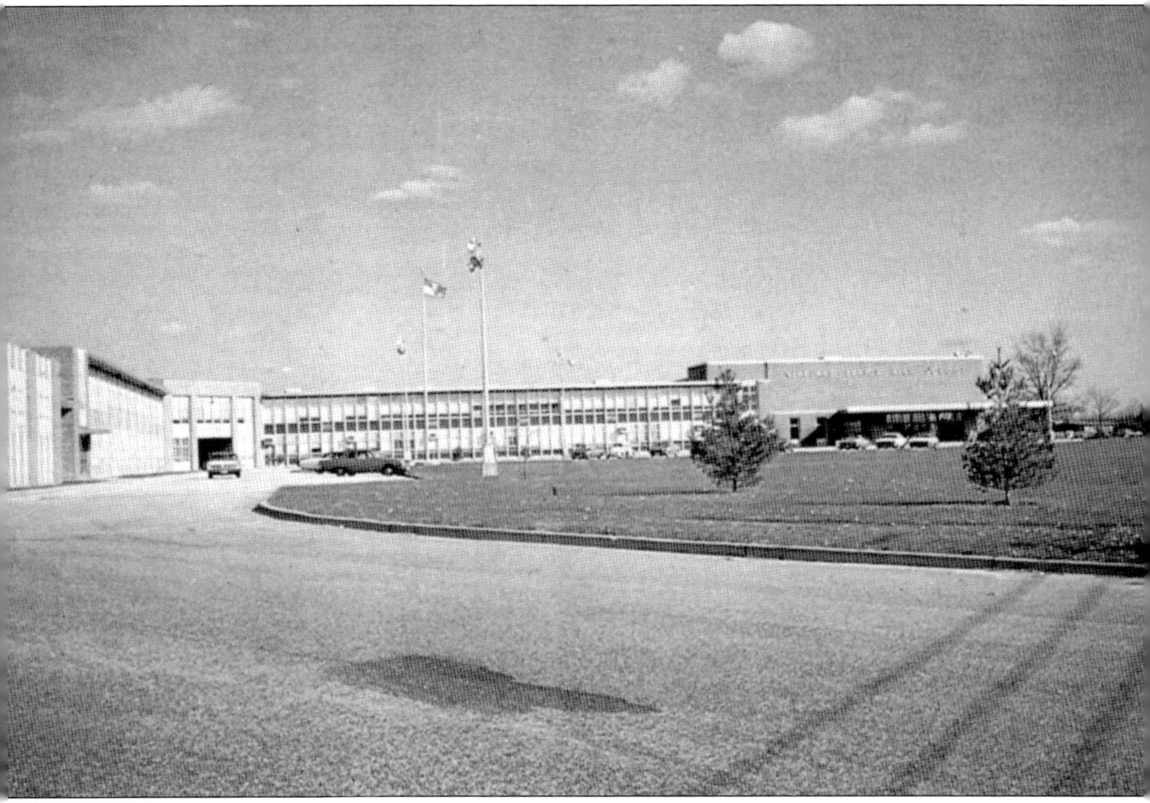

The current Vineland High School was completed in December 1963 at the cost of a little over $3 million. Situated on 48.5 acres at the intersection of Chestnut Avenue and Brewster Road, the school graduated its first class in 1964. As Vineland's population increased, a second high school was added to the campus. The buildings are designated VHS North (grades 9–10) and VHS South (grades 11–12).

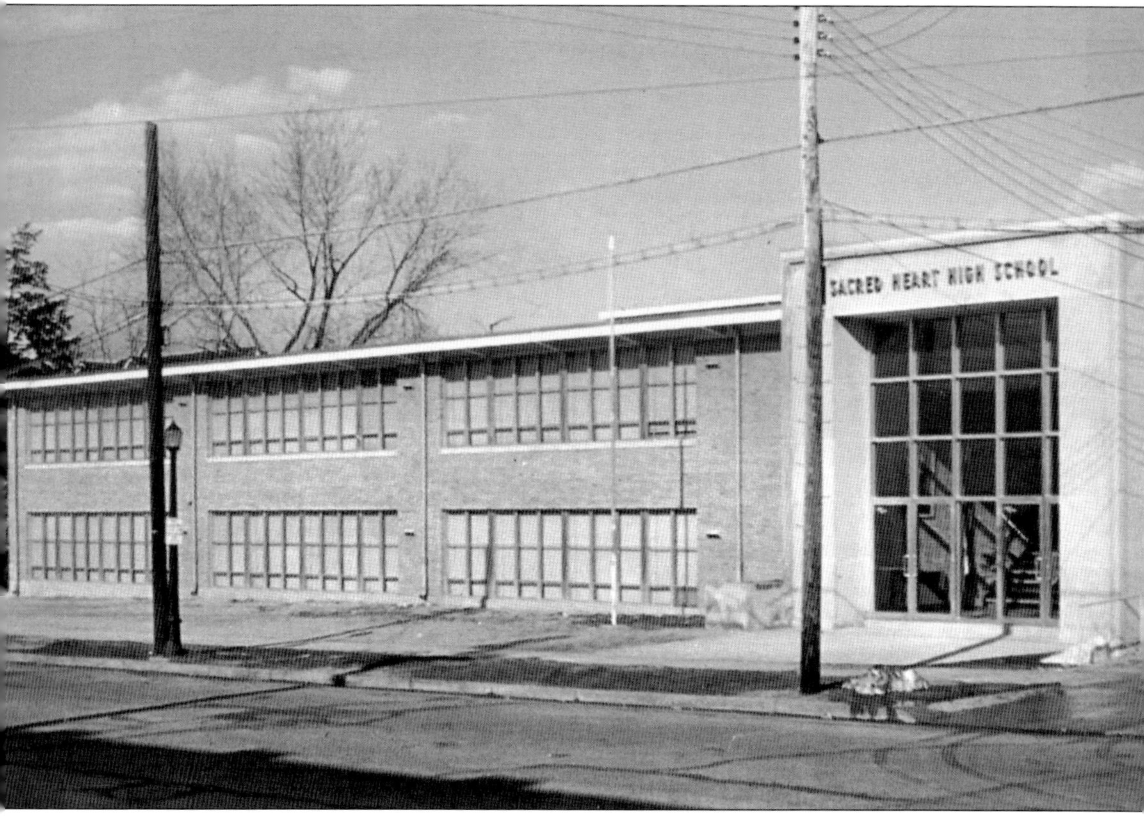

In 2013, many Vineland residents were upset by the closing of Sacred Heart High School, which had been an integral part of the downtown for generations. After the school opened in 1921, the enrollment soon increased to 375 students. Sacred Heart was expanded in 1927 and then enlarged again in 1955.

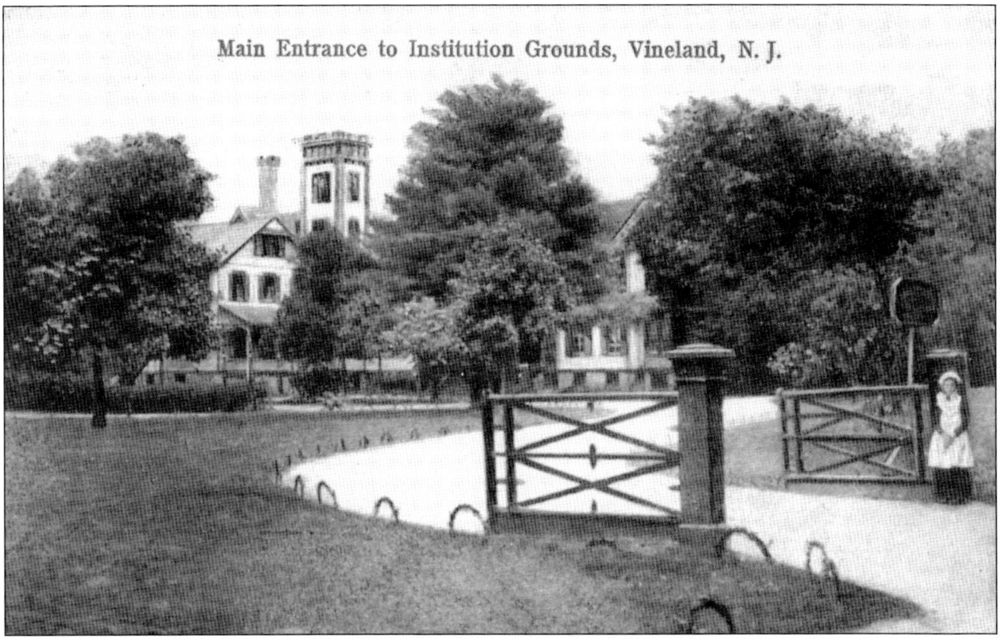

In 1888, New Jersey governor Robert S. Green empowered the state to send indigent mentally challenged females to "some suitable and convenient home." A yearly fee of $230 was appropriated for training and maintenance. Rev. Olin Garrison was assigned as the first superintendent, but he went on to devote more time across the street to the Vineland Training School for mentally challenged children. While many of the original buildings at the state school are still standing, parts of the facility have been modernized over the years.

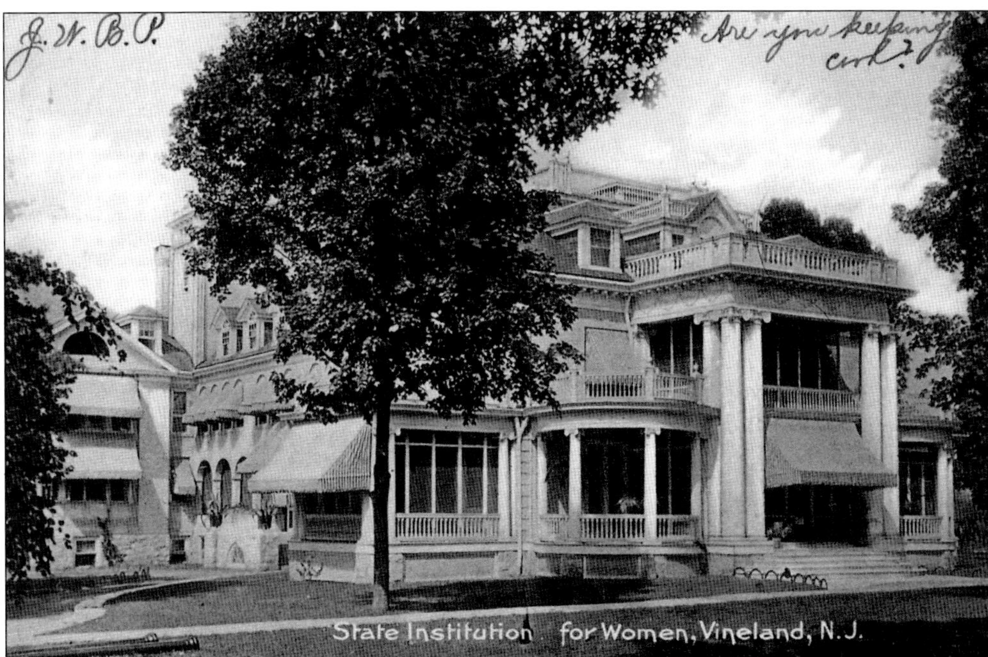

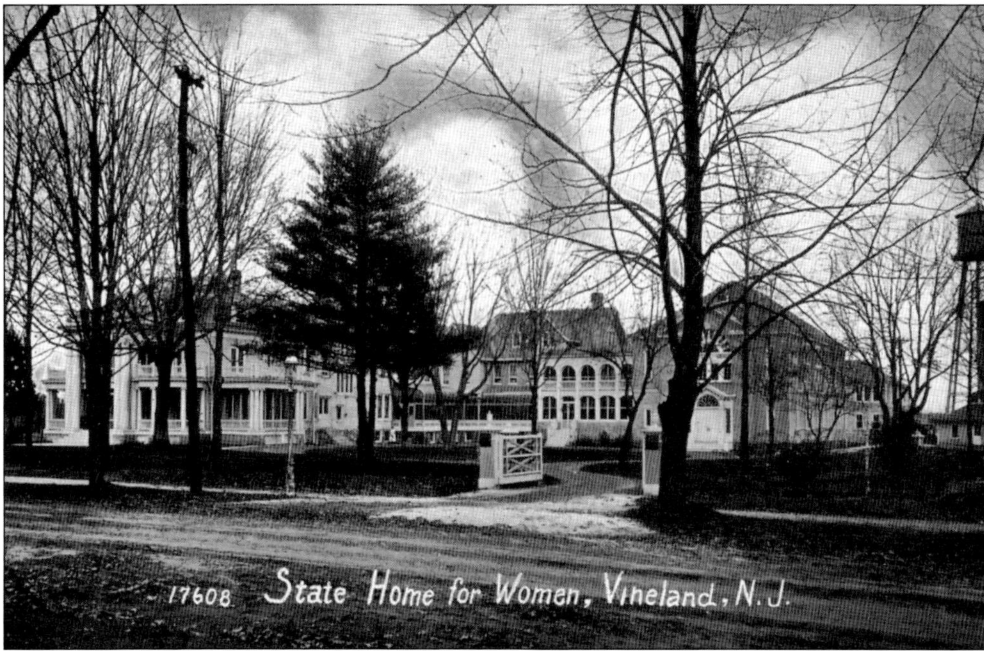

The Vineland Training School, located on a large plot of land that spanned from Main Road to Spring Road and from Landis Avenue to Chestnut Avenue, served a similar purpose as the state home. The school housed both males and females, who stayed in cottages with a housemother. For many years, it was also home to author Pearl S. Buck's daughter Carol Buck. The training school was later sold to other nonprofit agencies and remains in use today as Elwyn, a pioneer in training for the mentally challenged.

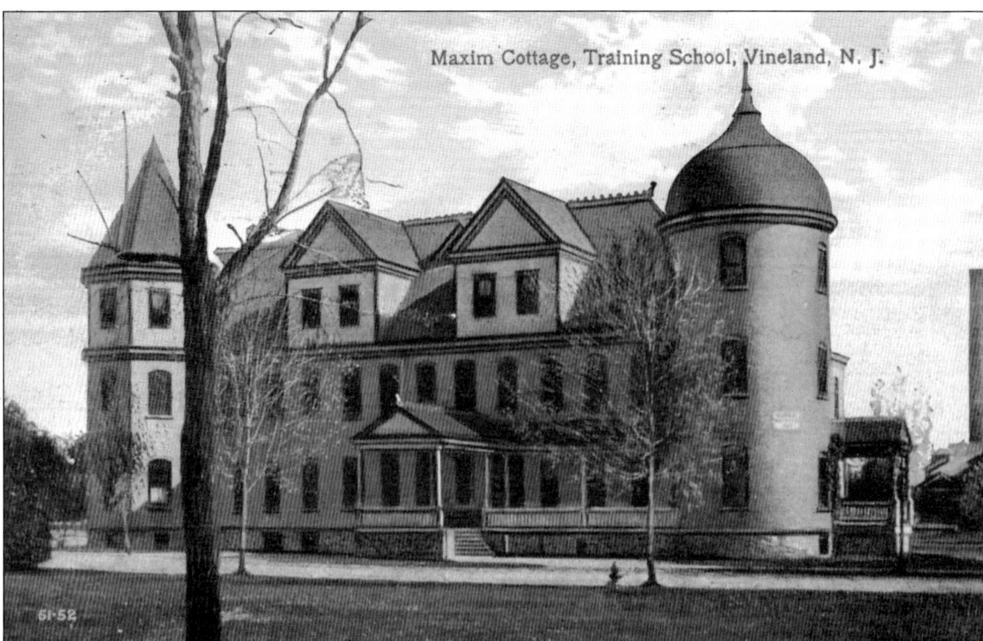

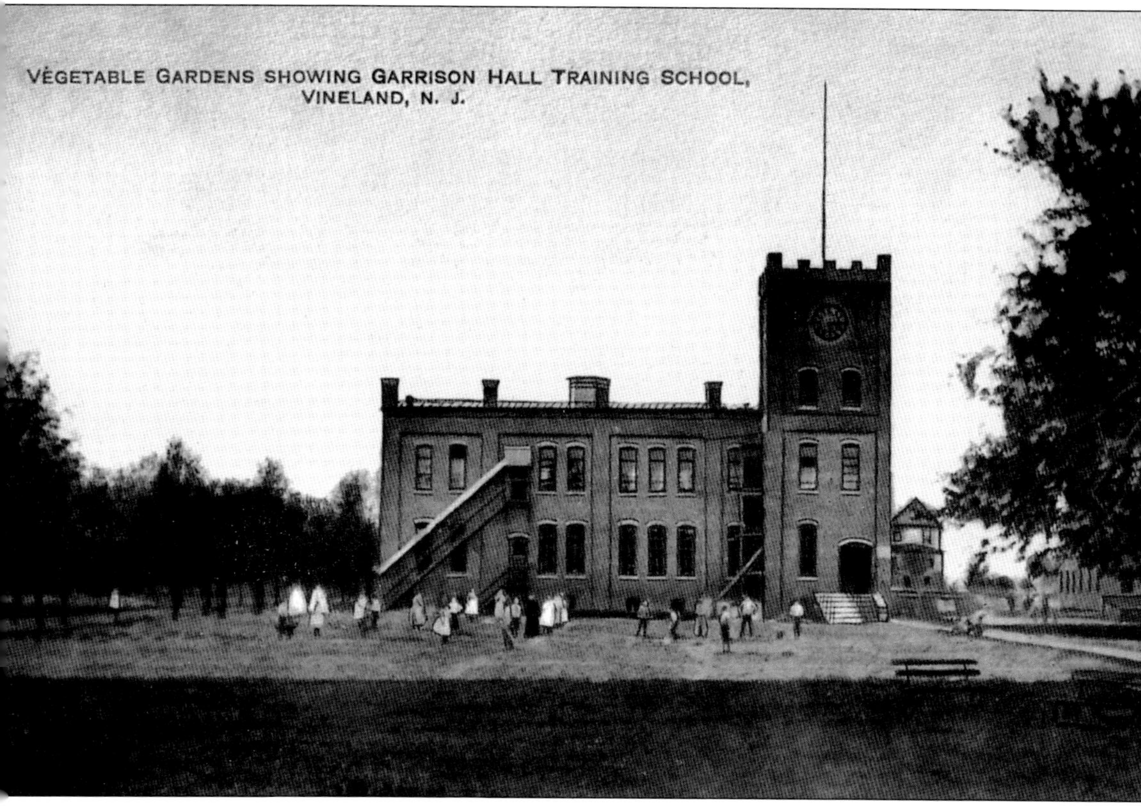

The Vineland Training School led the research field with new tests and groundbreaking research in the fields of IQ testing. The residents had the opportunity to learn new skills, such as basket weaving and agriculture, as well as animal husbandry. Open fields on the school grounds were used to grow crops to feed the students, while the Almond Road colony raised animals and drew the attention of the state agriculture department for its outstanding development and research.

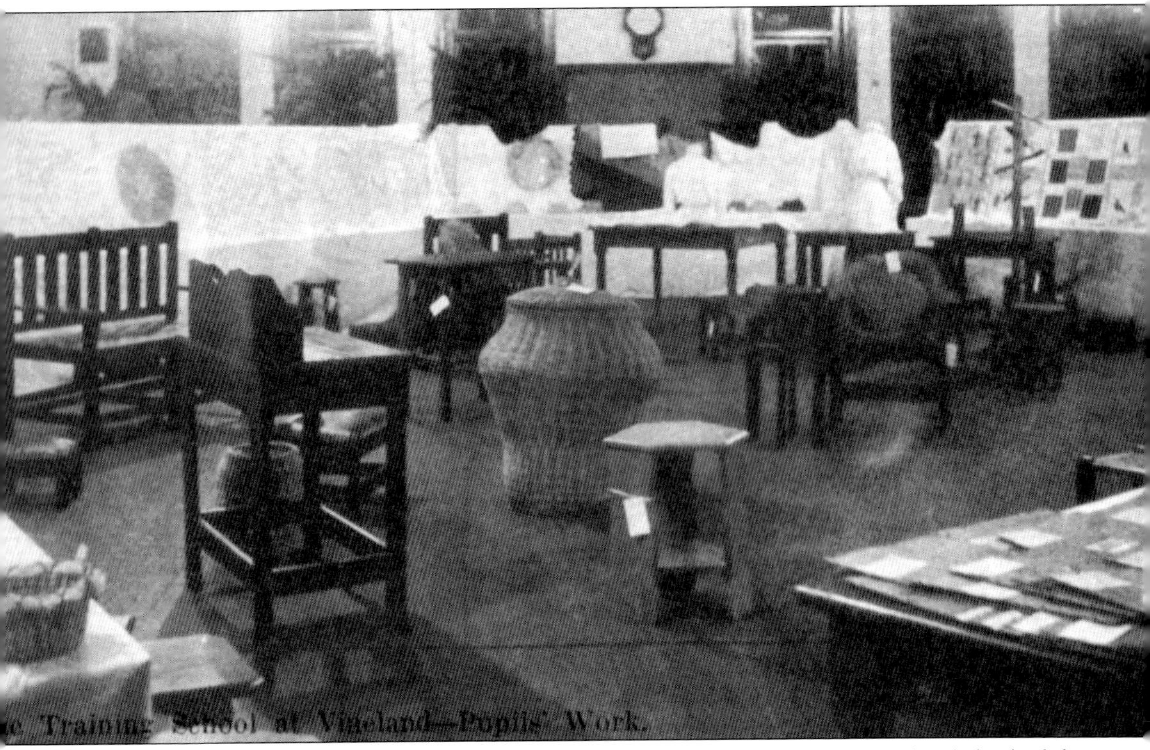

After it became an all-male institution, boys who lived at Vineland Training School also had the opportunity to participate in camping activities on the extensive grounds of the facility. Although the majority of the students were mentally challenged, some delinquents were sent there as an alternative to going to reform school or jail, in the hope that they would be rehabilitated.

Seven

Houses of Worship

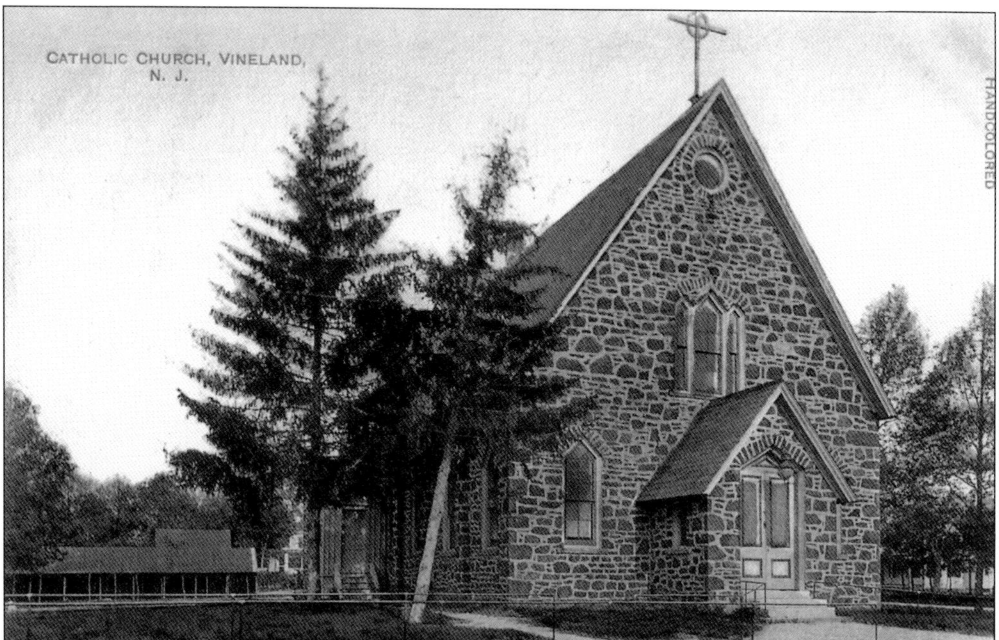

Vineland's first Catholic church was built in 1874 on South Eight Street on land donated by Charles K. Landis. The small brown sandstone church, called Sacred Heart, served its parishioners for more than 50 years. When the congregation grew too large, a new Sacred Heart Church was built in 1921 on Landis Avenue.

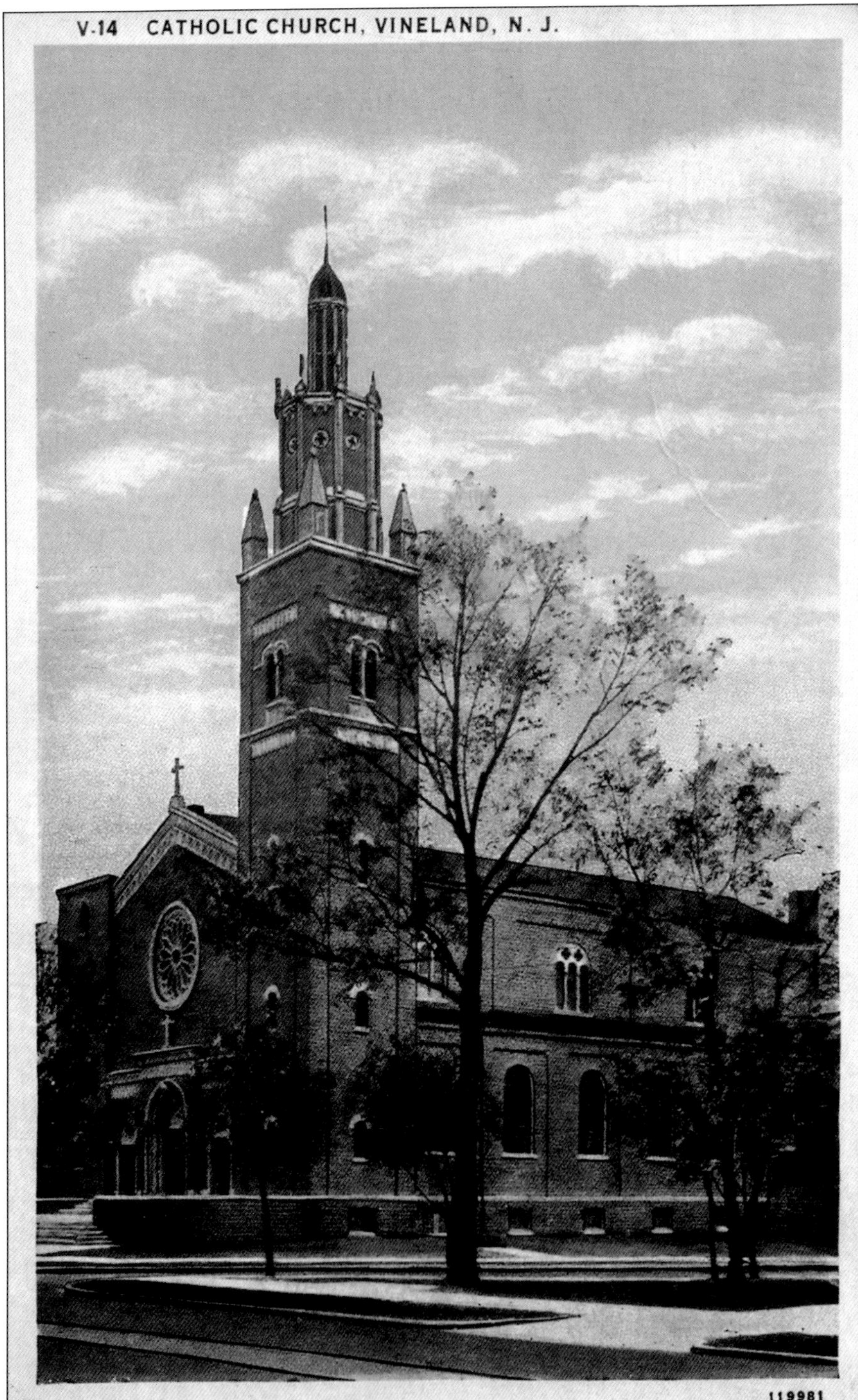

On July 7, 1920, parishioners passed a resolution to build a new Catholic church and school at the intersection of East Landis Avenue and Myrtle Street. Work began immediately on the imposing gray stone buildings, constructed for more than $73,000. Although the cornerstone was laid in August, the new buildings were not officially dedicated until May 1921.

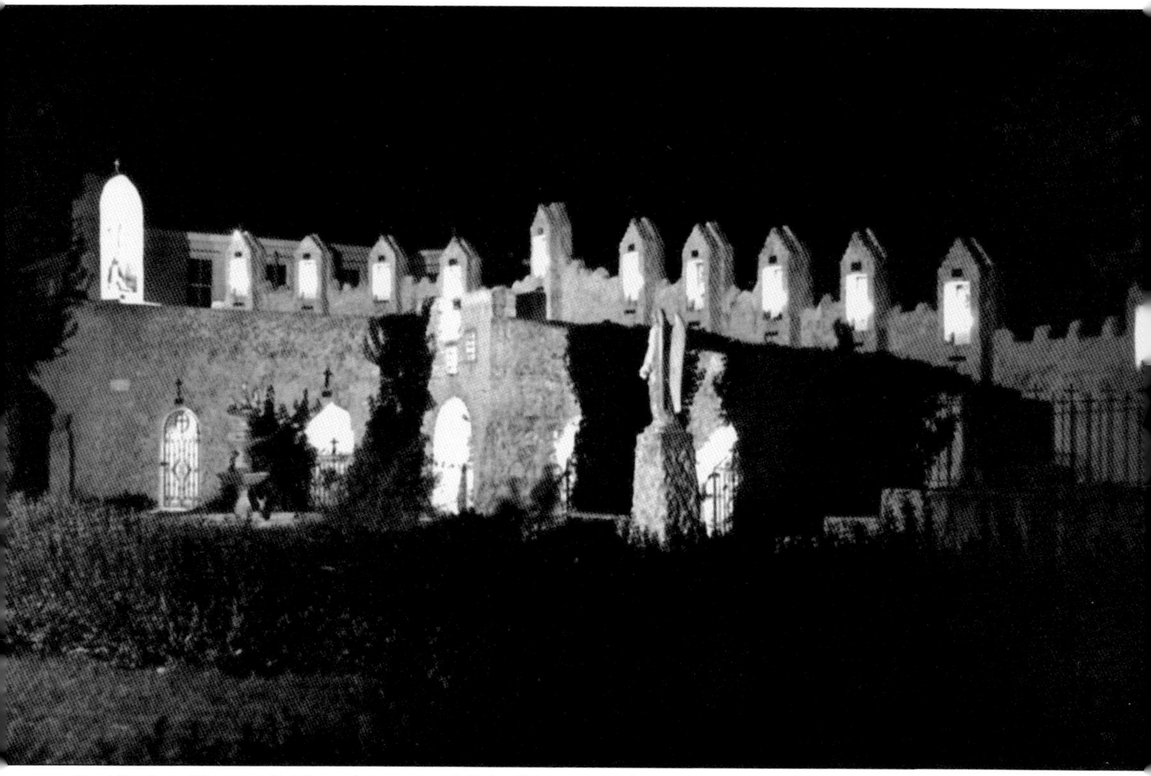

Our Lady of Pompeii Church was established in 1904 after Italian immigrants in the East Vineland colony of New Italy decided that it was time to organize a church close to their settlement. However, the old church was demolished in 1969 to make way for a larger, modern building. The grotto, which stands just east of the church, illustrates the Stations of the Cross.

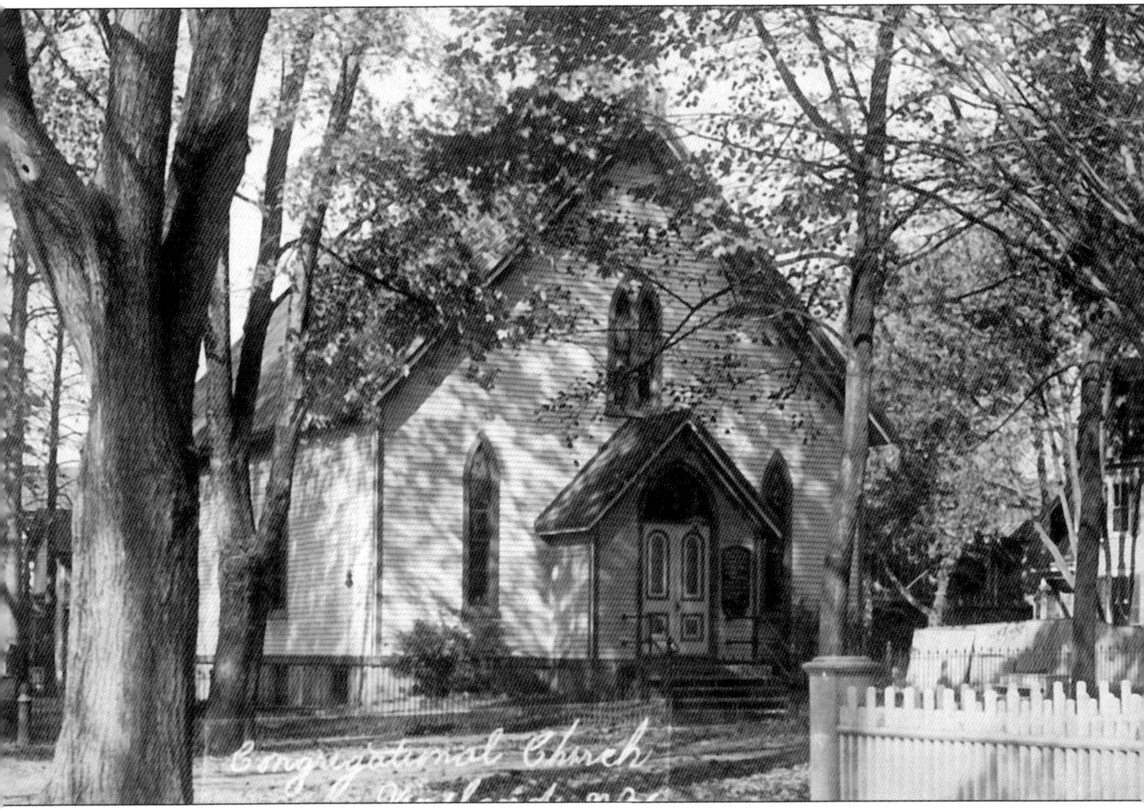

In 1868, devout South Vineland residents gathered together to build Lowber Chapel after regularly meeting for religious services at the home of Anna Barrows. Officially dedicated in June 1870, the chapel was destroyed by a suspicious fire four years later. In 1874, a new building was raised on Sherman Avenue and named the South Vineland Methodist Episcopal Church.

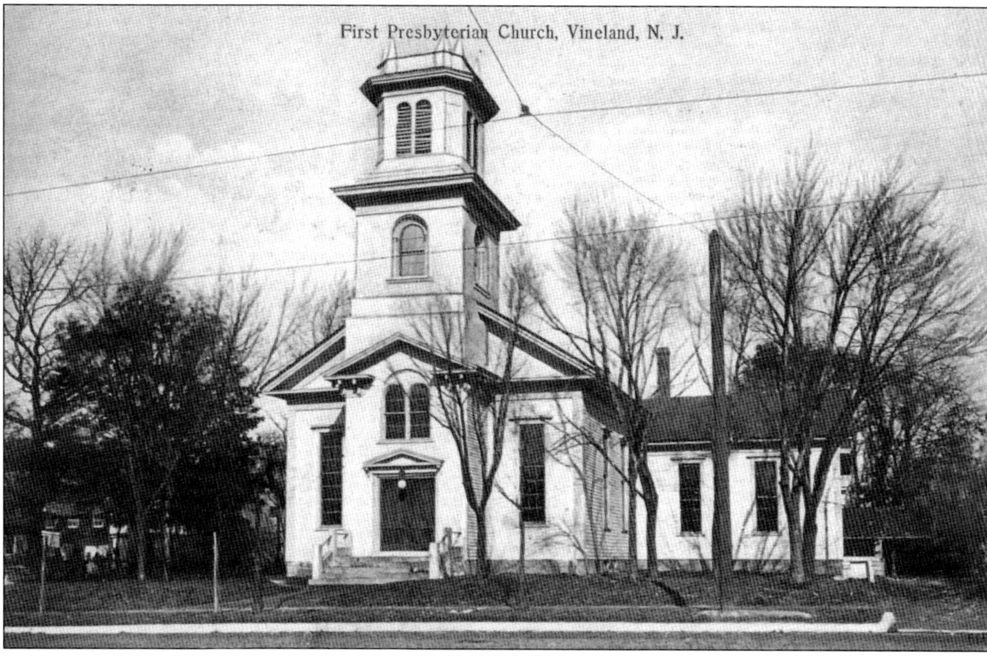

While the congregation first organized in 1863, two more years would pass before a new church for the Presbyterians of Vineland was built on Landis Avenue. Almost 50 years later, the original building was refurbished, followed by the dedication of the current church in June 1915. An article in the local newspaper notes that the new church was "a handsome well equipped house of worship with forty leaded stained glass windows." The impressive gray stone church still serves the community today.

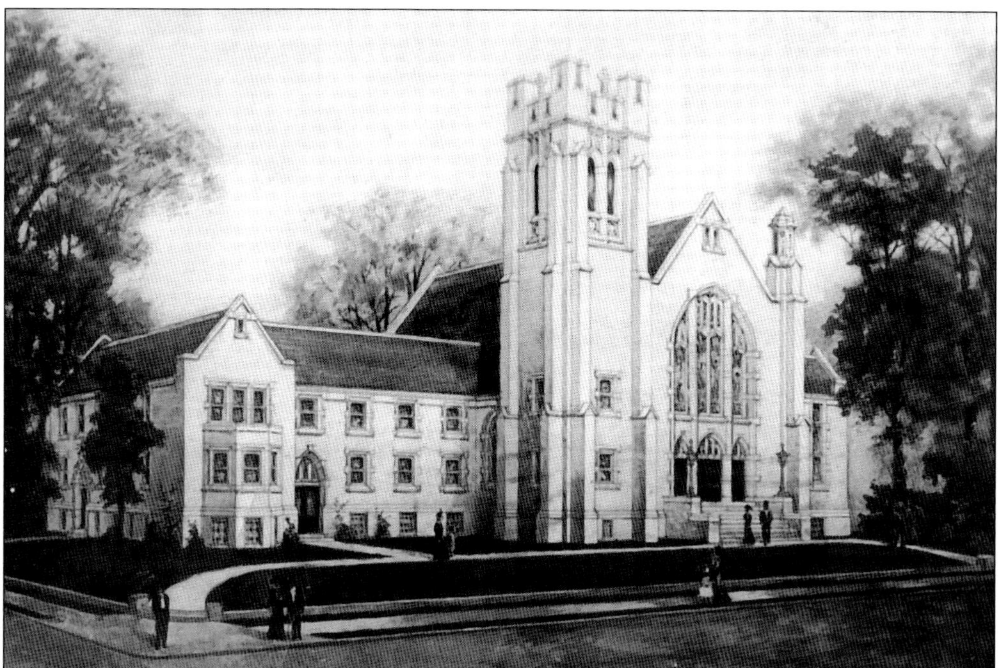

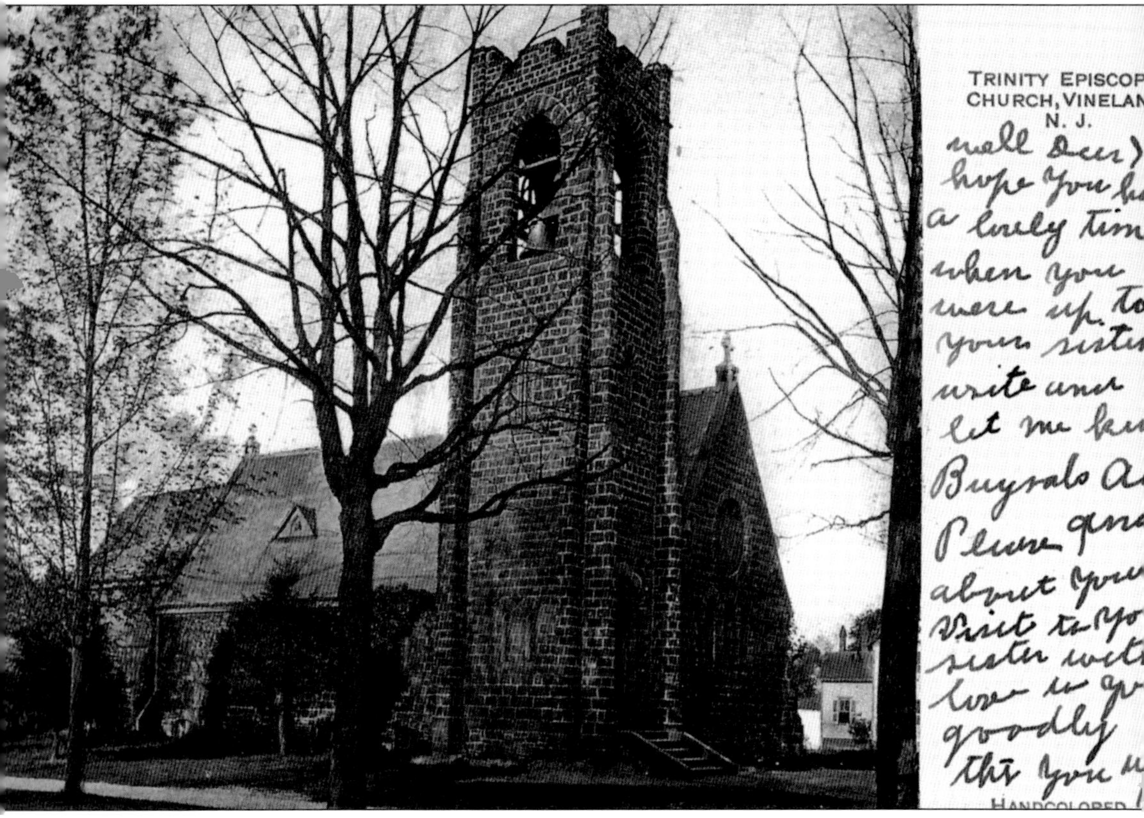

Trinity Episcopal Church was the first church built in Vineland, on land on Elmer Street donated by Charles K. Landis. The charming white clapboard structure opened its doors in November 1864 and was enlarged with a steeple that was topped with a bell donated by Landis. Unfortunately, a tornado struck in 1871 and completely destroyed the church, which was later rebuilt at the intersection of Eighth and Wood Streets.

A number of prominent Vineland residents, including town founder Charles K. Landis and Dr. Thomas B. Welch, the founder of Welch's Grape Juice, were parishioners at the First United Methodist Church, which was built in downtown Vineland in 1863. Landis had donated land for the church at the intersection of Landis Avenue and Seventh Street, just as he had done for most of the congregations in Vineland.

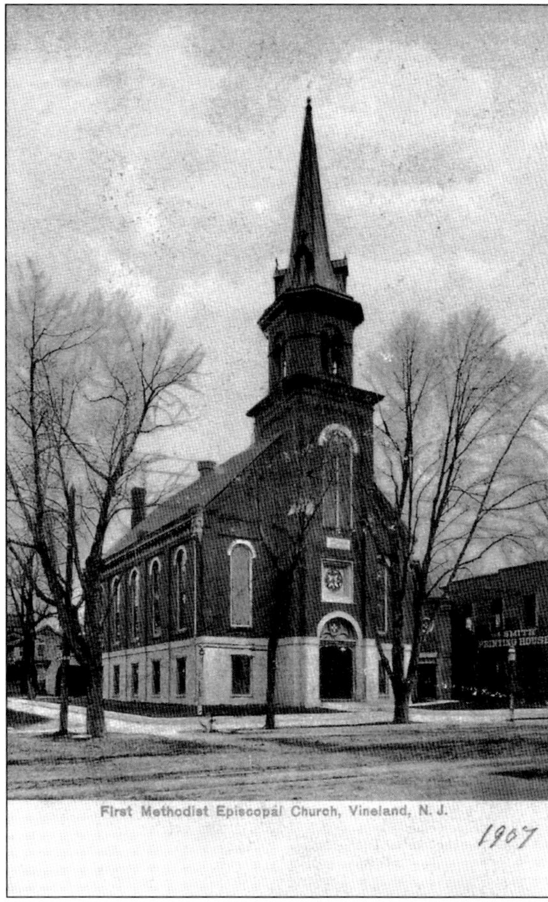

Unfortunately, the original, wooden First United Methodist Church was destroyed by fire in 1931, along with a number of the records of its early years. An imposing new Gothic Revival–style church of gray stone block was quickly raised the following year and remains in use today. The congregation celebrated the church's 150th anniversary in 2013.

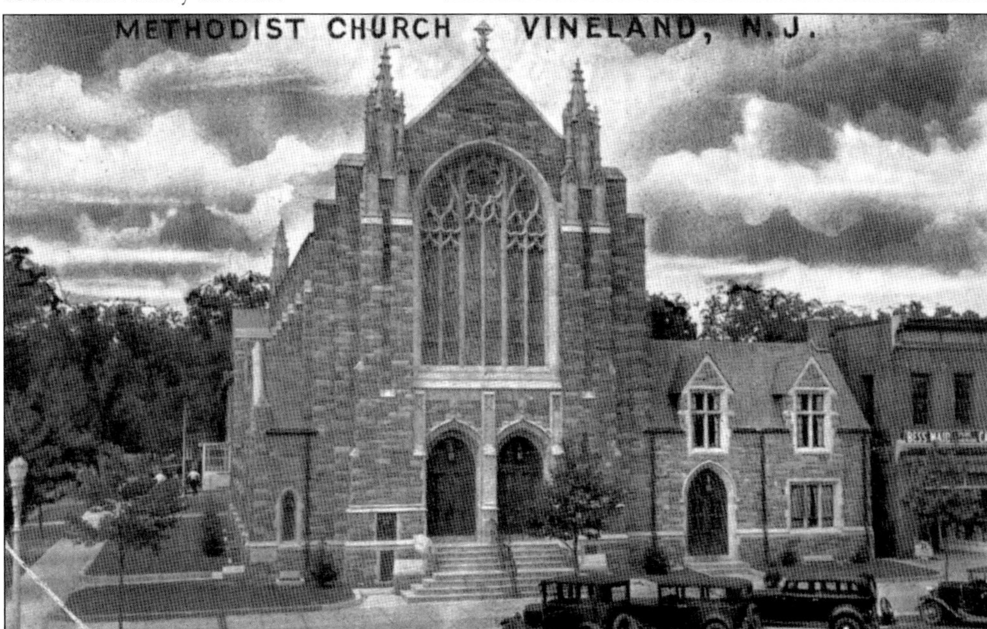

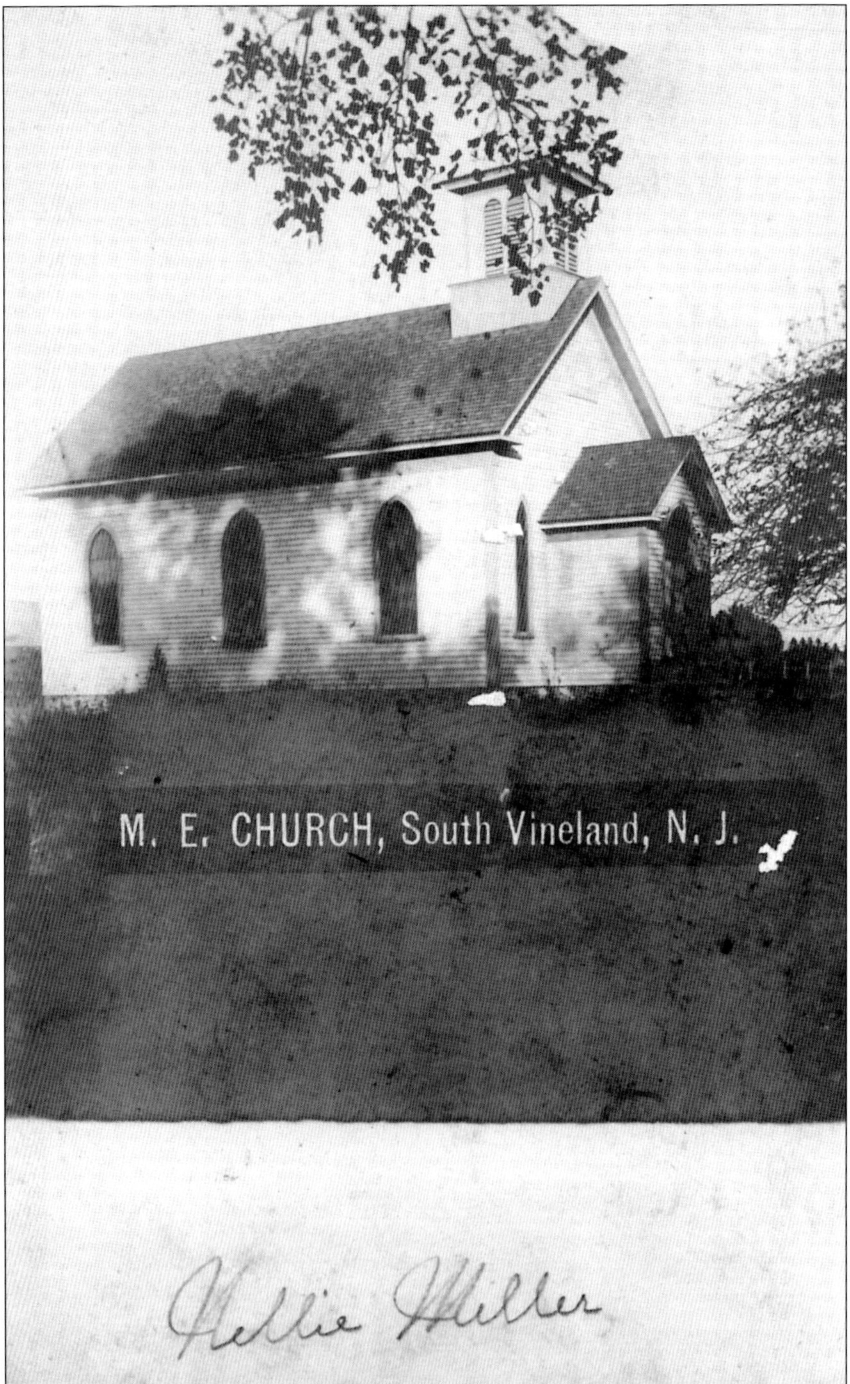

Since South Jersey residents were often isolated from one another by vast stretches of forest or farmland, the Methodist religion would send ministers known as circuit riders from place to place to hold religious services. In the early days, such services were often held in private homes. Later, when the settlements grew into towns, small wooden churches were built for services, which often lasted from morning to night.

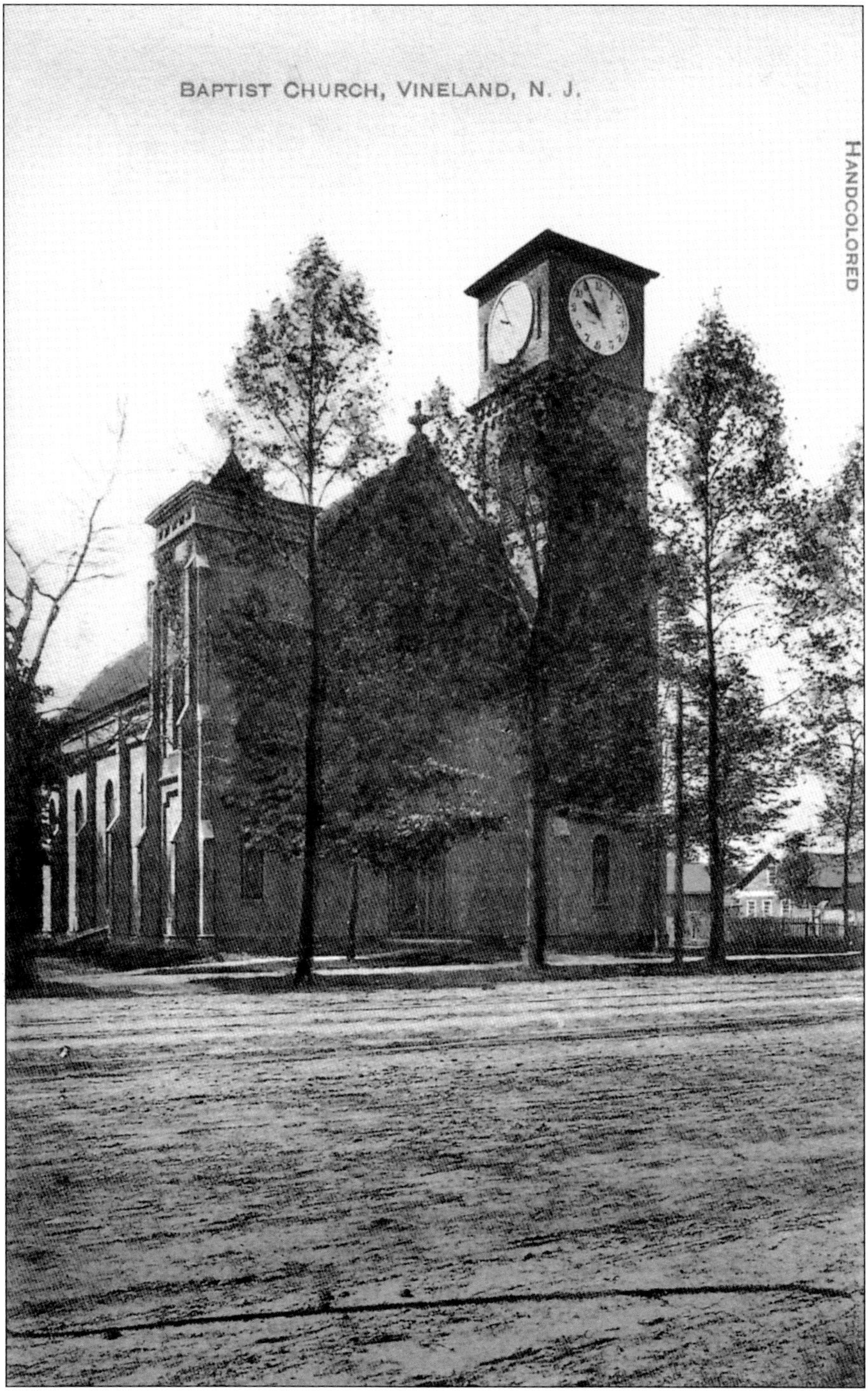

In 1865, a Baptist congregation was formed in Vineland. Three years later, it constructed the imposing, redbrick First Baptist Church on Landis Avenue near East Avenue. At the time, it was the largest church in town, with the capacity to seat more than 500 people. The clock tower was added in 1873. Although it is no longer used as a church, it still stands today as one of the oldest buildings in Vineland.

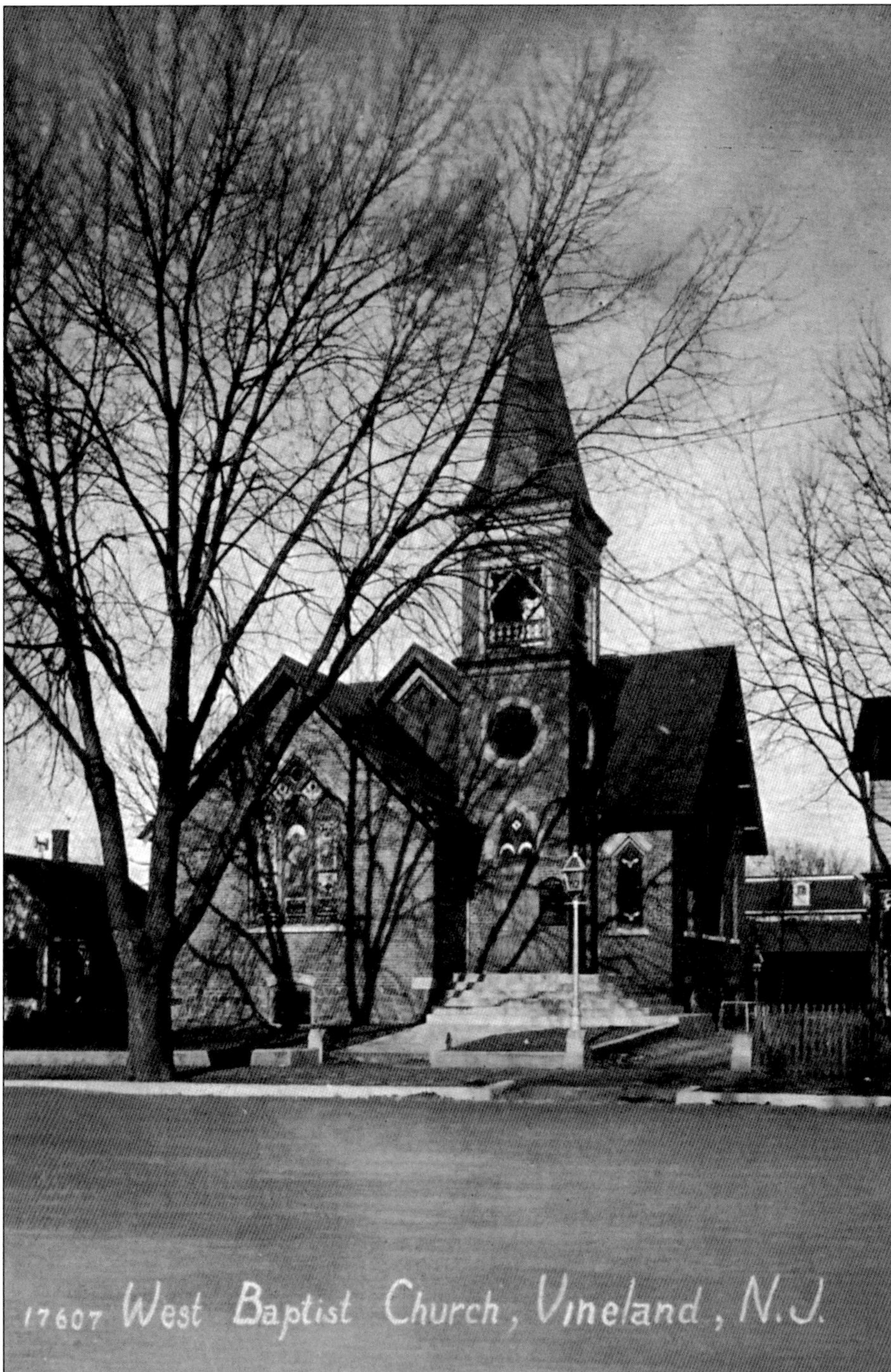

The West Baptist Church was formed in 1895 after several members of the First Baptist Church withdrew from the original congregation. Three years later, they built a church in the 400 block of Landis Avenue, which remained in operation until 1957, when it was forced to close due to declining membership.

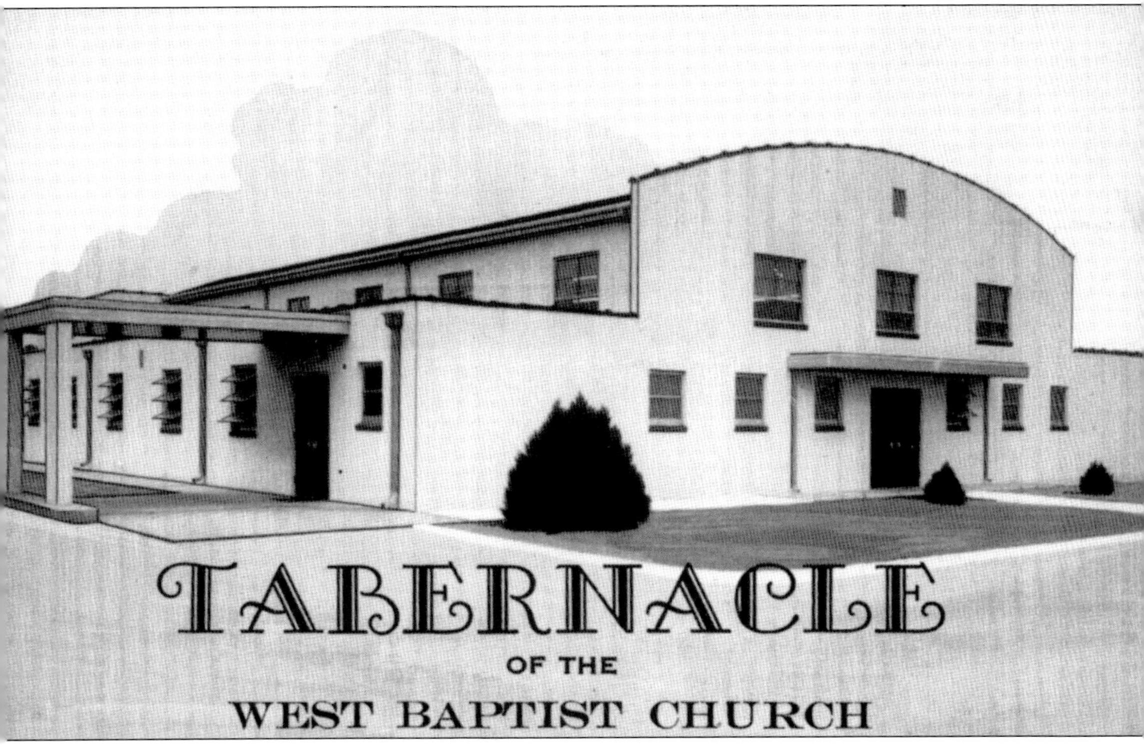

The Tabernacle, located on West Chestnut Avenue, was acquired in 1952 by the West Baptist Church. Unfortunately, membership in the church continued to decline, and, in 1994, the five remaining parishioners voted unanimously to sell all church properties.

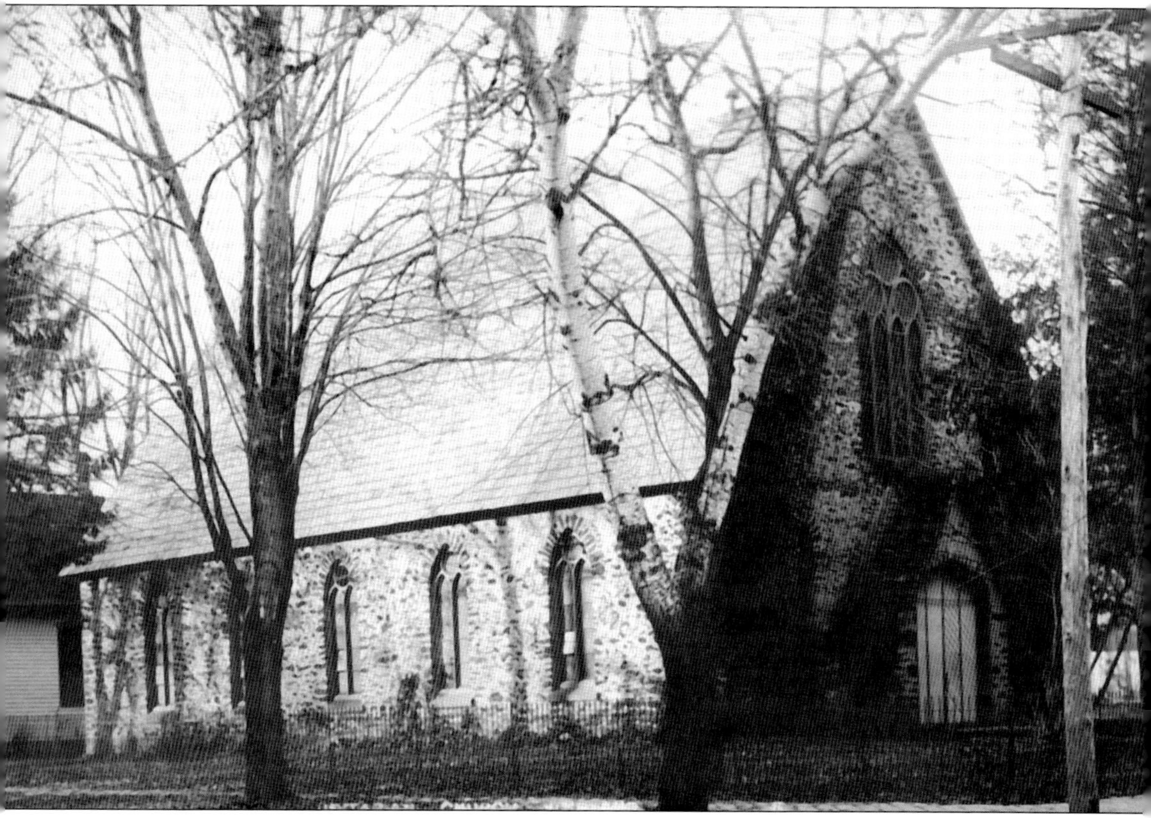

In 1868, a group of settlers from New England established the First Congregational Unitarian Church on the corner of Sixth and Elmer Streets, with William M. Gilbert serving as pastor. The liberal-minded congregation, who believed that individuals did not need ministers to intervene with God on their behalf, supported causes such as temperance, abolition, and women's suffrage. They erected the church out of Vineland sandstone, and it remained in use until the 1930s, when it was destroyed by fire.

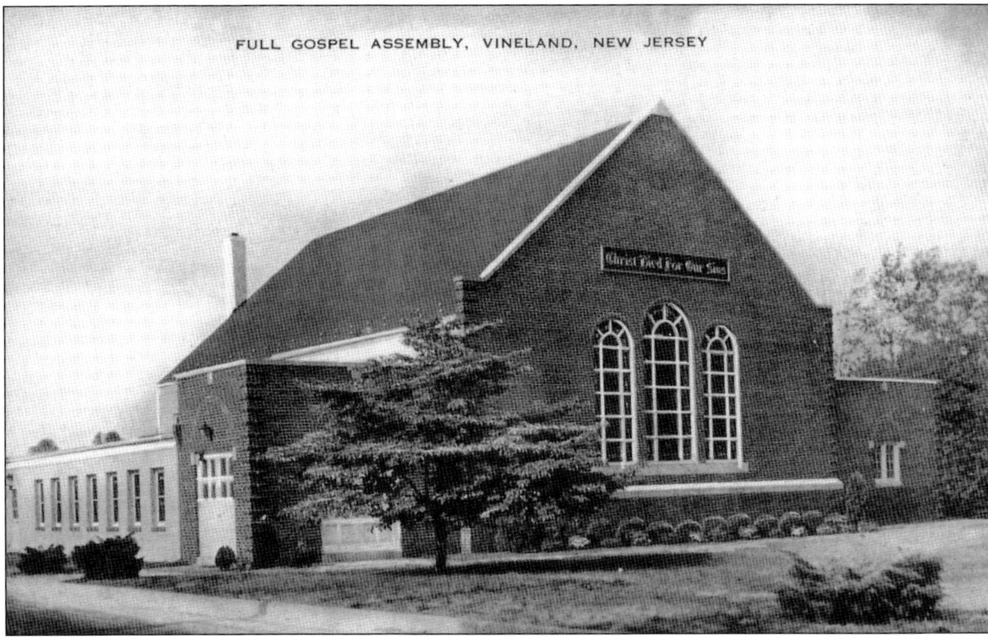

In 1910, George E. Laury held meetings at his Wood Street home, where like-minded Vineland residents could meet to discuss the teachings of the Bible. When the congregation expanded, it was incorporated into the Full Gospel Assembly of God in 1927. Services were then held at a church on North Sixth Street, but the growing congregation had moved to its current home on West Landis Avenue by 1951.

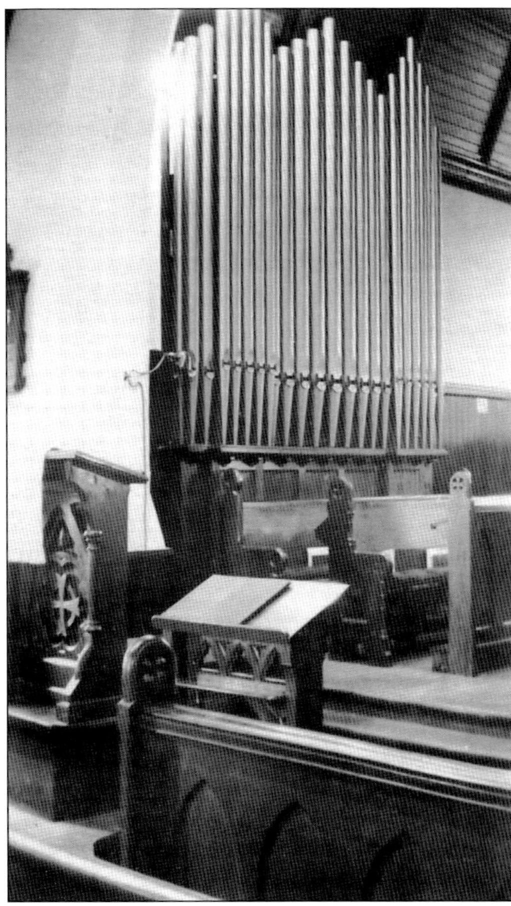

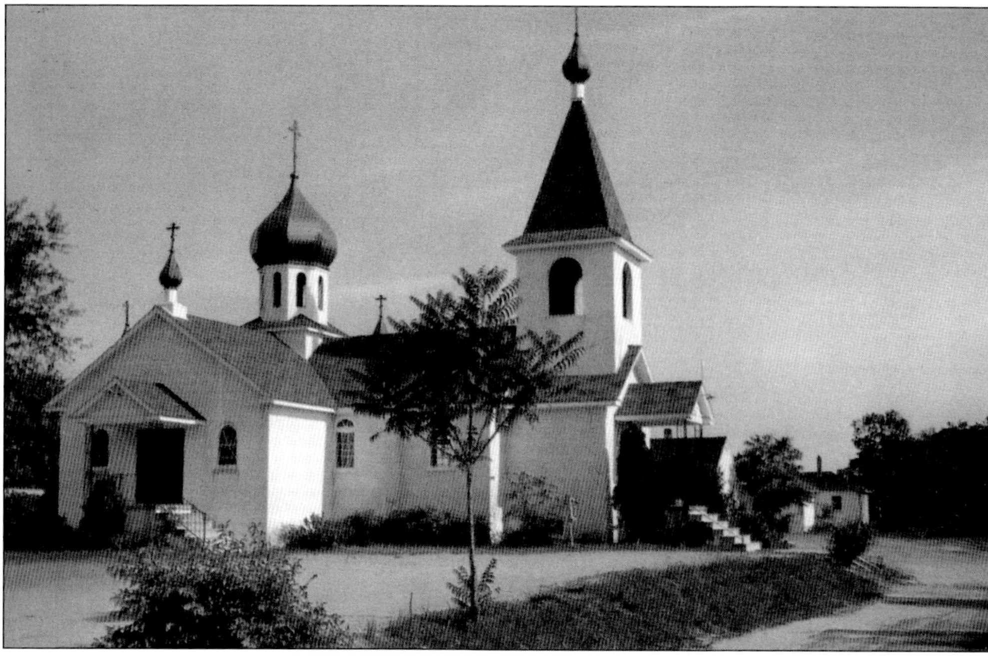

Russian immigrants, fleeing from poverty and unrest in their homeland, are believed to have settled in Vineland around 1914. In October 1947, they broke ground on West Landis Avenue for the Holy Trinity Russian Orthodox Church, but a harsh winter prevented them from completing construction before April 1948. The whitewashed structure, with its spires and blue onion dome, remains in use today by their descendants. The interior of the church reflects the traditional brightly colored religious mosaics typical of churches in their homeland.

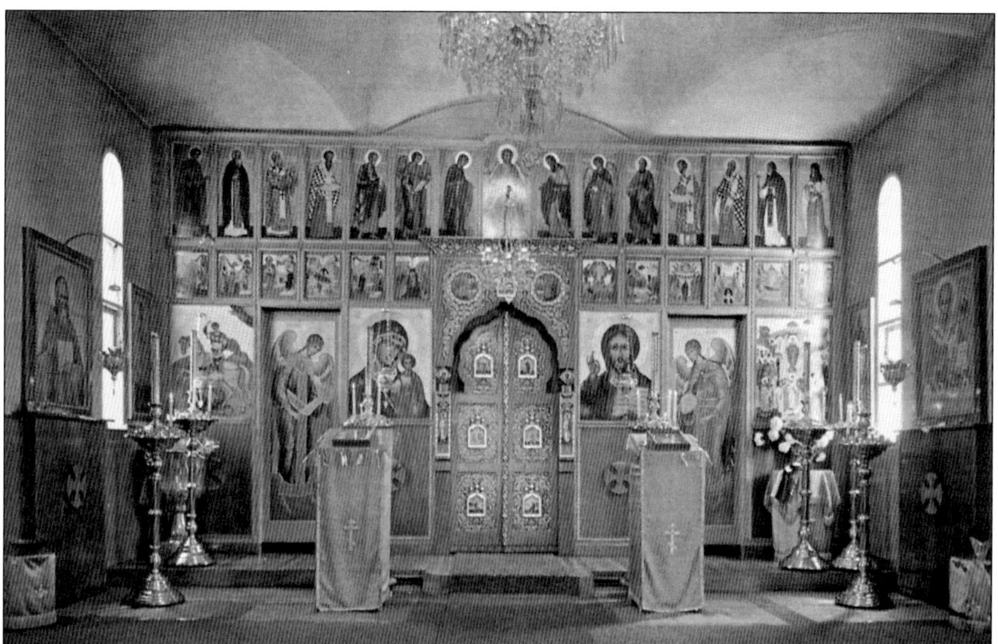

Eight

The Last Issues

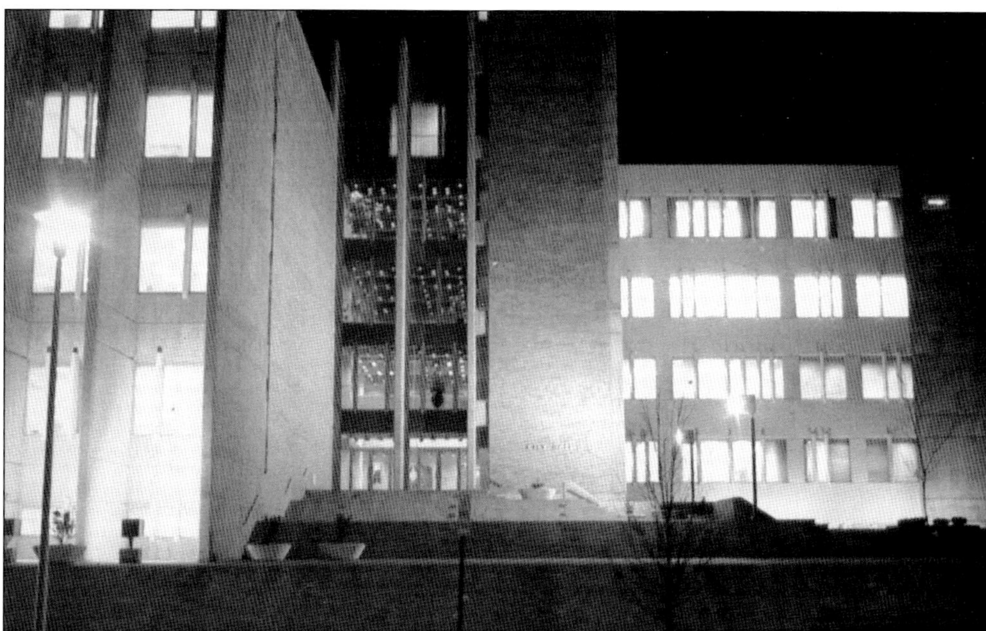

In keeping with its new position as the largest small town in New Jersey, Vineland officials decided to build a new city hall at the intersection of Seventh and Elmer Streets in 1970. The five-story, brick-and-glass building remains in use today, serving as home to the mayor, city council, and different municipal departments.

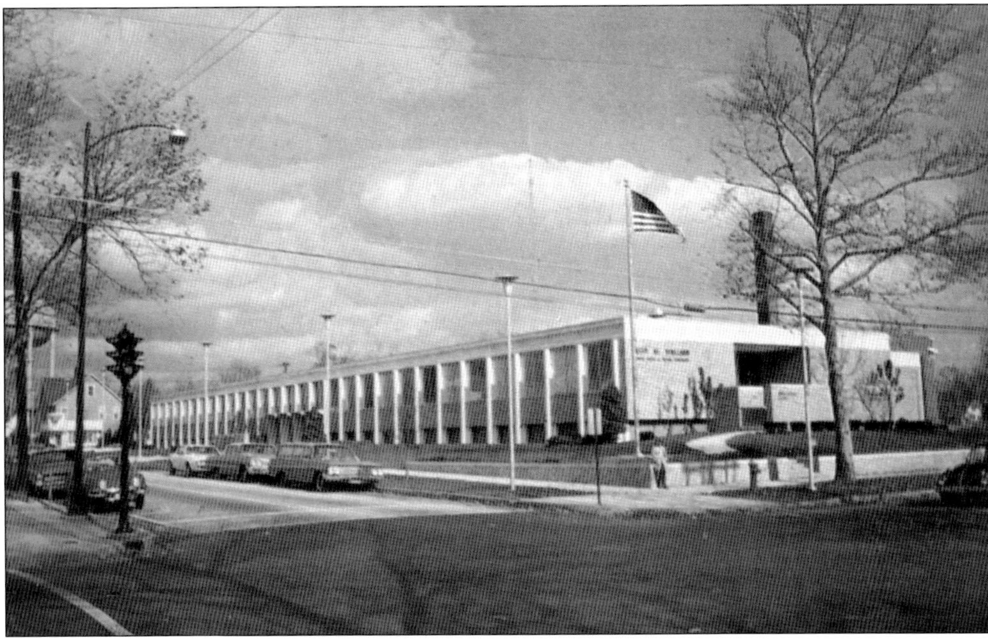

Although Vineland's police department was once headquartered at city hall, a separate building was constructed on the corner of Sixth and Elmer Streets in 1966 to accommodate the growing department. Vineland's first police force consisted of one constable who made his rounds on foot. Today, the department includes about 150 officers who patrol almost 70 square miles.

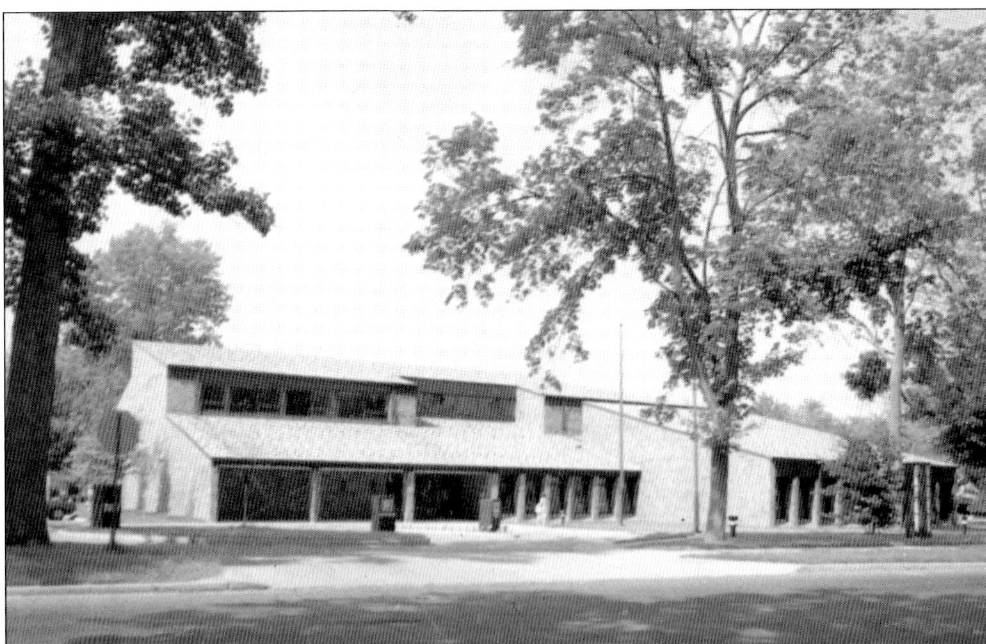

In the early 1970s, Vineland's public library moved to a spacious new home on East Landis Avenue to accommodate a growing collection and increased use by area residents. In addition to physically expanding, the new library allowed staff room to institute additional community services and programming for everyone from preschoolers to senior citizens.

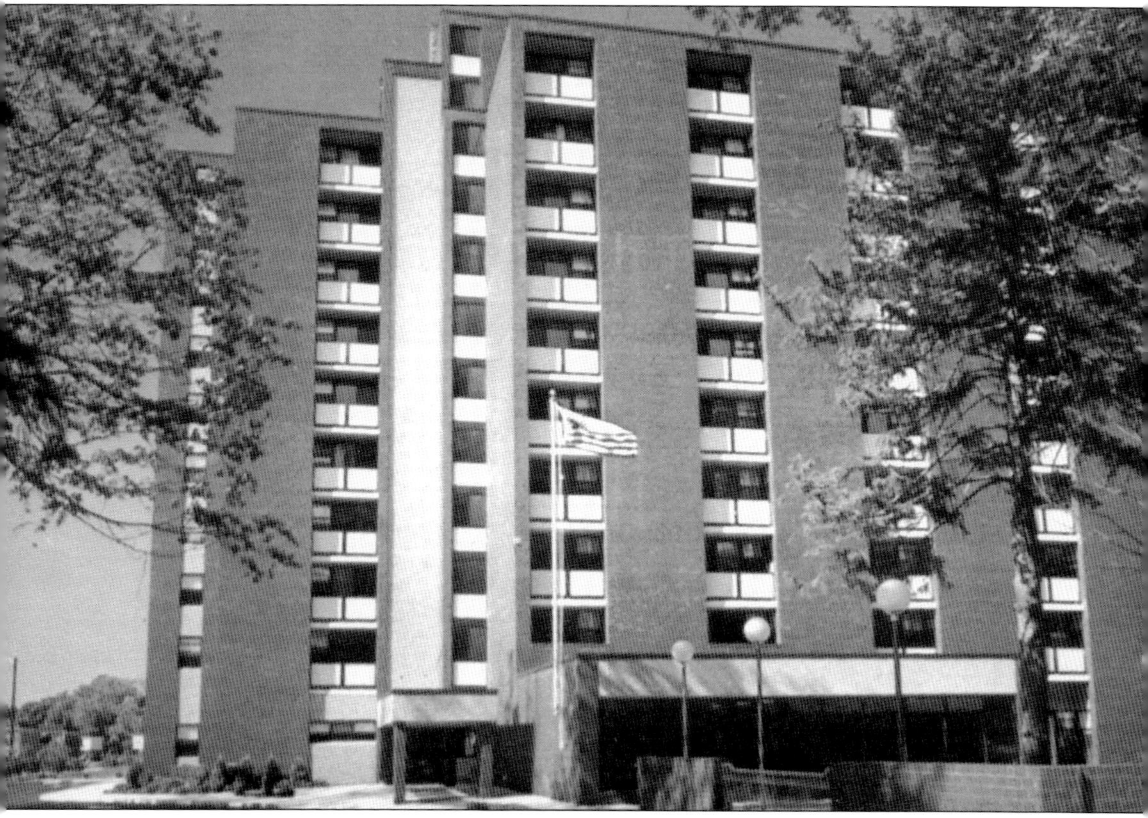

In the late 20th century, Vineland built its first senior citizen high-rise on East Landis Avenue. The brick-and-wood structure was radically different from anything else in the neighborhood, but it proved an immediate success. The location conveniently allowed older residents easy access to the downtown shopping district and the public library, which was situated just a few doors away.

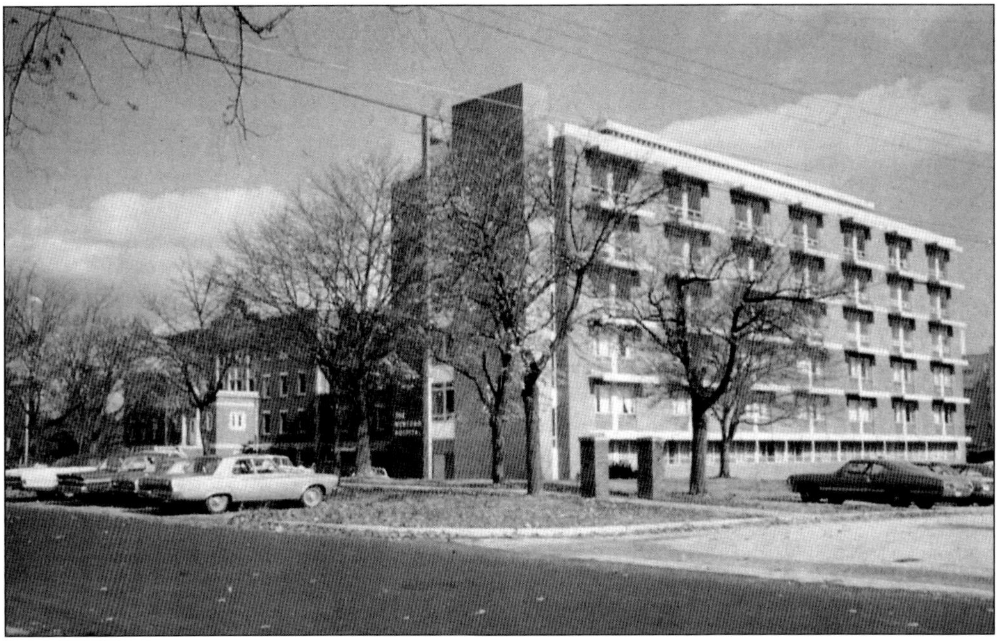

The original Newcomb Hospital, shown at left, was dwarfed by an addition constructed in the 1970s. The facility remained the primary health-care center for Vineland residents until it was replaced by South Jersey Healthcare (now Inspira) around 2005. While the Newcomb complex still stands, there has been no decision on its future use.

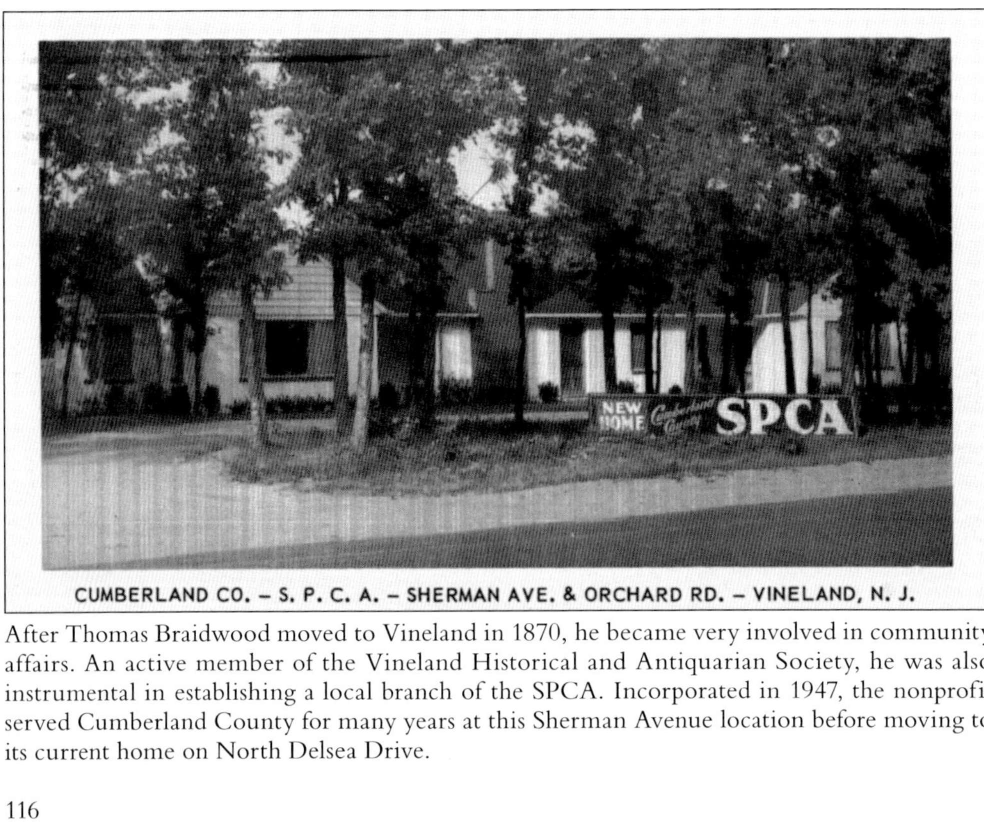

After Thomas Braidwood moved to Vineland in 1870, he became very involved in community affairs. An active member of the Vineland Historical and Antiquarian Society, he was also instrumental in establishing a local branch of the SPCA. Incorporated in 1947, the nonprofit served Cumberland County for many years at this Sherman Avenue location before moving to its current home on North Delsea Drive.

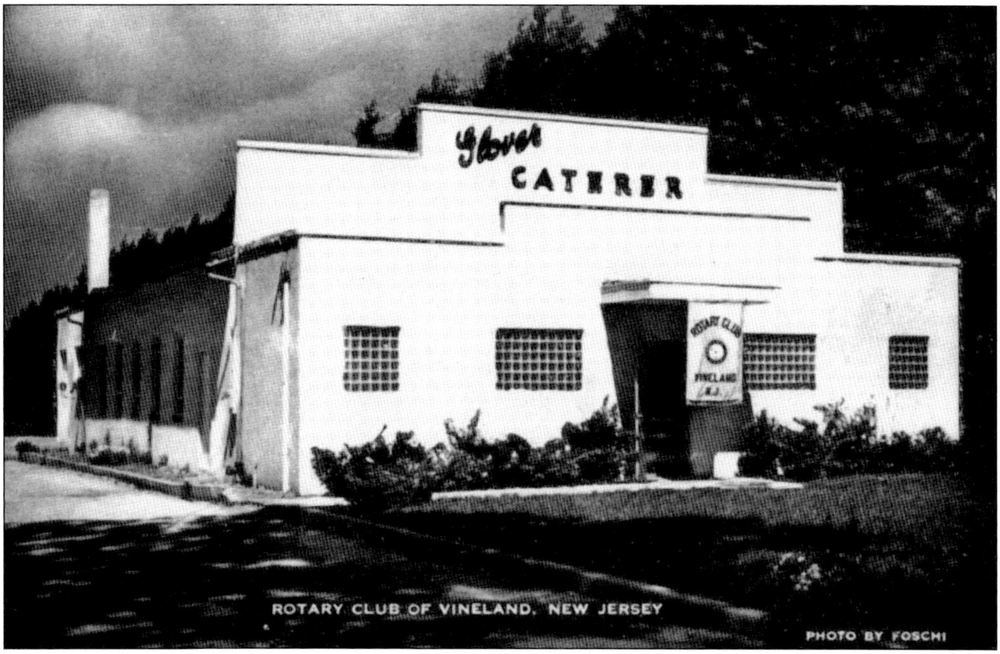

From Glover's Caterers on North Main Road to the Gift Mart on South Delsea Drive, Vineland's business community offered local residents a wide variety of choices that covered all of their shopping needs. In the days before shopping malls, small, family-owned businesses provided their customers with everything from lumber and paint to flowers and freshly grown food from area farmers. In the 1950s, Vineland was still primarily an agricultural community, with family-owned farms located around the business center of town.

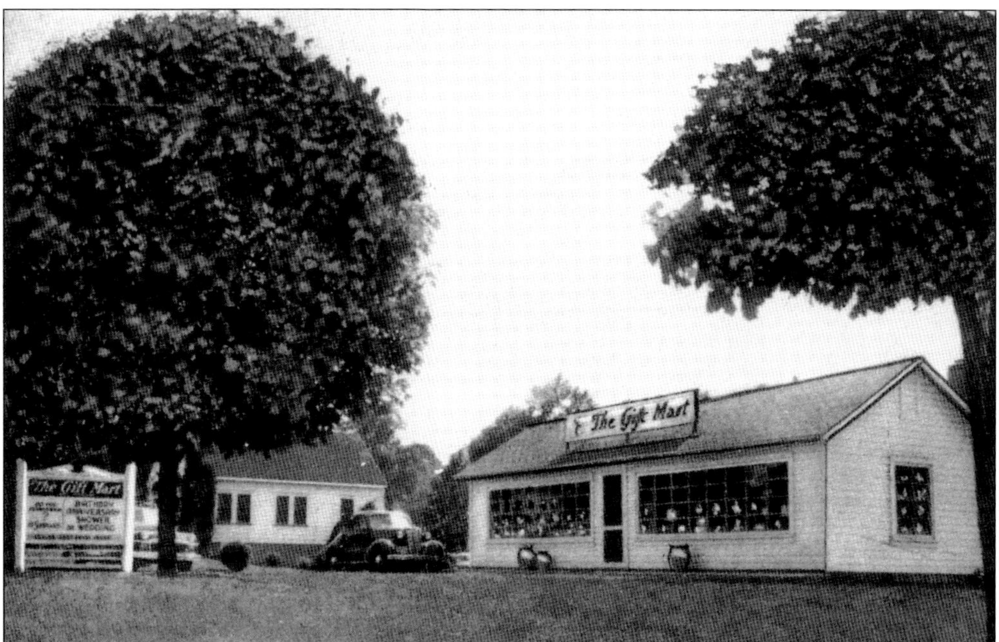

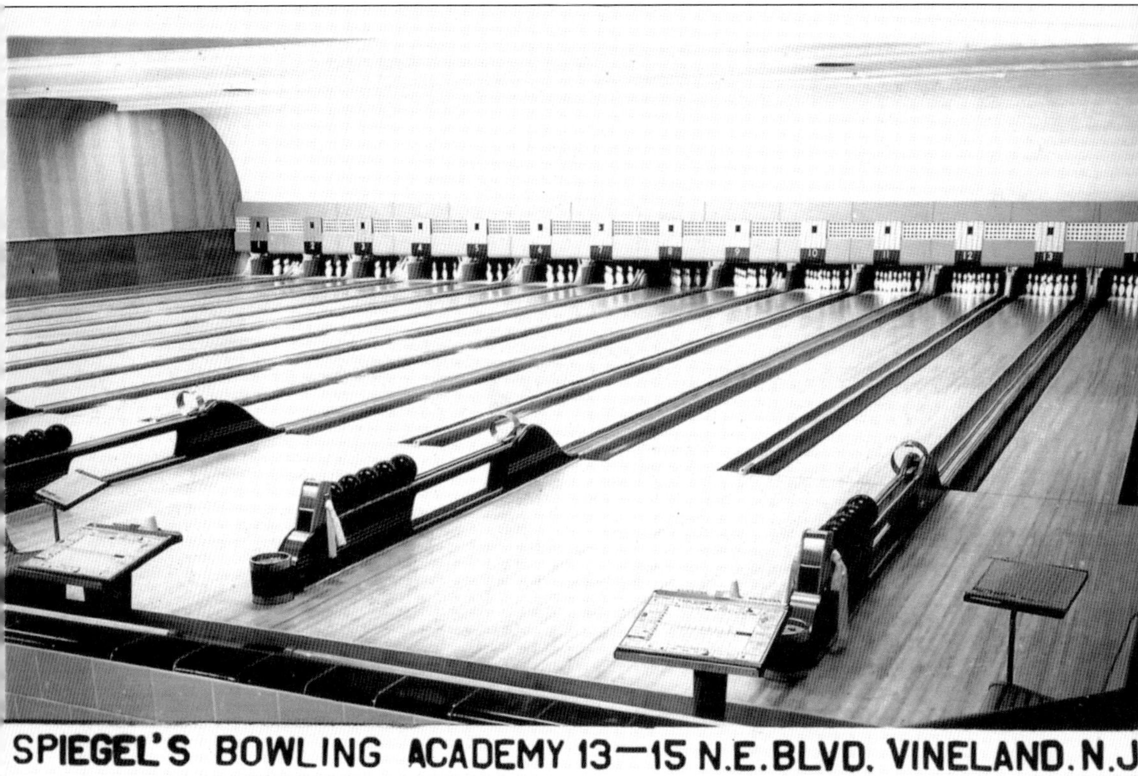

Vineland's first bowling alley, Spiegel's Bowling Academy, on North East Boulevard, was a popular spot for local residents in the 1950s, who gathered there to bowl in leagues or with friends. Although the alley eventually closed, a number of Vineland residents still have fond memories of the place where they learned to master the 7–10 split.

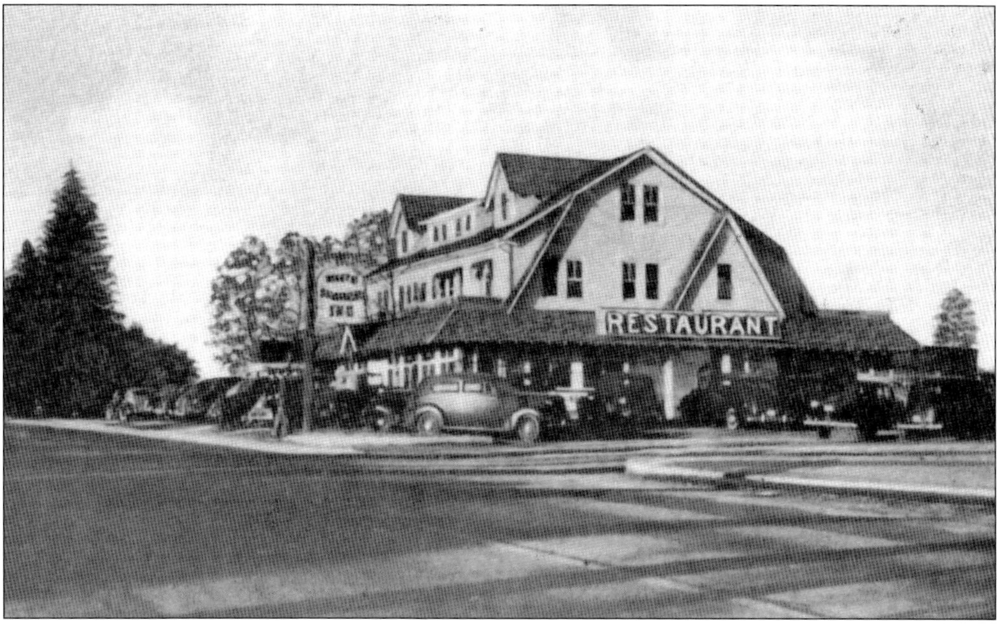

By World War II, the White Sparrow Restaurant was a very popular local eatery. At the intersection of Park Avenue and Delsea Drive, it offered a selection of Chinese and American favorites to its patrons. Open for lunch and dinner, the restaurant also offered live music and dancing on the weekends to the generations of customers that followed until it was destroyed by fire in the early 1980s.

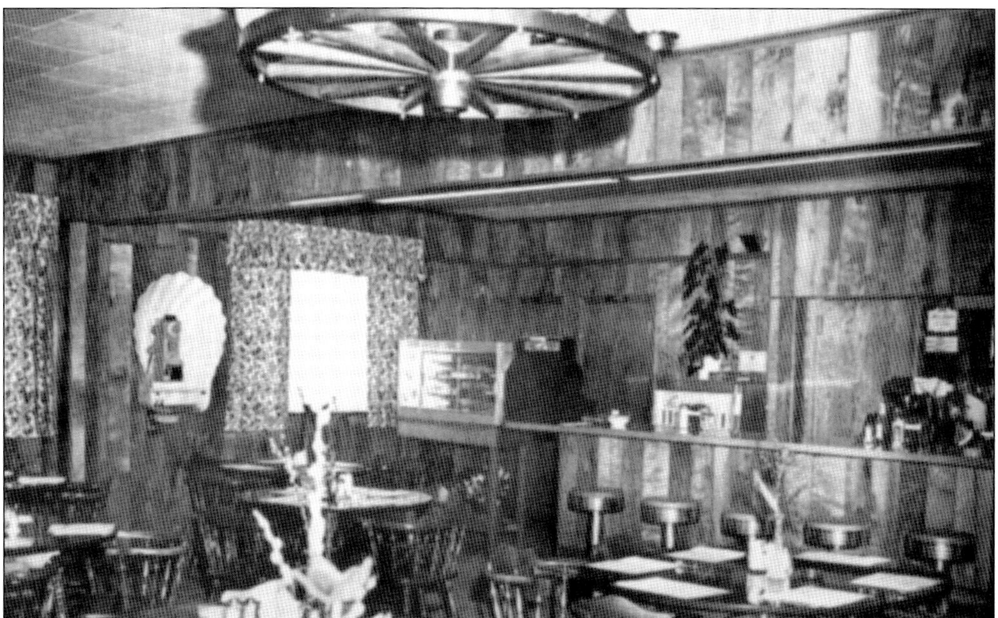

A number of smaller restaurants also thrived in Vineland during the first half of the 20th century, including Goss' Diner, at the intersection of West Landis Avenue and Mill Road. The cozy diner, run by Lou and Dee Chamberlain in the 1950s, offered chicken pot pie as a special for its customers every Friday night.

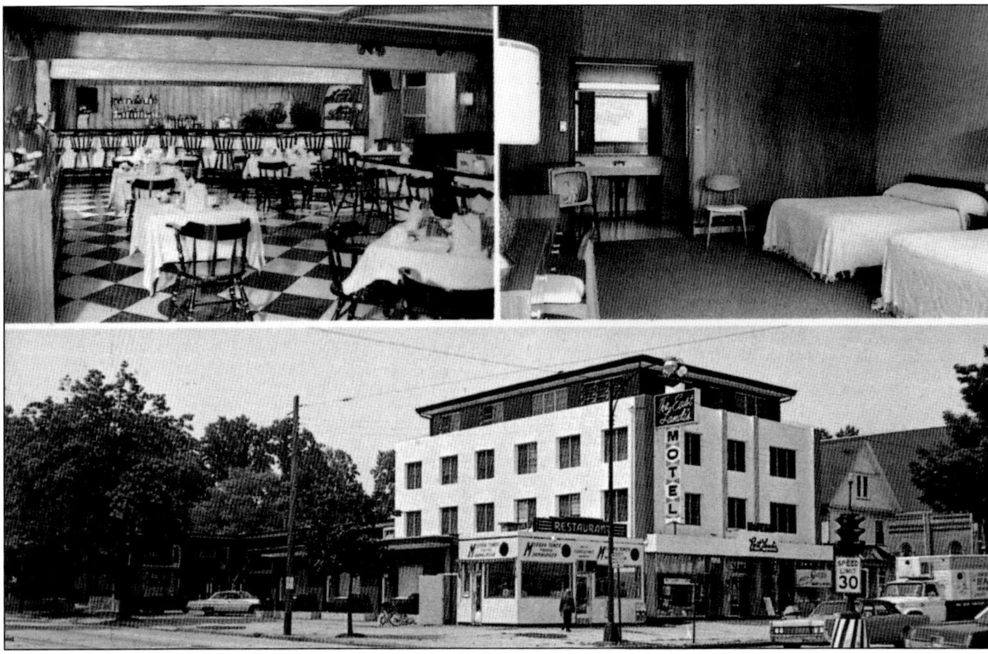

In the 1970s, the East Landis Motel acquired competition from the Imperial 400 Motel, which opened directly across the street from it at the intersection of Landis and East Avenues. Although the more traditional East Landis Motel was less distinctive than the Doo-Wop architectural style of the Imperial 400, both businesses attracted weary travelers for many years until they were later converted to residential motels.

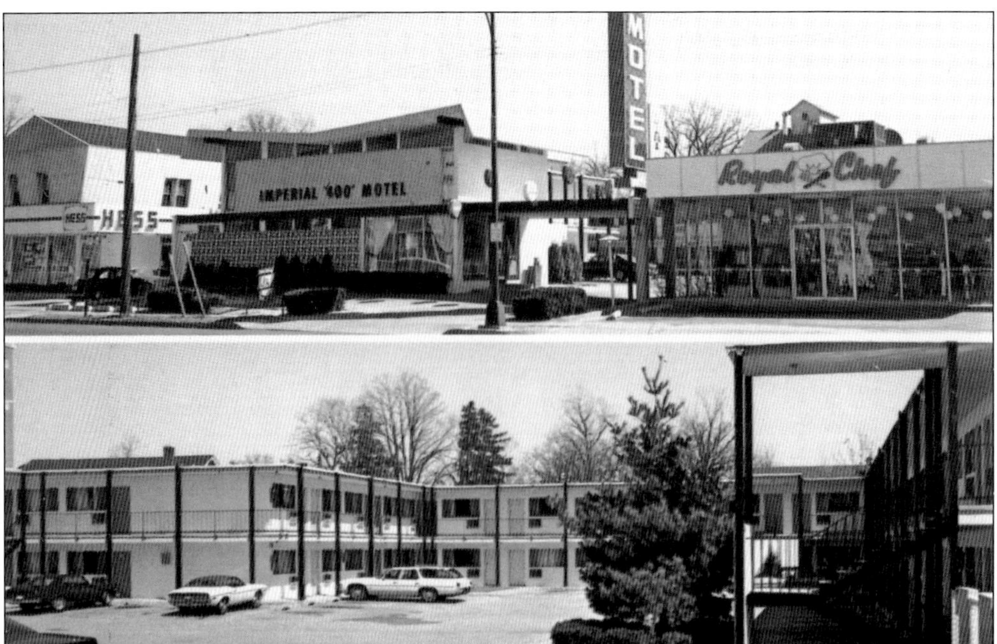

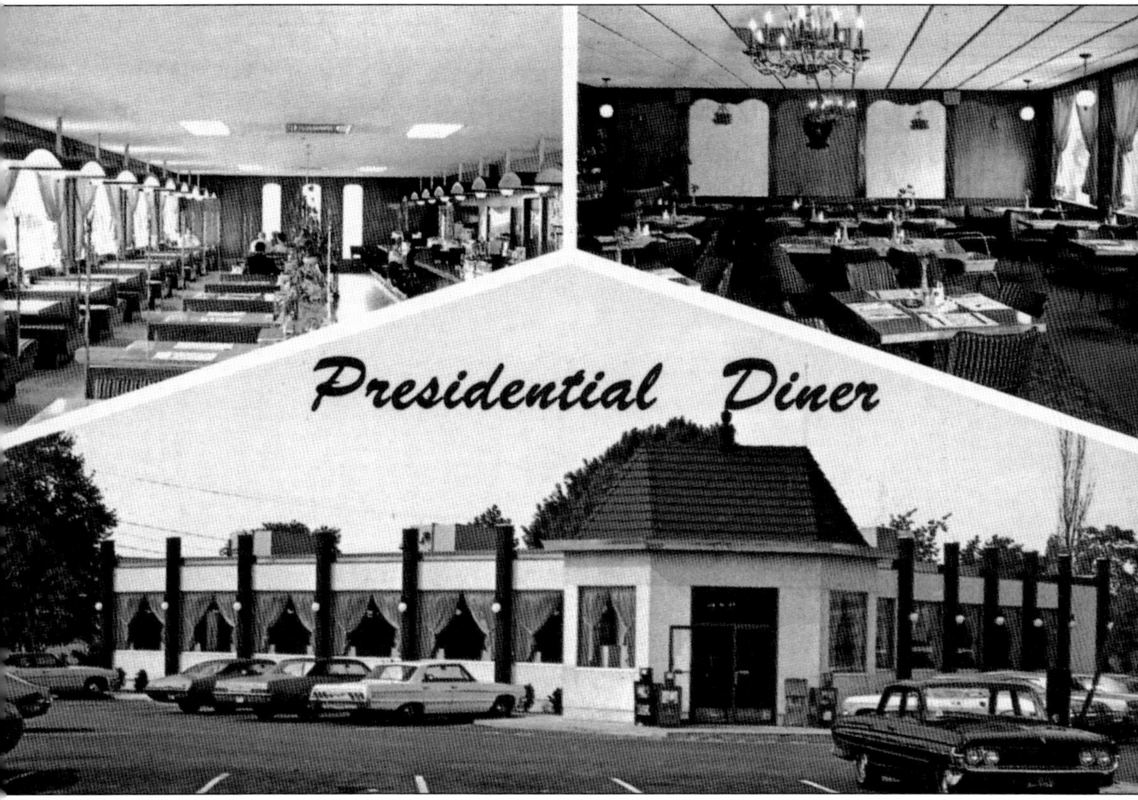

After the Circle Restaurant closed its doors at the intersection of Delsea Drive and Landis Avenue in 1969, the popular restaurant was reborn a few years later as the Presidential Diner. In addition to enjoying a wide variety of meals for breakfast, lunch, and dinner, patrons at the Presidential could also sneak in a late-night snack.

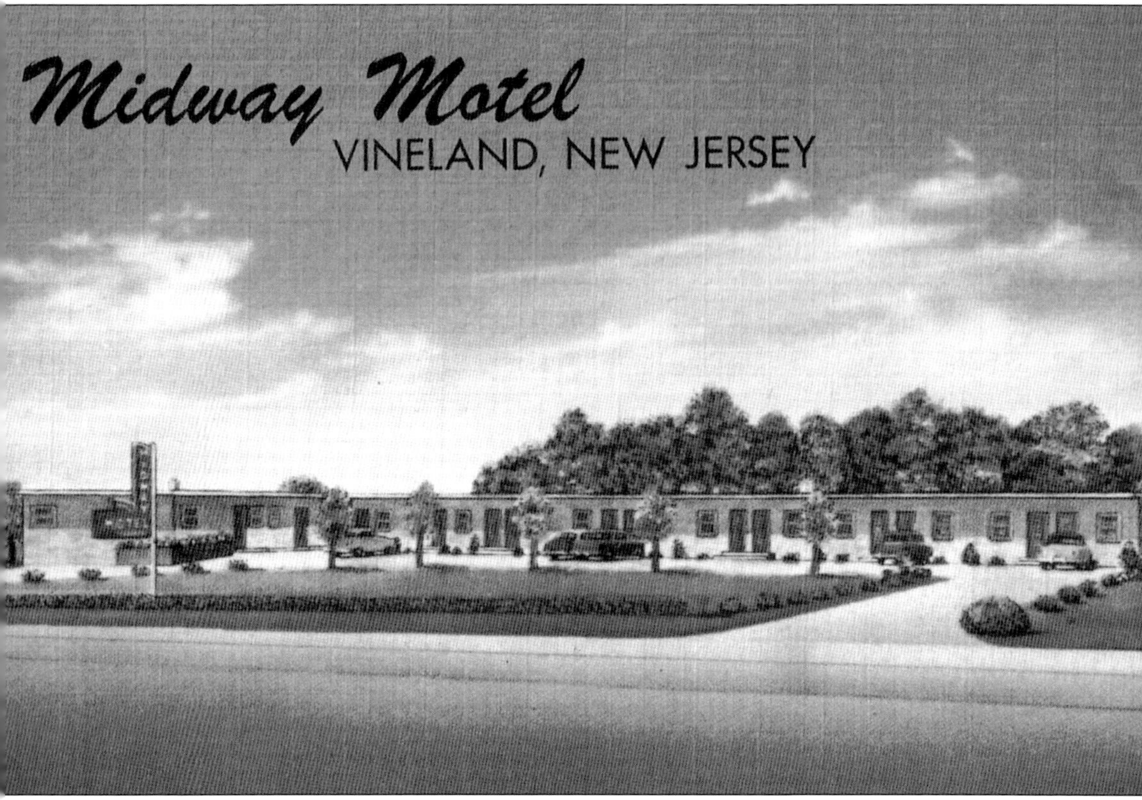

In the 1960s, the Midway Hotel was a classic example of the updated roadside cottages that dotted New Hersey's highways. A popular stop for travelers, its cozy rooms offered all of the amenities, as well as a private swimming pool, topped by the AAA seal of approval.

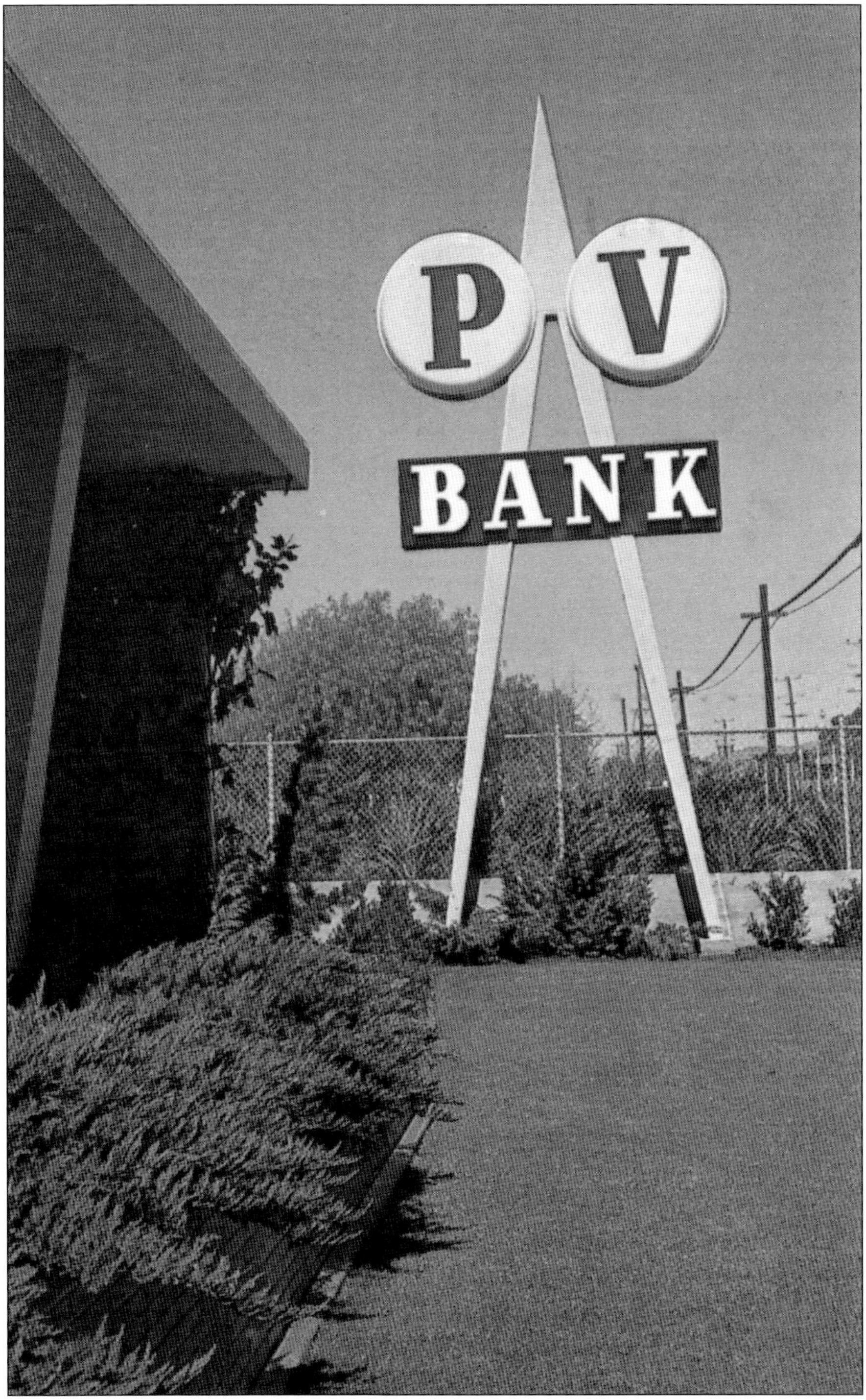

Like a number of Vineland businesses, PV Bank and the Branson and Doerr Ford dealership have long since disappeared from the landscape. However, in recent years, there has been an effort to draw new businesses to the town, which has seen a resurgence of interest in its center city business district.

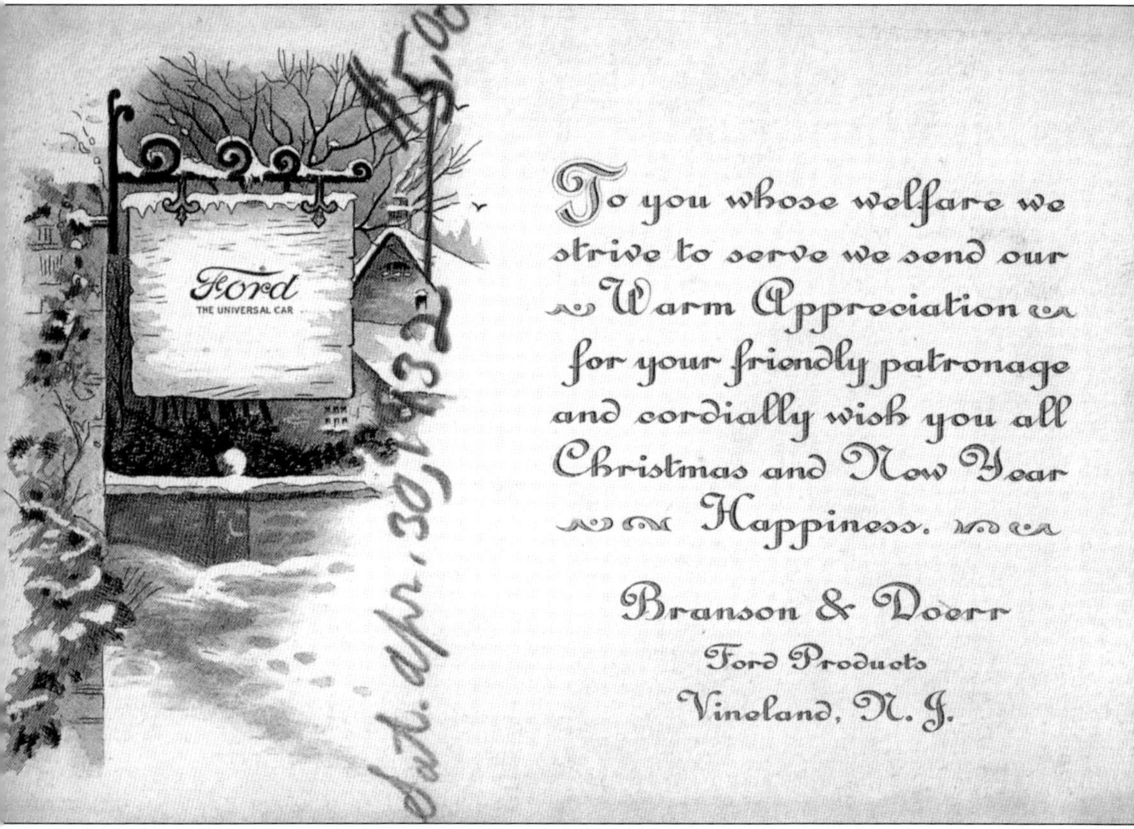

The Branson and Doerr Ford dealership, on West Landis Avenue, was a popular business in the 1930s, where local residents could purchase what was then the best-selling car in America. At that time, Fords ranged in price from about $395 for a coupe to $1,400 for a top-of-the-line touring car.

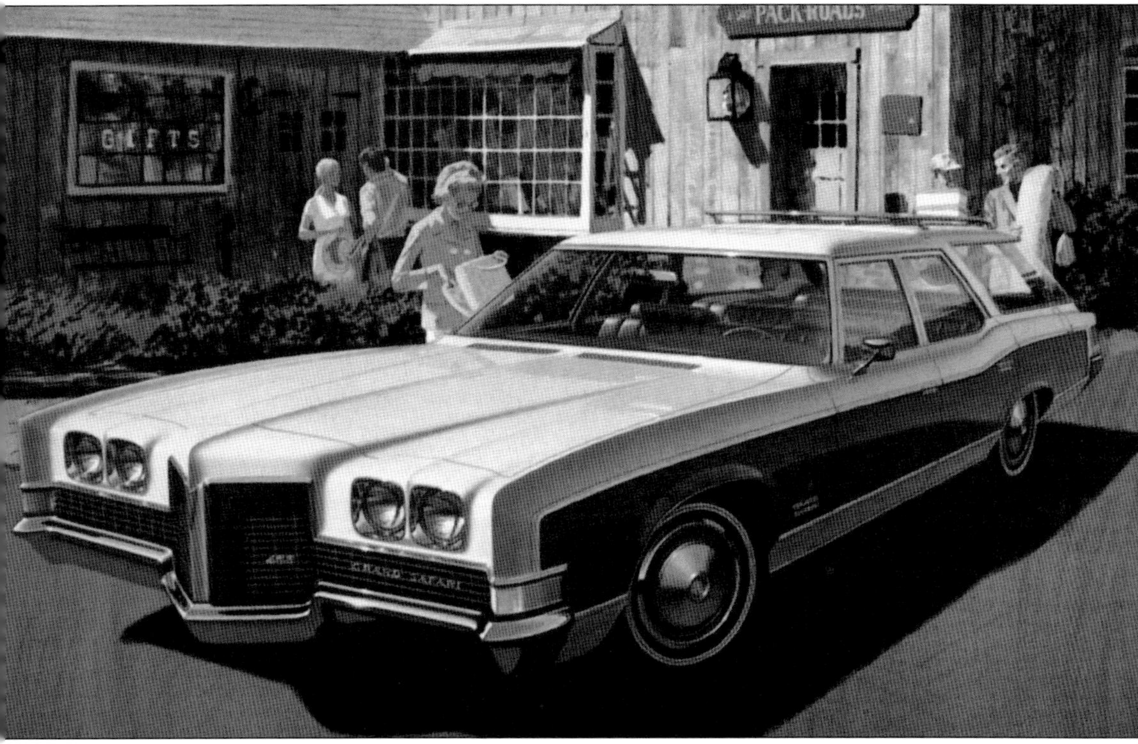

Landis Avenue remained a shopping district by day well into the 1960s, as families continued to shop there for clothing, food, and other necessities. A day of shopping was often followed by a snack at J.J. Newberry's lunch counter or a freshly made cherry Coke at a local drugstore.

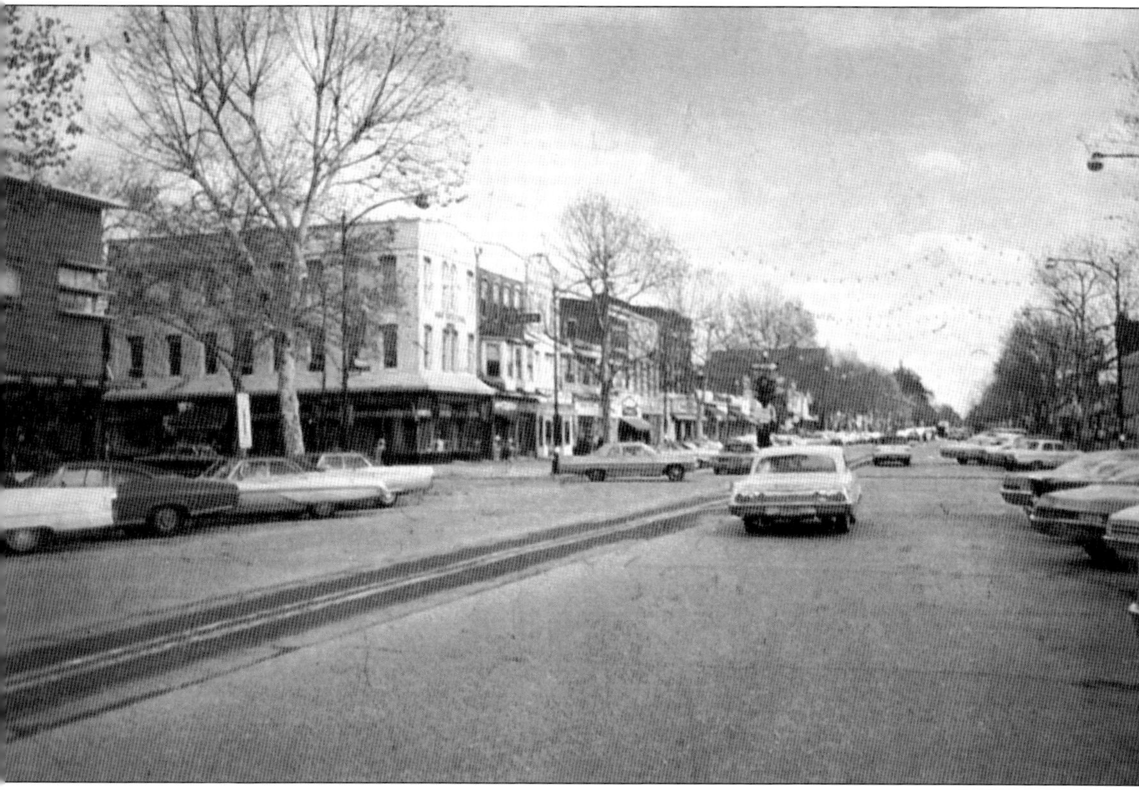

In the 1960s, Landis Avenue was a gathering place on the weekends for teenagers, who would ride it from East Avenue to the traffic circle at Delsea Drive and back again, especially on hot summer nights. In those days, American-made muscle cars could often be found with their hoods popped open while their owners compared engines. Though Landis Avenue has changed a lot in the intervening years, Vineland's downtown has remained a significant part of life for local residents. Like all of Vineland's history, records and artifacts of the business district have found a home at the Vineland Historical and Antiquarian Society.

Bibliography

Landis, Charles K. *The Founder's Own Story of the Founding of Vineland, New Jersey.* Vineland, NJ: Vineland Historical and Antiquarian Society, 1903.

———. *Vineland, New Jersey, and its Attractions.* Philadelphia: n.p., 1880.

Vineland Historical and Antiquarian Society. *Vineland.* Images of America. Charleston, SC: Arcadia Publishing, 2011.